AFRICAN POLITICAL THO

African Political Thought

Guy Martin

palgrave
macmillan

AFRICAN POLITICAL THOUGHT
Copyright © Guy Martin, 2012.

First published in 2012 by PALGRAVE MACMILLAN® in the United States—a division of St. Martin's Press LLC, 175 Fifth Avenue, New York, NY 10010.

Where this book is distributed in the UK, Europe and the rest of the world, this is by Palgrave Macmillan, a division of Macmillan Publishers Limited, registered in England, company number 785998, of Houndmills, Basingstoke, Hampshire RG21 6XS.

Palgrave Macmillan is the global academic imprint of the above companies and has companies and representatives throughout the world.

Palgrave® and Macmillan® are registered trademarks in the United States, the United Kingdom, Europe and other countries.

ISBN: 978-1-4039-6633-9 (hardcover)
ISBN: 978-1-4039-6634-6 (paperback)

Library of Congress Cataloging-in-Publication Data is available from the Library of Congress.

A catalogue record of the book is available from the British Library.

Design by Scribe Inc.

First edition: December 2012

10 9 8 7 6 5 4 3 2 1

Transferred to Digital Printing in 2013

This book is dedicated to the memories of
Emmanuel Hansen (1937–1987)
and
Claude Ake (1939–1996)

Perfect gentlemen, stellar scholars, esteemed colleagues,
valued friends, and faithful companions
in our unrelenting struggle for a better Africa;
May your spirit live on and continue to inspire present and future
generations of African scholar-activists and citizen truly dedicated
to the advent of a new African and a free Africa.

CONTENTS

Acknowledgments

The genesis of this book may be traced back to my experience teaching African political thought over a period of ten years (1993–2003) at various academic institutions (Clark Atlanta University, University of Virginia, and Spelman College). I soon came to realize that the instructor wishing to put together a collection of readings on the subject needed to delve into an extremely broad range of sources and materials widely scattered in many books, articles, and primary sources dealing with African history, anthropology, sociology, philosophy, politics, biography, and literature. This led me to the firm conviction that a single thematic volume that would synthesize the state of knowledge of African political thought was badly needed, hence this textbook, which constitutes—to the best of my knowledge—the first such enterprise.

Many individual and intellectual debts have been incurred in the long and arduous process leading up to the completion of this project. My interest in the subject of African political thought was first aroused when I was a graduate student at the School of Oriental and African Studies, University of London, in 1969–70; I was encouraged by my then advisor, Donal Cruise O'Brien, to embark on a comparative study of the political thought of Kwame Nkrumah and Sékou Touré, which eventually became the subject of my Master's thesis. I pursued this interest while a doctoral student in political science and African studies at Indiana University at Bloomington (1973–76). It was in the late Émile Snyder's seminar on Francophone African literature that I developed a particular interest in the political thought of Frantz Fanon. It is due to Émile's encouragement and advice that a paper on that subject that I wrote for his seminar became my very first article, published by *Ufahamu* in 1974. While at Indiana University, I had the good fortune to attend the dissertation defense of my fellow senior student from Ghana, Emmanuel Hansen. Fortuitously, the topic was "Frantz Fanon's Social and Political Thought" (which was published as a book in 1977 by Ohio State University Press). From then on, Emmanuel and I became friends, and he was instrumental in bringing me (in the mid-1980s) into the African Association of Political Science (AAPS), of which he was a prominent and active member. As a member of the faculty at the University of Nairobi (Kenya), I became increasingly more personally involved in the activities of AAPS—whose executive committee I joined from 1985 to 1990—and also of the Dakar-based Council for the Development of Social Science Research in Africa (CODESRIA). As leading Pan-African academic institutional networks, both AAPS and CODESRIA provided ample opportunity to interact regularly with the "best and brightest" on the continent, notably Dani W. Nabudere, Mahmood Mamdani, Abdoulaye Bathily, Peter Anyang' Nyong'o, Emmanuel Hansen, L. Adele Jinadu, and Claude Ake. Over time, I became particularly close to the last three mentioned, and I recall fondly our endless and passionate discussions and debates over the fate of Africa that we had in the conference lobbies and lounges of Addis Ababa, Dakar, and Nairobi. I owe in great part my sustained interest in African political thought to the invaluable intellectual exchange that I had with these three exceptional African scholars, particularly Emmanuel Hansen and Claude Ake, who left us much too soon and to whom this book is dedicated. I should mention here that when Claude declined an offer from the American University (Washington, DC) in the fall semester of 1991 to start his own Centre for Advanced Social Science (CASS) in Port-Harcourt (Nigeria), I (on his recommendation) was offered and took up that position.

This project was initiated at Palgrave Macmillan in 2007 under the expert guidance and advice of an extremely talented editorial team, whom I wish to thank for its constant encouragement and support, and which included first Gabriella Georgiades, then Luba Ostashevsky (editors), and Joanna Mericle (editorial assistant). It eventually fell on Chris Chappell (editor) to take up the challenge of rekindling the flame, reviving my waning energies, and bringing this project to completion. All this Chris accomplished with impeccable professionalism, exceptional competence, and remarkable patience and understanding; for this I am grateful to him. Thanks are also due to Sarah Whalen (assistant editor), who was responsible for steering this project through its final stages.

However, I undoubtedly owe my greatest debt of gratitude to my spouse, friend, intellectual companion, and *alter ego*, Mueni wa Muiu. After having invited me to join her in the pathbreaking *Fundi wa Afrika* project—culminating in a book published by Palgrave Macmillan in 2009—she was a constant and crucial source of encouragement and support, gently (but firmly) prodding me to complete my own project when my energies were waning. It is no exaggeration to state that if it was not for Mueni, this book might never have seen the light of day. For this (and for much, much more), I am deeply and sincerely grateful to her. Needless to say, I am solely responsible for all the remaining errors of fact or interpretation that may be found in this work.

Acronyms

AAPC	All-African Peoples' Conference
AAPS	African Association of Political Science
AEF	*Afrique Équatoriale Française* (French Equatorial Africa)
AFRIGOV	African Centre for Democratic Governance
AHSG	Assembly of Heads of States and Government
ANL	*Armée do Libération Nationale* (National Liberation Army) [Algeria]
AOF	*Afrique Occidentale Française* (French West Africa)
AU	African Union
BCM	Black Consciousness Movement [South Africa]
BCP	Black Community Programs [South Africa]
BPC	Black People's Convention [South Africa]
CASS	Centre for Advanced Social Science
CCM	*Chama Cha Mapinduzi* [Tanzania]
CDRs	*Comités de Défense de la Révolution* (Revolutionary Defense Committees) [Burkina Faso]
CNR	*Conseil National de la Révolution* (National Revolutionary Council) [Burkina Faso]
CODESRIA	Council for the Development of Social Science Research in Africa
CPP	Convention People's Party [Ghana]
DRC	Democratic Republic of the Congo
FAS	Federation of African States
FLN	*Front de Libération Nationale* (National Liberation Front) [Algeria]
FRELIMO	*Frente de Libertação de Moçambique* (Front for the Liberation of Mozambique)
GPC	General People's Congress [Libya]
MNC	*Mouvement National Congolais* (Congolese National Movement) [DRC]
NATO	North Atlantic Treaty Organization
NUSAS	National Union of South African Students
OAU	Organization of African Unity
OCAM	*Organisation Commune Africaine et Malgache* (Common African and Malagasy Union)
ONRA	*Office National de la Réforme Agraire* (National Office for Agrarian Reform) [Algeria]

PAIGC	*Partido Africano da Independência da Guiné e Cabo Verde* (African Party for the Independence of Guinea-Bissau and Cape Verde)
PDG	*Parti Démocratique de Guinée* (Democratic Party of Guinea)
RDA	*Rassemblement Démocratique Africain* (African Democratic Union)
RENAMO	Mozambique National Resistance Movement
SASO	South African Students' Organization [South Africa]
UAS	Union of African States
UNIA	Universal Negro Improvement Association
US-RDA	*Union Soudanaise-Rassemblement Démocratique Africain* (Sudanese Union-African Democratic Union) [Mali]
WASU	West African Students' Union

INTRODUCTION

AFRICAN POLITICAL THOUGHT
FROM ANTIQUITY TO THE PRESENT

*For my part, the deeper I enter into the cultures and the political circles,
the surer I am that the great danger that threatens Africa is the absence of
ideology.*

—Frantz Fanon, *Toward the African Revolution*, 186

As a distinct field of study, African political thought is a relatively new discipline. It was only in the late 1960s that it emerged as different and distinct from other—notably Western—systems of thought. The pioneering works in the field—now outdated and mostly out-of-print—focused essentially on various aspects of African nationalism and African socialism.[1] To say (as Boele van Hensbroek does) that "the history of African political ideas is a neglected field of study"[2] is a major understatement. Based on my personal experience and that of many of my colleagues, I can confidently state that the instructor wishing to put together a collection of readings on the subject needs to delve into an extremely broad range of sources and materials widely scattered in many books, articles, and primary sources dealing with African history, anthropology, sociology, philosophy, politics, biography, and literature. As arguably the very first attempt to synthesize African political thought into one single thematic volume, the present textbook is designed to address this concern and fill this gap in the literature.

In essence, African political thought refers to the original ideas, values, and blueprints for a better Africa that inform African political systems and institutions from the ancient period (Kush, sixth century BCE) to the present. African political thought also refers to political theories and ideologies developed by various African scholars and statesmen, as enunciated in their speeches, autobiographies, writings, and policy statements, the main focus here being on the *ideas* rather than on the individuals. Political thought usually precedes and informs political action; the latter, in turn, influences political thought. Political theory and political practice are thus inextricably linked. In other words, African political thought provides practical solutions to political, economic, social, and cultural problems, and it varies according to historical circumstances and a constantly changing African and world political environment.

To be efficient, an ideology must reach large numbers of people by means of slogans and catchwords. It must publicize and popularize concepts and ideals that have to be comprehended and assimilated in the shortest possible time by ordinary citizens. The impact of ideology will depend greatly on the form, frequency, and intimacy of the communication between the leader who formulates this ideology and the popular masses to whom it is directed. Henry Bretton defines the ideological function of political leadership as follows: "The ideological function of political leadership is primarily to formulate and articulate guidelines for political and social behavior and to translate them into concrete plans and goals for state and society. To be reasonably effective, to release popular energies and direct them toward specific social objectives, the ideas must be manageable in practice, must be articulate, consistent, and socially relevant, and must be perceived by the opinion and action of leaders throughout the state in approximately the sense intended."[3] A major distinction must be made here between indigenous and modern African political thought. The former was developed during the so-called golden age of African history[4] and refers to the governance of ancient kingdoms and empires (such as Egypt, Kush/Nubia, Axum, Ghana, Mali, Songhay, and Kanem-Bornu), but it was also developed by such scholars as Ibn Khaldûn, Al Bekri, Ibn Battuta, and Leo Africanus, and it is associated with indigenous African political systems and institutions. Modern African political thought emerged in the late nineteenth and early twentieth centuries and was developed by African scholars such as James Africanus Horton, Edward Wilmot Blyden, and Kwame Nkrumah.

In the African context, Thomas Hodgkin uses the term *nationalist* broadly to refer to individuals, organizations, or groups who called on Africans to assert their rights and fight against European colonialism. According to Basil Davidson, African nationalism is a desire for personal emancipation—a search for equality, rights, self-respect, and full participation in the society. It is a continuous effort to rescue Africans from perceived inferiority as a result of colonialism.[5] Thus African nationalism is a broad and inclusive ideology within which more narrowly defined ideologies—namely, African socialism, African populism, and African Marxism (or Afro-Marxism)—are subsumed. African nationalism takes various forms. Some of the African nationalists—such as K. A. Busia, Nnamdi Azikiwe, and Kenneth Kaunda—were advocates of modernization, westernization, and capitalism. Others—such as Kwame Nkrumah, Ahmed Sékou Touré, and Julius Nyerere—believed in a distinctly African brand of socialism that fused indigenous African values and traditions with elements of the Marxist-Leninist ideology and gave prominence to the state in the economy in their quest for political, economic, social, and cultural transformation. Still other African nationalists who fall under the label of "African populists"—such as Thomas Sankara, Muammar Qaddafi, and Steve Biko—while agreeing with the basic tenets of African socialism, focus strictly on transforming their polity, economies, and societies for the benefit of their people and (contrary to the African socialists) are doers (i.e., action-oriented) rather than theorists. Note that while African socialism and African populism are primarily focused on the domestic political level, they also have an international (or foreign policy) dimension that links them to the ideology of Pan-Africanism and the policy goal of African unity, which essentially aim at the political, economic, and cultural union of Africans in Africa and Africans in the diaspora.

All the modern African authors/activists/statesmen surveyed in this book exhibit a number of common characteristics. First, they were both political thinkers and political statesmen/activists, linking theory and practice, as all major philosopher-kings have been throughout history. Second, they were all, to various degrees, influenced by the Marxist-Leninist ideology. Third, they were all truly dedicated to the welfare and well-being of their countries and people. As such, they were all dedicated African nationalists. Last, most of them died young. Some—like Frantz Fanon—died as a result of a fatal disease; others—such as Steve Biko, Amilcar Cabral, Samora Machel, Eduardo Mondlane, Patrice Lumumba, and Thomas Sankara—were brutally murdered by agents of the Western powers.

Note that each of these ideologies can be broken down into various tendencies. Thus there are moderate and radical forms of African nationalism and African socialism. As a result of the demise of the Marxist-Leninist and socialist ideologies in the post–Cold War era, African countries and leaders have, beginning in 1990, progressively (and officially) abandoned these ideologies, while others—like Libya's Muammar Qaddafi and Zimbabwe's Robert Mugabe—continued to implement African-populist policies (such as the land reform in Zimbabwe). In this period of political transition and turmoil, as well as ideological uncertainty—prematurely described as the "End of History" by Francis Fukuyama—African leaders are sorely in need of a new ideology that would guide the political, economic, social, and cultural development of their countries and people. In this regard, they would be well advised to get inspiration and guidance from African scholars who have developed original ideas for a new, free, and self-reliant Africa, most notably Cheikh Anta Diop, Joseph Ki-Zerbo, Claude Ake, and Mueni wa Muiu.

Besides the fact that this textbook is, to the best of our knowledge, the very first attempt to synthesize African political thought into one single thematic volume, what else makes it unique and original? For one thing, it is the first book in which indigenous African political ideas and values (from Antiquity to the nineteenth century) are examined in detail alongside modern African political ideas (from the nineteenth century to the present). Furthermore, it is—again, to the best of our knowledge—also the very first time that the emergence of Islamic values and ideas on governance between the second and eighth centuries in North, West, and Eastern Africa are studied in relation to indigenous African values and ideas on governance. Finally, contrary to existing works on the subject, this textbook focuses primarily on the *ideas* and the common themes that bind them, rather than on the *individuals*—whether scholars, activists, statesmen, or leaders—themselves.

A word of caution is necessary here to point out what is *not* covered in this book. First of all, African Marxist (or Afro-Marxist) regimes fall outside the purview of this book because they do not derive from an original ideology; they merely implement—or, sometimes, pretend to implement—Marxist-Leninist ideology and public policy in an African political context. Besides, such regimes have been the object of exhaustive study by a number of authors, most notably David and Marina Ottaway, Edmond Keller and Donald Rothchild, and Crawford Young, but also in the "Marxist Regimes Series" edited by Bogdan Szajkowski.[6] Second, *Négritude* and its advocates and critics do not figure in this book. *Négritude* is a cultural movement reasserting African culture, values, and traditions as part of the common heritage of mankind. This ideology emerged in Paris (France) in the 1930s among the African and Caribbean elites and was enunciated by such authors as Aimé Césaire (Martinique), Léon-Gontran Damas (French Guyana), and Léopold Sédar Senghor (Senegal), the latter becoming president of his country from 1960 to 1980. Over the years, *Négritude* has become a distinct subfield in the area of Francophone African cultural studies and literary criticism, and it has given rise to a vast body of work. The acknowledged doyen of this school is Francis Abiola Irele, author of many books on the subject.[7] By the same token, Léopold Senghor's specific brand of "African Socialism" is not covered in this book, as it has been abundantly dealt with elsewhere.[8] Finally, constraints of space forced us to, unfortunately, exclude a number of African scholars/activists/leaders worthy of study. These include Blaise Diagne, Samuel Ajayi Crowther, Alexander Crummel, Herbert Macaulay, and John Mensah Sarbah among the early West African nationalists; Nnamdi Azikiwe, Hastings Kamuzu Banda, Félix Houphouët-Boigny, Nelson Mandela, Tom Mboya, and Jacques Rabemananjara among the advocates of liberal democracy; Eduardo Mondlane, Gamal Abdel Nasser, Agostinho Neto, Oginga Odinga, and Robert Sobukwe among the socialist-populists; Robert Mugabe and John Jerry Rawlings among the populist-socialists; and Pathë Diagne, Cheikh Anta Diop, Joseph Ki-Zerbo, Anton Muziwakhe Lembede, and Walter Rodney among the Africanist-populists.

As we have noted previously, African political thought varies according to historical circumstances and a constantly changing African and world political environment. It is therefore important to note in this regard that various African political ideologies are associated with specific historical periods and time frames. Thus Pan-Africanism first emerged in the United States of America and the Caribbean in the 1920s with such intellectual/activist leaders as W. E. B. Du Bois, Paul Robeson, C. L. R. James, George Padmore, and Marcus Garvey. It was only with the Manchester Pan-African Congress of October 1945 that the Pan-African movement moved to Africa under the leadership of Ghana's Kwame Nkrumah. Similarly, the *Négritude* movement emerged in Paris in the 1930s among a French-speaking intellectual elite led by Aimé Césaire, Léon-Gontran Damas, and Léopold Sédar Senghor. In the same way, the period from 1945 to 1960 may be viewed as the heyday of African nationalism, just as the decade from 1960 to 1970 is when African socialism came to full bloom. The following decade (1970 to 1980) is when Marxist regimes flourished throughout Africa (Angola, Benin, Congo, Ethiopia, Guinea-Bissau, Madagascar, Mozambique, Namibia, and Somalia), while the early 1990s saw the demise of these regimes. The populist-socialists fall into three different categories. The first includes those intellectuals/activists who remained at the level of ideas, with limited or no policy experience at all (Frantz Fanon and Steve Biko). The second includes those leaders who were in power for only a few years and thus were unable to see their policies bear fruit: Thomas Sankara (1983–87) and J. Jerry Rawlings (1979–82).[9] The third group includes those statesmen who were in power for the longest time: Muammar Qaddafi (1969–2011) and Robert Mugabe (1980 to present). Finally, while there were early Africanist-populists (such as Cheikh Anta Diop, Joseph Ki-Zerbo, and Anton M. Lembede), the majority of the scholars associated with this school of thought—such as Claude Ake, Daniel Osabu-Kle, and Mueni wa Muiu—came to prominence in the early twenty-first century.

Chapter 1 is a broad survey of the ideas and values that shaped indigenous African political systems and institutions, from Antiquity to the tenth century. Section 1 deals with the conceptualization of political power: namely, the confusion between the secular and the sacred; the communal nature of property rights; the system of checks and balances and the limits on the use and abuse of political power by the rulers (chiefs, kings, and emperors) in the form of various advisory bodies (inner or privy council and council of elders) and village assemblies; the institutionalization of succession and the transfer of power; and the rules of war and the methods of conflict resolution. Section 2 focuses on the conceptualization of democracy in terms of individual and collective rights, the rule of decision making by consensus, the role of age sets, gender relations and the role of women in politics, indigenous concepts of justice and the law, relations between the rulers and the ruled, and village assemblies acting as the ultimate political authority. The particular focus of this chapter is on the earliest state formations in Africa—namely, Egypt, Kush/Nubia, Ghana, and Mali—though occasional reference is made to some later state formations such as Asante (Ghana).

Chapter 2 continues the survey of the ideas and values that shaped indigenous African political systems and institutions initiated in Chapter 1, with particular focus on the progressive emergence of Islamic values and ideas on governance, as well as the process of mutual cross-fertilization of such values and ideas with indigenous African values and ideas on governance between the second and eighth centuries in North Africa and the coastal city-states of Eastern Africa.

Section 2 of Chapter 2 is an overview of the conception of the state embodied in the concept of 'asabiyah, referring to the rise and fall of political systems and institutions outlined by the medieval North African scholar and statesman Ibn Khaldûn (1332–1406) in his *magnum opus* titled *The Muqqadimah* (1377). Section 3 examines how Islamic values and ideas on governance influenced indigenous African values and ideas on power and governance in various Islamic theocratic states that emerged in the Western

Sudan in the nineteenth century: namely, the theocratic state of the Futa Jalon (1725–76); Usman dan Fodio's Sokoto Caliphate (1808–37); the Fulani kingdom of Sheiku Ahmadu and his successors (1818–62); and the Segu Tuklor Empire of al-Haj 'Umar Tall (1852–93).

In Chapter 3, the ideas of the African advocates of modernization, westernization, and liberal democracy are examined. The first section is an overview of the image of Africa and Africans constructed by Europeans from the sixteenth century onward, informed by the theory of "Social Darwinism." The chapter then focuses specifically on the French colonial policies of assimilation and association, as well as on the British colonial policy of "Indirect Rule." The chapter also examines the rise of economic and political liberalism in nineteenth century Europe as a background for the rise of "Humanitarianism." The next section focuses on a small Western-educated intellectual elite that tried to reconcile Western systems of thought with African culture, values, and traditions, or Western liberalism with African democracy: Edward W. Blyden, James Africanus Horton, and Joseph Casely Hayford. The last section of Chapter 3 examines the ideas of two prominent African advocates of liberal democracy: an academic and one-time prime minister (1969–72), Kofi Busia of Ghana, and the "Father of Zambian Nationalism" and president of Zambia for 27 years (1964–91), Kenneth Kaunda.

Chapter 4 is a survey of Pan-Africanism as a political and cultural ideal and movement eventually leading to African unity. The chapter first shows how the Pan-Africanist leaders' dream for immediate political and economic integration in the form of a "United States of Africa" was deferred in favor of a gradualist-functionalist approach, embodied in the creation of a weak and ineffective Organization of African Unity (OAU) on May 25, 1963, in Addis Ababa (Ethiopia). The chapter then analyzes the reasons for the failure of the Pan-Africanist leaders' dream of unity, among which inter-African rivalries and the divide-and-rule strategies of the major Western powers figure prominently. The chapter shows that the successor organization to the OAU, the African Union, created in May 2001, is bound to know the same fate as the OAU because it is modeled on the European Union and thus not homegrown. The chapter then surveys past and current proposals for a revision of the map of Africa and a reconfiguration of the African states put forward by various authors such as Cheikh Anta Diop, Marc-Louis Ropivia, Makau wa Mutua, Arthur Gakwandi, Joseph Ki-Zerbo, Daniel Osabu-Kle, Godfrey Mwakikagile, Pelle Danabo, and Mueni wa Muiu. The chapter concludes with a brief study of Mueni wa Muiu's proposal for a reconfiguration of Africa into five subregional states, the Federation of African States (FAS). It is argued that only with the advent of FAS will Africa's "Dream of Unity" finally become a reality.

Chapter 5 is a survey of the political, economic, social, and cultural dimensions of the socialist-populist ideology from a distinctly socialist perspective. The statesmen affiliated with this ideology either were not in power at all (Cabral and Mondlane) or else ruled for only a short period of time (Ben Bella, Lumumba, Machel, and Neto). Furthermore, these leaders may be characterized as "democrats" in the sense that they were unable or unwilling to exercise authoritarian rule, they encouraged a form of participatory democracy, and they truly had the best interest of their people at heart. Three of the countries surveyed (Algeria, Guinea-Bissau, and Mozambique) achieved independence as a result of an armed struggle. This group includes Patrice Lumumba (Congo), Ahmed Ben Bella (Algeria), Amilcar Cabral (Guinea-Bissau), Agostinho Neto (Angola), and Samora Machel and Eduardo Mondlane (Mozanbique). For the reasons explained previously, the chapter shall focus exclusively on Lumumba, Ben Bella, Cabral, and Machel.

Chapter 6 continues the survey—started in Chapter 5—of the political, economic, social, and cultural dimensions of the socialist-populist ideology from a distinctly socialist perspective. This chapter, however, focuses on the statesmen (and regimes) who, in spite of the socialist rhetoric, have used the socialist-populist ideology (to various degrees) as an instrument of control and coercion, sometimes even as an instrument of terror (as in the case of Sékou Touré). These political systems are characterized by relatively authoritarian (sometimes totalitarian) regimes, a top-down system of administration, as well as state control over the economy. Kwame Nkrumah (Ghana), Ahmed Sékou Touré (Guinea), Modibo Kéïta (Mali), and Julius Nyerere (Tanzania) all fall in this category. The chapter begins with a study of the "Father of African Nationalism," Kwame Nkrumah of Ghana, who conceived his own philosophy and ideology for decolonization, which he called "Consciencism." The chapter then surveys the political ideas and policies of two key proponents of "African Socialism" in Francophone Africa: Ahmed Sékou Touré of Guinea and Modibo Kéïta of Mali. The chapter concludes with a survey of the political ideology and policies of another prominent advocate of "African Socialism," Mwalimu Julius K. Nyerere of Tanzania.

Chapter 7 is an overview of the political, economic, social, and cultural dimensions of the populist-socialist ideology from a distinctly populist perspective, from the early 1960s to the present. The intellectuals/ statesmen reviewed in this chapter were both theoreticians and practitioners who genuinely sought to improve the condition of their people by attempting to implement policies of political, economic, social, and cultural transformation. Sections 1 and 4 deal with those scholar-activists who remained essentially at the level of ideas, with very limited or no policy experience at all: Frantz Fanon and Steve Biko. In section 2, we shall focus on the case of one intellectual/statesman who, because of particular historical circumstances, was in power for a limited period of time and thus was unable to see his policies of political and socioeconomic transformation bear fruit: Thomas Sankara (Burkina Faso). The third section of this chapter shall examine one populist leader who (until his elimination by NATO forces) had been in power for a very long time (42 years): Muammar Qaddafi of Libya.

Chapter 8 reviews the ideas and values for a new, free, and self-reliant Africa put forth by African academics who have the best interest of the people at heart and thus advocate a popular type of democracy and development. However, unlike the populist-socialist scholars, these Africanist-populist scholars refuse to operate within the parameters of Western ideologies—whether of the socialist, Marxist-Leninist, or liberal-democratic persuasion—and call on Africans to get rid of their economic, technological, and cultural dependency syndrome. These scholars are also convinced that the solution to African problems lie within Africans themselves. Thus they refuse to remain passive victims of a perceived or preordained fate and call on all Africans to become the initiators and agents of their own development, with the ultimate goal of creating a "new African." It is interesting to note that all these individuals are first and foremost academics, deal strictly with ideas, and have not been directly involved in politics (although the majority are political scientists).[10] Some of the most prominent Africanist-populist scholars include Senegalese scientist Cheikh Anta Diop (1923–86); Burkinabè historian Joseph Ki-Zerbo (1922–2006); Nigerian political scientist Claude Ake (1939–96); Ghanaian political scientist Daniel T. Osabu-Kle; Tanzanian scholar-journalist Godfrey Mwakikagile; and Kenyan political scientist Mueni wa Muiu. Note that all these scholars are dedicated Pan-Africanists and many would shun the reference to their nationality, preferring to be simply called "Africans." For the reasons stated previously, the chapter will focus exclusively on the last four scholars mentioned: namely, Osabu-Kle, Ake, Mwakikagile, and Muiu.

The conclusion will summarize the concepts and ideas presented in Chapters 1 through 8. First, the ideas and values that shaped indigenous African political systems and institutions, from Antiquity to the late nineteenth century are examined. Particular attention is given to the conceptualization of political power and democracy; the development of Islamic concepts of governance between the second and eighth centuries in North and Eastern Africa; Ibn Khaldun's conception of the state as embodied in the concept of 'asabiyah; and indigenous values and ideas on power and governance in various state formations of West, Central, and Southern Africa between the fourteenth and the nineteenth centuries. Second, the ideas for modernization and westernization of the early West African nationalists of the late nineteenth–early twentieth centuries are reviewed. Third, we undertake a survey of Pan-Africanism as an ideal and instrument of foreign policy, from North America in the early twentieth century. Fourth, the political, economic, social, and cultural dimensions of the socialist-populist ideology during the early years of independence—particularly from the mid-1960s to the mid-1980s—are examined. Fifth, the political, economic, social, and cultural dimensions of the populist-socialist ideology from a populist perspective, from the 1960s to the present, are reviewed. Lastly, we undertake an overview of the more recent ideas for a new, free, and self-reliant Africa, with particular attention to the interconnectedness of the concepts of development and democracy in contemporary Africa. These ideas and concepts are put forth primarily by contemporary African academics—the Africanist-populists, who are convinced that the solution to African problems lie within African themselves—who advocate a popular type of democracy and development and call for the advent of a "new African."

CHAPTER 1

---⟡---

THE POLITICAL IDEOLOGY OF INDIGENOUS AFRICAN POLITICAL SYSTEMS AND INSTITUTIONS FROM ANTIQUITY TO THE NINETEENTH CENTURY

(5) Every individual has a right to life and to defend his/her personal integrity. Consequently, any attempt at taking someone else's life will be punished by death; (16) In addition to their daily chores, women must be involved in all levels of government; (22) Vanity is a sign of weakness, and humility a sign of greatness; (24) In Mali, never mistreat a foreigner; (25) In Mali, the envoy is always safe.

—Selected articles from the *Mande Charter* (1240)
[*La Charte de Kurukan Fuga*], 45, 47, 49, 51

INTRODUCTION

Highly advanced and sophisticated African civilizations, cultures, societies, and states—such as Ancient Egypt, Kush/Nubia, Axum, Ghana, Mali, and Asante—evolved throughout the continent from the ninth century before the Christian era (BCE) to the nineteenth century CE. African political systems and institutions were traditionally based on kinship and lineage (i.e., common ancestry), sanctioned by a founding myth. The lineage was a powerful and effective force for unity and stability in ancient Africa. Each lineage had its head, chosen on the basis of age, maturity, and relation to ancestors. The old (respectfully referred to as "elders") were often chosen as lineage heads because old age was usually associated with wisdom. Each ethnic group had its own system of government. In all indigenous African societies, political organization began at the lineage or village level. Religion defined moral duties and controlled conduct; it informed laws and customs, as well as accepted norms of behavior. In African systems of thought, religion is an essential part of life; indeed, religion and life are inseparable. What this description accurately portrays is "the belief held among African communities that the supernatural powers and deities operate in every sphere and activity of life. Religion and life are inseparable, and life is not comparted [*sic*] into sacred and secular."[1]

INDIGENOUS AFRICAN POLITICAL SYSTEMS AND INSTITUTIONS: FOUNDATIONAL PRINCIPLES AND DEMOCRATIC CHARACTERISTICS

In indigenous African political systems, the rules and procedures of governance were established by custom and tradition rather than by written constitutions. In addition, these systems were based on the *rule of law*—that is, respect for (and adherence to) customary ways of resolving disputes and upholding the traditions governing political behavior. More important, customary African laws were subject to full public debate and scrutiny; in fact, chiefs and kings could not promulgate laws without the consent of the councils. In Pharaonic Egypt—as in other indigenous African societies—every individual was equal before the law: "Pharaonic law remained resolutely individualistic. In relation to royal decisions and to legal procedure and penalties, men and women of all classes seem to have been equals before the law."[2]

Indigenous African political systems were democratic in many respects. First, they were based on an elaborate system of checks and balances; such institutions as the Inner or Privy Council and the Council of Elders acted as effective checks on the potential abuse of power by the leader (chief, king, or emperor).[3] Second, political succession was carefully institutionalized in such a way that family, clan, and ethnic competition for power was minimized and (physically or mentally) unfit leaders were automatically eliminated. Third, the basic political unit was the village assembly, where major decisions concerning the society were adopted and ordinary people were able to express their opinions, have their voices heard, and actively participate in a political decision-making process based on majority rule. A specific socioprofessional group (or caste)—such as the *griots* (or praise-singers) in the Western Sudan—were the custodians of tradition and the living historical memory of the society.

INDIGENOUS AFRICAN POLITICAL SYSTEMS AS SECULAR AND SACRED

In indigenous African societies, the social order was informed by the belief—passed on from generation to generation—that the ancestors constituted the link between the present, the past, and the future. The African concept of power fused the secular and the sacred. The leader was both a secular and religious leader and acted as intermediary between the living and the dead—between the people and their ancestors. The following quote from K. A. Busia perfectly captures the essence of this concept as it relates to the case of the Asante:

> In traditional African communities, it was not possible to distinguish between religious and non-religious areas of life. All life was religious . . . for in traditional African communities, politics and religion were closely associated. In many tribes, the chief was the representative of the ancestors. This enhanced his authority. He was respected as the one who linked the living and the dead . . . The most important aspect of Ashanti [Asante] chieftaincy was undoubtedly the religious one. An Ashanti chief filled a sacred role . . . The chief was the link between the living and the dead, and his highest role was when he officiated in the public religious rites which gave expression to the community values . . . This sacral aspect of the chief's role was a powerful sanction of his authority.[4]

The religious authority of the leader meant that he was also custodian of the land bequeathed to the group by the ancestors and held in sacred trust by the leader on behalf of the whole people; this explains why the land could under no circumstance be individually appropriated. While some indigenous African political systems were more elaborate and institutionalized than others— the so-called state societies—all of them had some form of centralized power and authority.[5]

POWER AND AUTHORITY IN INDIGENOUS AFRICAN POLITICAL SYSTEMS AND INSTITUTIONS

In indigenous African political systems, the power of leaders was derived from the founding ancestors and was hereditary in the sense that it was reserved for certain lineages by right of ancestry. Thus, in the Mali Empire, Kéïta was customarily the ruling clan by virtue of the fact that the empire was founded in 1235 by Sunjata Kéïta against tremendous odds.[6] Similarly, as documented by Elliott Skinner, in the Mossi kingdoms, political power was linked to closeness to the ancestors: "To the Mossi, the power to rule was intimately linked to closeness of descent from the royal ancestors. The supernatural power of these ancestors, and the vigilance they were believed to maintain over the affairs of their descendants, were regarded as important factors in Mossi government . . . Ritual and the supernatural thus played an extremely important role in the cohesiveness of the Mossi kingdoms and in the functioning of their governmental processes."[7] The leaders were customarily appointed by members of the royal lineage (who constituted the Inner or Privy Council). In the Mali Empire, in addition to the Kéïta ruling clan, the aristocratic clans represented in this council were Koulibaly, Soumano, and Konaté.[8] As the guardian of the social order and the "soul of the nation," the leader needed to be endowed with certain personal and moral qualities; he was expected to be strong, generous, humble, courageous, bold in warfare, and devout in everyday life. As they derived their power from their ancestors, African leaders were endowed with (and exercised) both religious and secular powers. Wealth and property did not belong to the leader personally, but rather to the office. Thus in the kingdom of Ghana (eighth to eleventh centuries), gold (the basis of the kingdom's wealth) was held in trust for the people by the king, who could not appropriate it for personal use. According to El Bekri, "All nuggets of gold that are found in the mines of this empire belong to the king; but he leaves to his people the gold dust that everyone knows. Without this precaution gold would become so plentiful that it would practically lose its value."[9] Similarly, in Asante (central Ghana), the "Golden Stool" was the symbol of the office of the *Asantehene* (Supreme Chief of the Asante) and was said to embody the spirit of the whole Asante nation. Thus the Golden Stool—presented to the Asante as enshrining the "soul of the nation"—constituted an emblem of unity and formed the religious basis of the Asante Confederation.[10] This explains why (as reported by Colin Turnbull) the outrageous demand on the part of a junior British officer to be allowed to sit on the Golden Stool was perceived as an insult that resulted in a bloody war between the Asante and the British: "What he [the junior British officer] did not know was that the Golden Stool was not a throne . . . to be sat upon. It was the sacred symbol of the unity of the Ashanti [Asante] nation, and it was believed to contain the soul of the Ashanti [Asante] people. Therefore what the officer proposed was . . . to defile the sacred stool, desecrate the soul of the nation, and so destroy its very existence."[11]

Another democratic feature of indigenous African political systems was the decentralization of political authority and the delicate balance between central and regional power, which allowed each lineage or village to manage its own affairs and gave ordinary people a say in local governance. Again, the Asante political system, as described by K. A. Busia, perfectly illustrates this situation:

> The Ashanti [Asante] were careful to prevent their chief from becoming tyrannical, and they developed a delicate balance between central authority and regional autonomy . . . In matters of administration, each lineage or village managed its own affairs . . . each chiefdom was run on a policy of decentralization, and there was a careful balance between the central authority of the chief on the one hand and the local autonomy of the component units of the chiefdom on the other. If the chief abused his power, his subordinate chiefs, the members of his Council, could destool him. On the other hand, if a subordinate chief or councilor tried to become too powerful, the chief could destool him . . . In the Ashanti system, the fact that each lineage, village, or part of a chiefdom managed as much of its own affairs as was consistent with the unity of the whole chiefdom enabled many to share in decision-making in local affairs; for the head of each unit was, like the chief at the center, obliged to act only on the concurrence and with the advice of his own local council.[12]

The African leader was fully accountable for his actions at all times. In theory, the leader ruled for life, but in practice, he ruled only as long as the people allowed it: "However autocratic a chief was permitted to appear, he really ruled by the consent of the people. There was a balance between authority on the one side, and obligation on the other."[13] The leader would be abandoned, be removed, or—in the worst-case scenario—be the victim of a ritual murder if he did not perform according to customs and expectations or if his people so wished, irrespective of how long he had been in office. Thus

K. A. Busia describes the circumstances leading to the customary "destool-ment" (i.e., removal) of the chief in Asante in the following manner:

> The Ashanti [Asante] had a constitutional practice which ensured that the will of the people was given consideration. They had ultimately the constitutional right to destool a chief. As the fundamental principle was that only those who elected a chief could destool him, a destoolment required the consent of the elders. Sometimes they initiated a destoolment themselves when, for example, a chief repeatedly rejected their advice, or when he broke a taboo, or committed a sacrilegious act . . . A chief was also destooled if he became blind, or impotent, or suffered from leprosy, madness, or fits, or if his body was maimed in a way that disfigured him.[14]

Similarly, aggrieved or oppressed peasant subjects could always "vote with their feet" by deserting the village to create a new one, leaving the chief alone (a social death sentence in African culture). In most African societies, natural disasters (such as droughts, famines, and epidemics) were generally attributed to the fact that the chief or king had not ruled well and thus should be deposed or killed (regicide). Ritual murders of kings deemed morally or physically unfit to rule were commonly practiced among the Serer of Senegal, the Junkun and Yoruba of Nigeria, and the Shilluk of the Nilotic Sudan.

CHECKS AND BALANCES IN INDIGENOUS AFRICAN POLITICAL SYSTEMS AND INSTITUTIONS

An elaborate system of checks and balances ensured that the power and authority of the African leader was strictly circumscribed. In exercising his functions and discharging his duties as the ultimate political, legal, and reli-gious authority—essentially the maintenance of law and order and the man-agement of public affairs for the good of the community—the leader had to take the advice and counsel of two key advisory bodies: the Inner or Privy Council and the Council of Elders. The Inner or Privy Council represented the aristocratic clans and constituted the inner circle of the chief: relatives and friends, as well as prominent members of the community. This system is well described by K. A. Busia in the case of Asante: "The political system of the Ashanti [Asante] . . . had checks and balances. The chief . . . was given a Council to hold him in check. The chief was bound by custom to act only with the concurrence and on the advice of his Council. If he acted arbitrarily, and without consultation and approval by his Council, he could be deposed . . . Those who elected the chief, also had the power to depose him if he did not perform the duties of his office satisfactorily."[15] The Inner or Privy Council was appointed (and thus could be dismissed) by the leader. On the other hand, the Council of Elders represented the non-aristocratic lineages and the commoners and thus could not be dismissed by the chief. This body reached its decisions by consensus and aimed at unanimity rather than majority. Failure on the part of the leaders to consult with the Council of Elders could result in their removal.[16]

At the village level, ordinary African people acted as the ultimate judge and final authority on contested issues. Thus the Village Assembly was convened whenever the Council of Elders could not reach unanimity on a contested issue. In Bantu societies (Central and Southern Africa), Village Assemblies also ratified all new laws. Meeting procedures in the Village Assemblies were essentially democratic. First, the chief—addressing the assembly through a spokesman—would explain the purpose of the meeting, merely stating the facts. The chief's advisors would then open the debate, followed by headmen and elders. Then, anybody else wishing to speak or ask questions (commoners, women, etc.) could do so. Decisions were usually taken by consensus; if that proved impossible, majority rule prevailed. Total freedom of expression—in the form of open debate and free dissent—was the rule. Thus African political systems were truly democratic in the sense that they allowed ordinary people to have their voice heard and influence political decision making: "The Ashanti [Asante] system provided opportunities for the 'commoners,' those who were ruled, to express criticism, either through their lineage heads, or through a chosen leader recognized as spokesman for the commoners; through him the body of free citizens could criticize the government and express their wishes . . . in the last resort, they could depose their rulers."[17]

THE ROLE OF WOMEN IN INDIGENOUS AFRICAN POLITICAL SYSTEMS AND INSTITUTIONS

Women played a key role in African societies, as well as in African political systems and institutions. In Ancient Egypt, women were master of their homes and senior to their husbands, and children were named after them.[18] In general, honors were showered on the mothers, wives, and daughters of the king. It is interesting to note that there were four women pharaohs in Ancient Egypt: Nitokris, Sebeknefru, Hatshepsut, and Tauosre. Women played a key role in the political system. Also noteworthy is the fact that Ahmosis-Nefertari (under Amenhotep I) and Ahhotep (under Amasis) wielded considerable influence in political and religious matters.[19] One of the most intriguing characters of the New Kingdom (1580 to 1085 BCE) was the ambitious Queen Hatshepsut, only child of Queen Ahmosis and Thoutmosis I and the very first female monarch in world history. In the fifth year of her reign, she was powerful enough to declare herself supreme ruler of the country. The two peaceful decades of her reign were prosperous ones for Egypt. She gave priority to the country's internal affairs, commissioned a number of important building projects, and revived—after a military expedition—the trade to Punt (present-day Somalia), which had lapsed for several hundred years.[20] According to Maspéro (quoted by Cheikh Anta Diop), Hatshepsut's rights of succession were superior to those of her male relatives (husband, brother, and father), as she claimed Amon-Re as her "father." Consequently, she appeared, in the eyes of the people, as the legitimate heir to the ruling Egyptian dynasties. One could conclude from this that in Ancient Egypt, women naturally inherited political rights.[21]

In Kush—the ancient Nubian rival kingdom of Egypt—the queen mother played a crucial role in the political system. In religious matters, the queen was second only to the king. Queens could also act as co-regents when they assumed power after the death of their husbands. Sometimes, queen mothers directly assumed political office. According to Hakem, many of these queen mothers became famous, and "in Greco-Roman times, Meroe was known to have been ruled by a line of *Candace, Kandake* or queen-regnant." These *Kandake* were extremely powerful figures, often able to act as the full-fledged rulers of the kingdom and, in such cases, to be buried with full royal rituals.[22]

The Mande Charter stipulates that because they are mothers, women should always be treated with respect; it also rules that in addition to their domestic duties, women should also be part of the political decision-making process.[23] Maninka women enjoyed a high social status and a high degree of freedom. Thus, until the middle of the fourteenth century, the first wife of the *mansa* (emperor) of Mali was the second most senior person in the politico-administrative hierarchy of the empire. The key province of Jenne was under her direct authority.[24]

CUSTOMARY LAW AND CONFLICT RESOLUTION IN INDIGENOUS AFRICAN POLITICAL SYSTEMS AND INSTITUTIONS

In African societies—as in any other society—disputes arise in any family or social group with regard to property. Various mechanisms and institutions were created to resolve these disputes. In Africa, individual attachment to lineages always carried the potential risk of transforming personal disputes into broader group conflicts, as was often the case among the Ganda (Uganda) and the Nuer (Sudan). As a result, the principles of custom, tradition, and fairness were paramount, and particular emphasis was placed on the peaceful resolution of disputes and the promotion of social harmony. Thus the Arusha of Tanzania strongly believed that disputes should be settled peacefully "by persuasion and by resort to the established procedures for settlement." Similarly, the Tallensi of Ghana abhorred killings and the violent resolution of conflicts. During the *Golib* festival, all feuds and hostilities between clans were prohibited, and "the themes of food, harmony, fecundity, and the common interests of the people as a whole" were emphasized.[25]

Peace and security prevailed in most indigenous African states. Thus the Mande Charter specifically states that in Mali foreigners should never be harmed and that the security of foreign envoys is inviolable.[26] Ibn Battuta's observations on the Mali Empire are pertinent in this regard: "Among these qualities [of the Blacks] there is also the prevalence of peace in their country, the traveler is not afraid in it, nor is he who lives there in fear of the chief or of the robber by violence."[27] The maintenance of peace within most African communities was based on four fundamental legal principles: settlement of disputes by deliberation and discussion, rather than by force; correction of wrongdoing by compensation (except in serious offences such as murder); assessment and adjudication by elders, who were considered to be impartial; and fairness.[28] Thus the Mande Charter ruled that two inviolable principles should prevail in relations among the people of Mali: *sanankunya* (joking relation) and *tanamannyonya* (blood pact). As a result, respect of the other and peaceful settlement of disputes were the rule.[29]

CONCLUSION

This chapter began by observing that advanced African civilizations, cultures, societies, and states—such as Ancient Egypt, Kush/Nubia, Axum, Ghana, Mali, and Asante—evolved throughout the continent, from the ninth century BCE to the nineteenth century CE.

Indigenous African political systems and institutions were traditionally based on *kinship* and *common ancestry*. These systems were based on the *rule of law*, and the rules and procedures of governance were established by custom and tradition. In these systems, succession was institutionalized in such a way that family, clan, and ethnic competition for power was minimized. The African concept of power fused the secular and the sacred; the leader was both a *secular* and *religious leader*, and he acted as intermediary between the living and the dead—between the people and their ancestors.

Indigenous African political systems were essentially *democratic* in the sense that (1) they were based on an elaborate system of checks and balances according to which advisory bodies—such as the Inner or Privy Council and the Council of Elders—acted as effective checks on the potential abuse of power by the leader (chief, king, or emperor) and (2) through the agency of the *village assemblies* these systems allowed ordinary people to have their voices heard and influence political decision making. Moreover, the African leader was accountable for his actions at all times. In theory, the leader ruled for life, but in practice he ruled only as long as the people allowed it. In addition, *women* played a key role in African societies, as well as in Indigenous African political systems and institutions.

Indigenous African political systems did not all follow the same pattern of state formation. Each differed depending on the conditions facing it, resource availability, military strength, leadership style, population, types of state, and size. In indigenous Africa, power and authority varied from highly centralized (kingdoms and empires) to highly decentralized structures of governance. States were either centralized under one leader or federal systems in which the people in the periphery paid tribute to the leader. The reference to "indigenous" should not be read as a nostalgic "golden age," but rather as a way of analyzing which institutions can be modified to be incorporated in a reconstituted modern African state.

FURTHER READING

Ayittey, George B. N., *Indigenous African Institutions* (Ardsley-on-Hudson, NY: Transnational Publishers, 1991).

CELTHO, *La Charte de Kurukan Fuga: Aux sources d'une pensée politique en Afrique* [The Mande Charter of 1340] (Paris: L'Harmattan/SAEC, 2008).

Davidson, Basil, *The African Genius: An Introduction to African Cultural & Social History* (Boston: Little, Brown and Co., 1969).

Diop, Cheikh Anta, *Precolonial Black Africa* (Chicago: Lawrence Hill Books, 1987).

Fyle, C. Magbaily, *Introduction to the History of African Civilization; Volume I: Pre-Colonial Africa* (Lanham, MD: University Press of America, 1999).

Harris, Joseph E., *Africans and Their History*, 2nd revised edition (New York: Meridian/Penguin Books, 1998).

Shinnie, Margaret, *Ancient African Kingdoms* (London: Edward Arnold, 1965).

CHAPTER 2

THE INFLUENCE OF ISLAMIC VALUES AND IDEAS ON INDIGENOUS AFRICAN POLITICAL SYSTEMS AND INSTITUTIONS FROM THE TENTH TO THE NINETEENTH CENTURY

Through the nineteenth-century revolution Islam was transformed into a social and political force which ushered in a new age because its relationship to indigenous civilizations was changed . . . The new states foundered, not primarily because they coincided with increasing European penetration, but because they could not transcend the basic African organization of society . . . These states fell to pieces because they were not based on indigenous institutions.

—J. Spencer Trimingham, *A History of Islam in West Africa*, 233

ISLAMIC VALUES AND IDEAS, THE ISLAMIC EMPIRE, AND INDIGENOUS AFRICAN VALUES AND POLITICAL IDEAS, SYSTEMS, AND INSTITUTIONS

Born in Mecca (on the Arabian Peninsula) at the beginning of the seventh century, Islam had, by 1100, ceased to be an exclusively Arab religion. Indeed, "the new faith showed the capacity to win over and assimilate ethnic elements of the most diverse origins, fusing them into a single cultural and religious community."[1] Islam was able to acclimatize itself in various regions of Africa and among such diverse peoples as the Berber, Fulani, and Somali nomads; the Soninke and Hausa traders; and the aristocracy and ruling clans of Ghana, Mali, Songhay, Kanem, and Bornu. This explains why many historians have called the period from the seventh to the eleventh century "the Islamic age."

ISLAMIZATION OF STATES AND SOCIETIES IN NORTH AFRICA, EASTERN AFRICA, AND THE INDIAN OCEAN ISLANDS (SEVENTH TO FIFTEENTH CENTURY)

With the spread of Islam between the seventh century and the end of the eleventh century, Egypt became the site of a powerful Fatimid empire, the most important transit point for trade between the Mediterranean and the Indian Ocean, and one of the main centers of cultural life. Egypt was also the starting point of the Arab conquest of the Maghreb, which led to the Islamization of North Africa and the emergence of a typically Islamic form of governance, the Caliphate. Furthermore, Egypt was the final destination of many African slaves imported from Nubia, Ethiopia, and the Western and Central Sudan from the ninth century onwards.[2] It should be noted in this regard that, throughout this period, a significant number of Africans converted to Islam as a way of protecting themselves against being sold into slavery.

In the Maghreb, it was not until the end of the seventh century that the conquering Arabs eventually subdued the majority of the Berbers, who then adopted Islam while resenting the political domination of the Arabs. The Berbers played a key role in the spread of Islam in both North Africa and the Western Sudan in two main respects. First, their democratic and egalitarian traditions led them to adhere to the teachings of those Islamic sects that preached those values, infusing Islam in the Maghreb with a spirit of reform and populism—such as Sufism—exemplified by the great movements of the Almoravids and the Almohads of Northwest Africa. Second, the Berber traders progressively introduced the Islamic religion, culture, and values first among the commercial classes and then among the ruling élite in sub-Saharan Africa. A second wave of Islamization of the Western Sudan occurred in the eleventh century, with the rise of the Almoravids, a Berber reformist religious movement whose spirit survived for centuries until the nineteenth-century holy wars (*jihads*). The emergence in the ninth century of the first major North African states—such as the kingdoms of Fès, Tahert, Tlemcen, and Qayrawan—is closely linked with the development of the gold trade originating in the Western Sudan (empire of Ghana, then Mali). This trade—gold being exchanged for the salt and copper of the Saharan mines (Taghaza, Tawdeni, and Takkeda)—became a major source of revenue and wealth for the states of the Maghreb acting as intermediaries between sub-Saharan Africa and North Africa and Europe. Thus the Western Sudan became progressively integrated into the Muslim world not by force (there was no Arab conquest of the area) but through commercial and cultural contacts.[3] After the rise of Islam, there emerged on the East African coast and in the Indian Ocean a vast commercial network controlled by Muslims, mostly Arabs and Persians. After the Fatimids of Egypt began to develop their commercial relations with the Indian Ocean, East African coastal settlements—such as Lamu, Mombasa, Zanzibar, and Sofala—played an increasingly important role in this commercial network. Thus Islamic religion and culture progressively fused with indigenous African culture, leading to the emergence and blossoming of the Swahili culture in the next centuries. From the tenth century on began a new period of Islamic penetration of Ethiopia by Muslim merchants that led to the foundation of the first Muslim states in southern Ethiopia. Thus, in the first five centuries of the Islamic era, many regions of Africa had come, directly or indirectly, under the influence of the new Islamic empire.

Finally, it is important to remember that the accounts of Muslim Arab scholars who travelled to the states of the Western Sudan between the ninth and the fourteenth century—such as Al Bekri, Ibn Battuta, and Ibn Khaldûn—constitute an essential and unique source of information about these kingdoms and empires.[4] However, Zakari Dramani-Issifou rightly cautions against the biases inherent in the accounts of the Arab (and other foreign) scholar-travelers. These biases—coupled with an insufficient knowledge of African culture and traditions—have sometimes led to an insidious "Arabization" and "Islamization" of African history, as well as to a "genealogical snobbery" whereby the only noble origins were deemed to be those of the East, preferably related to the Prophet, his family, or his companions. The pitfalls of African historiography are accurately identified by Dramani-Issifou:

> The oral transmission of their [African cultures and societies] knowledge, the implicit nature of their rich and ancient cultural life, means that factual evidence concerning them is often derived from external sources; in this instance, the evidence comes from Arab historiography which is marred by prejudice and by ideological assumptions which must be identified and clarified. If this is not done, there is once again the risk that the history of Africa will seem to be a history without any inherent originality and will appear, for a long period of time, as an "object-history," the history of a land that was conquered, exploited and civilized.[5]

In this sense, one could argue—following Élikia M'Bokolo—that the history of the Islamization of Africa from a distinctly African perspective is still in its infancy.[6]

Islam proclaims the equality of men and women. The Prophet Muhammad proclaimed that "women are fully men's sisters before the law." In law, Muslim women have enjoyed a legal status far superior to that enjoyed by women in other religious systems but equal to that enjoyed by women in indigenous African societies (such as Ancient Egypt and Kush). As was the rule in those societies, Muslim women have always had the right to initiate legal proceedings without referring to their husbands and administer their property independently of them. It is the husband (rather than the woman) who is required to pay the bride a certain sum and give her certain gifts—which become the wife's personal property—as dowry.[7] Some chronicles indicate that wealthy women traders formed part of the elite of Timbuktu and that the famous Sankore mosque (renown throughout the Muslim world) was built by one of them—a very wealthy and prominent Tuareg (Berber) woman.[8]

By 715, the Arab state (the Caliphate) comprised a vast territory that became the core of the Islamic world. Under the Umayyads, the Arabs formed the exclusive ruling class, and Muslim Arabs were exempted from paying taxes while all non-Muslims were subject to taxation. Unable to cope with the complex administrative problems arising from the continuing expansion of the empire, the Arabs adopted the administrative systems already existing in the provinces and left their running in the hands of the converted indigenous people. The contradictions resulting from the monopoly of political and economic power by the Arab ruling class while the indigenous minority (even though it was Muslim) was excluded led to a crisis that ended in the fall of the Umayyads and the rise to power of a new dynasty, the Abbasids, centered in Iraq. The Abbasid revolution was engineered by all the non-Arab Muslims, who claimed their fair share in the community; it inaugurated an Islamic empire in which Arabs lost their privileged status and in which distinctions followed religious (rather than national) lines. However, Arabic continued to be the language of the state, arts, sciences, and literature employed widely by the non-Arab—including African—peoples. In political terms, the end of the eleventh century heralded the definitive preponderance of the Berbers—Almoravids and Almohads—in North Africa. By the end of the century, the Fatimids had lost their Maghreban provinces but retained their hold on Egypt. Between the tenth and eleven centuries, the Indian Ocean trade shifted gradually to the Red Sea, to the benefit of Egypt, which became, for many years to come, the main center of the transit trade between the Mediterranean and the Indian Ocean.[9]

Islam is a missionary religion according to which the spreading of the truth and the conversion of "unbelievers" were considered a duty by the founder of the religion and the whole community. Ideologically, Islam discourages compulsory conversion. Islamic political theory requires control of the polity for the Muslims, but it does not require bringing every subject of the Muslim state into the fold. The Muslims were more interested in incorporating non-Muslims into the Islamic state than in their immediate conversion. Thus, while conversion was desirable from a religious point of view, it was not necessary from a political point of view. Over time, the Arab conquest resulted in the Islamization of the majority of the North African population. "The rule of Muslim Arabs created political, religious, social and cultural conditions that favored conversions to the religion of the politically dominant group without there being any need to employ force."[10]

ISLAMIZATION OF STATES AND SOCIETIES
OF THE WESTERN AND CENTRAL SUDAN
(EIGHTH TO EIGHTEENTH CENTURY)

The Islamization of sub-Saharan Africa was not the result of external conquest by Muslim invaders; rather, it was due to the influence of Muslim Arab merchants. The conquest of African societies by local Islamized states was a significant factor only in the Lake Chad region and in southern Ethiopia.

From the eighth century on, Ibadi merchants from Tahert, Wargla, and southern Tunisia traveled to various Western Sudanese towns such as Ghana, Gao, Awdaghost, Tadmekka, Ghayaru, Zafunu, and Kugha. The Kharidjites of the Sufri sect were ruling Sidjilmasa, one of the most important northern termini of the caravan trade until the tenth century. The Ibadite dynasty of the Banu Khattab in Zawila (in the Fezzan) dominated the northern end of the important trade route from Libya to the Lake Chad Basin. Thus one may safely assume that the centuries-long presence and missionary activities of these merchants in the most important Western Sudanese centers exercised a profound religious influence on the local people, with the local traders—such as the Dyula, the Soninke, the Hausa, and the Dyakhanke—being the first converts to Islam. In general, this early Islam in the Western Sudan was of a "mixed" nature and contained many elements of various pre-Islamic faiths, including remnants from Berber and other indigenous African religions.

Islam as a religion born in the commercial society of Mecca provides a set of ethical and practical rules closely related to business activities. This moral code helped to regulate and control commercial relationships and constituted a unifying ideology among the members of different ethnic groups, thus helping to guarantee security and credit, two of the main requirements of long-distance trade.[11] This situation is well captured by A. G. Hopkins: "The 'blueprint' for the formation of a moral community of businessmen was provided by Islam, which was closely associated with long distance trade in West Africa from the eighth century onwards. Islam helped maintain the identity of members of a network or firm who were scattered over a wide area, and often in foreign countries; it enabled traders to recognize, and hence to deal readily with, each other; and it provided moral and ritual sanctions to enforce a code of conduct which made trust and credit possible."[12] Thus Islam in West Africa first appeared not as mass conversion in a broad area but rather in a series of urban commercial and political centers while the peasant majority in the countryside was barely influenced by the religion. Since its emergence in West Africa, Islam has always had to contend with non-Islamic customs and practices. For most converts, the acceptance of the new religion had never meant a complete abandonment of beliefs, practices, and rituals associated with indigenous African religion. As El Fasi and Hrbek cogently put it, "In fact, many accepted Islam because early Muslim leaders were liberal in their interpretation of what constituted the profession of Islam and were therefore very tolerant of some non-Islamic practices."[13]

After the merchants, the second social groups in West Africa to be converted to Islam were the rulers and sections of the aristocracy or ruling elite. The first ruler in the Western Sudan to become Muslim—even before the rise of the Almoravid in the 1030s—was War-Dyabe (d. 1040) of the Soninke kingdom of Takrur on the lower Senegal. According to Al-Bakri, in Gao, Dya Kosoy adopted Islam around 1009; however, Islamic influence in Gao (originating in Tahert) has been traced as far back as 776–83. Al-Bakri also clearly shows that while Islam was the official royal religion, the majority of the population continued to adhere to indigenous African beliefs, and court ceremony—as in other Western Sudanese states—remained essentially traditional.[14] Similarly, the king, royal family, and court of one of the earlier chiefdoms of the Maninka, Malal, converted to Islam early (definitely before 1068) while the rest of the people continued to adhere to their indigenous beliefs. In the Central Sudan, the first ruler to convert to Islam was the *mais* of Kanem in the eleventh century. That century witnessed the spread of Islam in the Western and Central Sudan. From the lower Senegal to the shores of Lake Chad, Islam was adopted by various chiefs, kings, and emperors, thus gaining official status in a number of African states and societies. The eleventh century also saw the conversion to Islam of Ghana, the most powerful of the Western Sudanese states at that time.[15]

According to Nehemia Levtzion, two major trends—typified by Gao and Takrur—dominated the development of Islam in West Africa between the tenth and nineteenth centuries: "The kings of Gao and Takrur set the example for two trends in the development of Islam in West Africa: that of a symbiotic relationship between Islam and the traditional religion represented by Gao, as against the militant Islam of Takrur, which aimed at the imposition of the new religion in all its vigorousness, forcing the subjects to adopt Islam . . . and waging the holy war against the infidels."[16] Recent historical research reveals that rather than being conquered by the Almoravids as was previously thought, the Soninke of Ghana in fact maintained friendly relations with them, became their allies, and were peacefully persuaded by them to adopt Sunni Islam as the official religion of the Ghana Empire. The most important achievement of the Almoravid intervention (1076–77) was undoubtedly the conversion of the king and his court.[17] Furthermore, the Islamized Maninka and Soninke merchants—respectively referred to as *Wangara* and *Wakoré* in the Arabic sources—gradually established their commercial network in the Sahel and south of it, toward the tropical forest. Thus they in fact substantially helped to spread Islam to non-Muslim parts of the Western and Central Sudan where neither Arabs nor Berbers ever penetrated. The Diakhanke Soninke of Dyakhaba adopted the Maninka language and developed a closely knit community in which religious and commercial activities went hand in hand. Other southern traders of Soninke origin who adopted the Maninka language were the Dyula, as well as the Marka of the Niger Bend.

In the Mali Empire, the Islamization of the rulers occurred at the end of the thirteenth century among the ruling clan of the Kéïta founded by Sundiata Kéïta (1217–55). Sundiata's son and successor, Mansa Uli, performed the pilgrimage to Mecca. Under his rule, Mali expanded and took control of the trading towns of Walata, Timbuktu, and Gao. The Islamic character of the empire was strengthened in the fourteenth century under Mansa Musa (1312–37) and his brother Mansa Suleyman (1341–60), who encouraged the building of mosques and the development of Islamic learning. The general security prevailing during the heyday of the Mali Empire was favorable to the expansion of trade in the Western Sudan.[18]

An important development was the emergence and growth of a local clerical class (*ulama*) in the main political and commercial towns such as Jenne,

Timbuktu, and Gao. Until the sixteenth century, the majority of Muslim scholars in Jenne and Timbuktu—many of them world-renowned experts in Islamic science—were Sudanese, who also held senior public offices. Among the most prominent Timbuktu scholars specializing in jurisprudence, philosophy, and theology were Mahmud ben Omar Aqit (1463–1548), Muhammad Bagayokho (1523–94) and his brother Ahmad, Mahmud Kati, and Ahmed Baba (d. 1627). As El Fasi and Hrbek point out, this was an important factor in the indigenization of Islam in Africa: "The establishment of a class of learned Muslim scholars and clerics of Sudanese origin was an important event in the history of Islam in Africa south of the Sahara. It meant that from then on Islam was propagated and spread by autochthons armed with the knowledge of local languages, customs and beliefs . . . In the eyes of the Africans Islam ceased to be the religion of white expatriates and, because it was now carried by Africans themselves, it became an African religion."[19]

The factors that led to the progressive Islamization of the states and societies of the Western and Central Sudan are both internal and external. Externally, since the economic function of these empires was the control and exploitation of the trade (gold for salt) with North Africa, the ruling class had a vested interest in adopting Islam in order to establish and maintain good relations with its North African clients and partners. Internally, the dilemma of the Islamized ruling dynasty was to secure the allegiance of clans and peoples still governed by indigenous African values and beliefs. As noted by El Fasi and Hrbek, "a universal religion such as Islam seemed to offer a suitable solution; an effort was made to implant it at least among the heads of other lineages and clans and to establish a new common religious bond."[20] Thus in order to be recognized as legitimate in the eyes of their people and maintain their people's loyalty, the Western Sudanese rulers had to acknowledge the local traditions, customs, and beliefs of the majority of their non-Muslim subjects who traditionally looked up to them as intermediaries with their ancestors; the leaders thus did not have the political power to enforce Islam or Islamic law. This helps explain the numerous indigenous rituals and ceremonies observed by Arab travelers at the courts of Muslim emperors like the *mansas* of Mali and the *askiyas* of Songhay—men who were commonly considered to be devout Muslims.

In Hausaland in the Central Sudan (extending from northern Nigeria to the Lake Chad Basin) under the reign of Sarki Yaji of Kano (1349–85), Wangarawa and Fulbe (Fulani) missionaries came from Mali bringing the Muslim religion. By the second half of the fifteenth century, a strong Islamic tradition was established in the cities (and major trading centers) of Zaria, Katsina, and Kano. Islam at that time was not generally accepted and was still infused with many local customs and practices: "It [Islam] became the religion of small communities of traders and professional clerics; the court circles were influenced superficially, whereas the masses of people continued in their traditional beliefs. But gradually Islamic concepts and attitudes became more pervasive creating a situation of 'mixed' Islam."[21] The Hausa traders became—after the Dyula—the second most active commercial class and a main vector of the spread of Islam in Central and Western Sudan. By the sixteenth century, the position of Islam had been further improved by the policies of Askya Muhammad Toure of Songhay as well as the exodus of the *mais* from Kanem to Bornu and the long rule of Idris Alaoma. In the same century, both Bagirmi and Wadai became Muslim states. After having resisted the spread of Islam for centuries—including Askya Muhammad Toure's *jihad* of 1498–99 against them—the Mossi people of the Niger Bend only started to be penetrated by Muslim merchants (Yarse) after the seventeenth century, and it was only in the nineteenth century that some Mossi were converted. After the decline of the Mali Empire in the fifteenth century, the Maninka lived in small *kafu* (chiefdoms) without central administration and without urban life while the Bambara formed an island of indigenous religion. Islam was then abandoned by the political class and was only represented by the traders (Dyula) or the clerics (*moriba*).[22]

By the sixteenth century, Islam was firmly established in the Western and Central Sudan, from Senegal to the Lake Chad Basin. The ruling classes of all the states of the region—large and small—were at least nominally Muslim. In all the towns and in many villages of the area lived communities of African Muslims of various ethnic origins, traders and clerics with a broad outlook and in contact with Muslim states and communities in North Africa. Although the majority of African peasants remained untouched by this universal religion, Islam had become, after so many centuries, part and parcel of the culture and society of West Africa.[23]

The period from the seventh to the sixteenth century saw the progressive Islamization of the states and societies of North Africa, the Western and Central Sudan, Ethiopia and Somalia, the East African coastal areas, and the Indian Ocean islands. With the exception of North Africa—where it was the result of Arab conquest—Islam was spread peacefully by first Arab then Berber and other indigenous African traders. As a result, Islam was an essentially urban phenomenon found in all the (major and minor) commercial and political centers. Islam was adopted by the merchant classes as well as by the rulers, ruling elites, and aristocracy of all the states and societies of these regions; it also gave rise to a cosmopolitan class of Muslim clerics and scholars (*ulamas*). However, the rural areas and the majority of the population (mostly peasants) remained largely untouched by the new religion and continued to adhere to their indigenous African beliefs.

Islam as a religion and way of life is one of the fundamental aspects of African civilization. According to the Quran, all Muslims belong to the same community (*umma*) characterized by fraternal solidarity among believers who are all "brothers" and duty-bound to adhere to an ethical code of conduct characterized by justice, hospitality, generosity, and honor; the *zakal* (alms for the poor and orphans) is one of the five pillars of Islam. This spirit of community is clearly compatible with indigenous African values, culture, and tradition, such as giving the greeting of peace to members of the community and strangers alike or giving alms to the poor and food to the hungry. It must be noted that the act of embracing Islam is an individual one, but it is also an irreversible one. As noted by Zakari Dramani-Issifou, "it is a *social* conversion which denotes the act of joining a community of a new type and severing links with other types of socio-cultural community. This is a fundamental point at issue for the relations between the Muslim world and the societies and cultures of Africa."[24] Islamic law (*shari'a*) includes the Quranic prescriptions supplemented by the rules of jurisprudence. Historically and geographically, two different Islamic legal schools of jurisprudence prevailed in different regions of Africa. The west (Maghreb and Western Sudan) was, from the eleventh century onwards, deeply (and almost exclusively) influenced by the more formal and intransigent Maliki school (Malikism), while the more liberal Shafi'ism was generally predominant in Egypt, the Horn of Africa, and on the East African coast. In the eleventh century, Islam developed in two directions that had a profound influence on the relations between Islam and African societies. On the one hand, Sunnism tended to impose, through the law, uniformity on the authority of the state, education, and a single Muslim rite. On the other hand, mystic currents of thought—Sufism—sought to express religious feeling through asceticism and rejection of the world. In the twelfth century, Sufi brotherhoods—such as the Kadiriyya and the Shadhiliyya—began to appear, notably in Morocco. Sunnism (which was dominated by Malikism) made the Muslim community more intransigent in its dealings with African cultural traditions. Conversely, Sufism successfully spread the cult of holy men, which took on the role of healers and diviners, thus Islamizing some very ancient aspects of the culture and daily life of Africans. Thus developed first in the Maghreb and then (particularly after the seventeenth century) in West Africa the character of the *marabout*, a cleric and learned scholar of Islam also acting as a magician, healer, and (more important) a living intermediary between mere mortals and Prophet Muhammad, who is in direct contact with God. The emulation of the Arab religious and cultural model posed a real danger to African societies; should Africans renounce their culture and traditions and adopt Arab culture and values instead? In other words, could Islamization lead to Arabization? According to Dramani-Issifou, the process whereby Islam became established as a social system in Africa has its own, unique dynamics: "It was a meeting between peoples, cultures and societies of different traditions, a meeting the results of which depended on the extent to which each side was able to distinguish between what was merely cultural and what was of general religious significance, and this was ultimately a question of the permeability of African societies and cultures, which were in no sense passive, to the new influences that came from the east."[25]

In North Africa, the Berbers tenaciously struggled against certain forms of Islamization; they were able for a long time to retain some of their indigenous traditions as well as a certain linguistic autonomy. Thus, in certain tribes of Kabylia or the Atlas, the Berbers preserved their language and their customs. Furthermore, Berber law is characterized by customary law, as exemplified by the collective oath as a means of proof as well as the administration of justice by judge-arbiters or village assemblies. In fact, some of these features were reflected in the organization of the Almohad Empire. After the major confrontation of the eighth century between Arabs and Berbers, the strategically vital process of territorial and political integration of the latter into the House of Islam (*Dar al-Islam*) was complete. As the case of the Ibadites demonstrates, relations between Saharan Berbers and sub-Saharan Africans were excellent; these relations were characterized by genuine mutual religious tolerance, as well as by open-mindedness and understanding toward indigenous African cultural and social practices. The introduction of the Muslim social system into indigenous African societies was a very long and gradual process, as the case of the gold miners and blacksmiths clearly shows. In the empires of Ghana and Mali, the numerous producers of gold and iron did not convert to Islam, continued to practice indigenous religion and magical rites, and were exempted from the tax that was imposed on the nonbelievers. In Takrur, Ghana, and Mali, ironworkers became progressively divorced from the ruling elite and lost their political influence; they were feared on account of their economic and magical powers, and they gradually formed a group hemmed in by prohibitions that became socially isolated. This led, in the eighteenth century, to the emergence of the socially exclusive concept of "caste." Thus the reasons for the non-conversion to Islam of the gold miners and blacksmiths of West Africa their activities were necessary for the economic prosperity of the states, and their religious and magical powers were an essential source of power, authority, and legitimacy for the Western Sudanese rulers.[26]

The sub-Saharan African societies that were penetrated by Islam were essentially agrarian cultures based on oral tradition; they had functional links with the land and all the constituent elements of their natural environment (such as air, water, and minerals). While in the Arabo-Islamic world the keystone of the social structure was the nuclear family—man, wife, and children—the extended family, consisting of the descendants of a common ancestor bound together by kinship and territorial ties, was the basic component of indigenous African societies. In addition, African indigenous societies had a holistic concept of culture and religion according to which all the constituent elements of the culture, religion, and society were interlinked and constituted a whole whose elements could not be dissociated without destroying the entire balance of their life. Communal bonds were shared by all their ancestors, the living, and the unborn children in an unbroken generational chain in perfect harmony (and in a sacred bond) with their natural environment (the soil, the bush, the waters), which provided food and was the object of worship. In general, the African retained his or her vision of the world as a vast confrontation of (natural and supernatural) forces that were to be exploited or exorcised. Cheikh Anta Diop notes that there is a metaphysical convergence between indigenous African beliefs and the Muslim faith. Both believe in the existence of an "invisible world"—peopled by various types of genies—which duplicates the real world. This dual conception of the world is common to both religions. This, Diop argues, explains why Africans so easily and comfortably fit into the Islamic faith.[27]

The Arab Muslim conception of nuclear family and urban wealth con-
flicted with the indigenous African conception of community of land, work,
and harvests, however. While among the Arab people, Islamic law was based
on the patrilineal family, indigenous African societies were essential matrilineal: descent was traced through the female ancestors, and the mother/
woman played an essential role in the transmission of property. The pressure to change the matrilineal rules of succession in favor of the patrilineal
practices imposed by the Quran was a cause of extreme tension between
indigenous African law and Islamic law. From a social point of view, the Africanization of Muslim names marked a simple and gradual transfer from the
indigenous African community to the Muslim community (*umma*). Thus, in
the Western Sudan, Muhammad became Mamadu. African and Islamic moral
values also came in conflict with regard to the behavior and customs of African women. What was considered "immoral" by the Arab-Muslim travelers—
the laxity in the behavior of women, the nudity of adolescent girls, the failure
of women to wear the veil—was seen as perfectly normal in African culture
and society. This leads Dramani-Issifou to the (somewhat exaggerated and
possibly flawed) conclusion that "at all these levels underlying their respective and hardly compatible forms of organization, the differences between
Arab-Muslim societies and African societies, whether they were Muslim or
otherwise, remained un-reconciled between the twelfth and the seventeenth
centuries. They no doubt tended to see these opposing forms of social life
as indicating an incompatibility between Islam and African religion."[28] A
point of convergence between indigenous African and Islamic sociocultural
customs is constituted by the age-grades and essential rites of passage from
childhood to adulthood in indigenous African societies and the "ceremony
of the turban"—whereby a young adolescent becomes a responsible member
of the Muslim community—in Muslim societies.[29]

In the Western Sudan (as in Takrur and Mali from the tenth century), *Dar
al-Islam* coexisted with *Dar al-Kafr* (the land of the nonbelievers, or infidels). In the former, administrators appointed by the African leaders resided
in the urban centers, while in the second, the peasant majority constituted a
source of agricultural labor whose conversion was not considered essential or
urgent. Sub-Saharan African rulers and their Muslim advisers attempted to
achieve political and social integration on the Islamic model. As the case of
the conversion of a king of Malal in the eleventh century—as recounted by
al-Bakri and al-Dardjini—clearly illustrates, the exercise of political power by
the leader was based on indigenous religion and the consent of the people.
Acting in accordance with indigenous African political tradition and practices, the king of Malal, the ruling clan, and the aristocracy—but not the
commoners and peasants—adopted Islam after a drought in order to obtain
of the God of the Muslims (acting as a substitute for the God of the Ancestors) the rain that was necessary for the survival of his people. According to
Dramani-Issifou, the price of the conversion was a heavy one: "the destruction of all the instruments of the ancestral religion; the hounding of sorcerers,

the devastation of age-old traditions. The response of the people was unexpected: 'we are your servants, do not change our religion!'"[30]

This example shows that the African leaders borrowed from Muslim society—which, like indigenous African religion, believed in a single God—what was convenient for the effective administration of their kingdoms and helped them sustain their legitimacy and consolidate their power; it also demonstrates that these experiments in "modernization" constituted a series of attempts to establish a balance between indigenous African traditions and the requirements of Islam.[31] There is also some evidence that the Islamized chiefs and kings found themselves in a delicate position between an influential, urban Muslim minority and the majority of the people (commoners and peasants) steeped in indigenous religion. As Levtzion rightly observes, "They [Islamized kings] were thus obliged to hold a middle position between Islam and the traditional religion; they were neither real Muslims nor complete pagans. From this middle position some chiefs or dynasties might turn towards the true Islam, while others might fall back to regain closer relations with their traditional religion."[32]

In the Western Sudan, the empire of Mali became a major economic, political, and diplomatic power in the fourteenth century, when Islam triumphed. According to Joseph Ki-Zerbo, "as a devout Muslim [Emperor Kanku Musa] expanded the influence of Islam. His brand of Islam incorporated elements of indigenous beliefs and magical rites imported from Arab countries. Furthermore, the peasant masses continued to adhere to their indigenous beliefs, and this was tolerated by the emperor in exchange for their loyalty and their taxes."[33] However, Islam significantly contributed to maintaining the cohesion (and thus the unity) of the vast, multiethnic Mali Empire. In Songhay, Askiya Muhammad Ture, who succeeded Sonni Ali Ber in 1493 by means of a *coup d'état* and ruled until 1528, acted as both a religious and secular leader and endeavored to achieve political and social integration according to the precepts of the Quran. With the support of the "Muslim party" (Timbuktu Muslim scholars), he made the pilgrimage to Mecca in 1496 and was invested with the title of caliph (*khalifa*) with spiritual authority over the whole Western Sudan. He proceeded to introduce Islamic values into the society as well as Islamic principles and rules of governance. Almost all the ministers of state, provincial governors, army commanders, and judges were Muslims. The emperor relied almost entirely on the advice of prominent Muslim scholars in matters relating to the administration of the empire. At the request of the *askiya*, one of them, Al-Maghili, wrote a kind of handbook of the perfect Muslim prince.[34] According to Dramani-Issifou, however, Askiya Muhammad Ture was no more successful than the emperors of Mali who had preceded him "in distancing himself from the African traditions which enjoined him to retain the ancestral attributes inherited from the time of the Shi: a drum, sacred fire, precise regulations concerning dress, hairstyle, regalia, the catching of the ruler's spittle, the existence in the higher administration of the *Hori farima*, in other words the high priest of the worship of ancestors and genies."[35]

In Bornu, the rulers (*mai*), traditionally regarded as true living gods, filled their courts with learned Muslim clerics. Islamic justice was dispensed by the Muslim judges (*kadi*) only in the urban areas, while indigenous African law continued to be administered to the African majority in the country. Muslim scholars—such as Muhammad Bagayokho, Mahmud Kati, and Ahmed Baba of Timbuktu—belonged to a very small intellectual elite thinking and writing in Arabic and facing a mass of believers in African indigenous religion, whom they considered themselves duty-bound to convert to Islam. It was under the rule of the Soninke leader Sonni Ali Ber (1464–92) that the sharpest conflict between Islam and indigenous African traditions and beliefs occurred. Sonni Ali Ber was a master of the southern Songhay religion of *holé*; he was also *dâli*, a master geomancer with strong powers of divination and a reputation for invincibility in battle. The "emperor-magician"—as Sonni Ali was known—could thus predict the future; he was master of the present and the acknowledged religious leader of his community, which he was able to protect through his *korté* (magical charms).[36] This explains why Sonni Ali could not bear to see his supernatural powers, recognized by the majority of his subjects who adhered to indigenous African beliefs, challenged by the (mostly foreign) Muslim scholars of Timbuktu; this group led the wealthy, cosmopolitan, Muslim urban populations of that city and others (such as Jenne and Walata) to act as independent merchant republics. The reign of Sonni Ali Ber was marked by the bringing into line of Timbuktu, the supremacy of Gao, and the revival of African indigenous religion against Islam. Apart from two brief interludes that witnessed a revival of Islam—the reigns of Askiya Muhammad I (1493–1528) and Askiya Dawud (1549–82)—the end of the sixteenth century was marked by the Moroccan conquest (1591), the collapse of the political system and institutions of the empire, the disorganization of the society, and the decline of the urban centers. Popular resistance to the Moroccan invasion in the last decade of the sixteenth century took the form of small, independent states that abandoned Islam and reverted to African indigenous religion, most notably the *Songnanke* cult (magician-healers) in Dendi (southwestern Songhay). The Moroccan occupation and the subsequent disintegration of the Songhay state created a political vacuum and social and religious disarray that eventually led, during the late seventeenth century, to the emergence of the Bamana kingdom of Segu (1712–1860), whose leaders and people exclusively adhered to indigenous African beliefs. Bamana religion (*Batair*) was expressed through rituals in age-sets and secret societies, whose members served as intermediaries between the spiritual and temporal worlds.[37]

Between the eleventh and eighteenth centuries, elements of the Islamic religion, culture, and values became progressively fused with indigenous African religion, culture, and values to produce a mixed religion retaining aspects of both. This process may rightly be described as the Africanization of Islam. The conversion of the African rulers and ruling elite to Islam was not always heartfelt, deep, and unconditional; it was essentially a matter of economic and political expediency, and the African leaders retained elements of indigenous values, beliefs, traditions, and decorum in order to ensure the loyalty of their citizens. This process of mutual cross-fertilization of Islamic religion and culture with indigenous African religion and culture is well captured by Nehemia Levtzion: "The long, peaceful process of the Islamization of Africa was paralleled by the Africanization of Islam; Islam was integrated into African societies, and though foreign in origin it became one of the African religions. While winning over converts, Islam also assimilated African traditional elements."[38]

IBN KHALDÛN'S CONCEPTION OF POLITICAL POWER AND THE STATE: 'ASABÎYAH

'Abd-ar-Rahmân Abu Zayd ibn Muhammad ibn Muhammad ibn Khaldûn al-Hadrami—commonly known as Ibn Khaldûn—hailed from an aristocratic Muslim Yemeni family of mixed Arab and Berber ancestry originally settled in Andalusia (Southern Spain) and that later emigrated to Tunis, where Ibn Khaldûn was born in 1332. Ibn Khaldûn was steeped in the Mediterranean culture of the fourteenth century, at the intersection of African, Berber, Christian, Jewish, and Muslim influences. Having received a broad education from the best scholars of the time in Islamic law and jurisprudence, as well as in Arab philology and literature, he travelled widely throughout North Africa and the Western Sudan and rose to high positions in government, law, and academia in Tunisia, Morocco, Algeria, Spain, and Egypt, eventually becoming Chief Malakite Judge and lecturer at Al-Azhar University in Cairo, where he died in 1406. From his privileged vantage point as a philosopher-statesman directly involved in the turbulent politics of Medieval North Africa as soldier, diplomat, minister, or adviser, Ibn Khaldûn was in a unique position to not only observe and analyze but also influence events. His prolific scholarship reflected an encyclopedic knowledge of history, anthropology, sociology, geography, economics, jurisprudence, and politics. His *magnum opus*, titled the *Muqaddimah* (1377), was hailed by British historian Arnold Toynbee as "undoubtedly the greatest work of its kind that has ever yet been created by any mind in any time or place."[39] N. J. Dawood puts it best: "The *Muqaddimah* . . . can be regarded as the earliest attempt made by any historian to discover a pattern in the changes that occur in man's political and social organization. Rational in its approach, analytical in its method, encyclopedic in detail . . . and seeking, beyond the mere chronicle of events, an explanation—and hence a philosophy—of history."[40] Indeed, many contemporary scholars—such as Yves Lacoste—consider Ibn Khaldûn to be the founding father of the scientific study of the social sciences in general and of history in particular. Ibn Khaldûn anticipated critical themes in modern political thought. To the extent that he turned from considering how things ought to be to studying states and societies as they really are, he may also be considered to be the founding father of political realism. Two centuries before Hobbes, he located the vital force of human behavior and thus society in passions, not reason. Although Ibn Khaldûn's philosophy of history was grounded in material-empirical reality, it also embraced political philosophy and religion. His thought thus represents a unique instance in the transition from classical to modern theory.[41]

Ibn Khaldûn's conception of historical evolution fundamentally opposes two main social groups: nomads and sedentary people. Because they are endowed with *'asabîyah*—which enables the tribal chief to build an empire— only nomadic societies can evolve into states. The author's concept of *umran* (loosely translated as "civilization") is heuristic and includes all the dimensions—political, economic, social, and cultural—of human activity. Ibn Khaldûn introduces a fundamental distinction here between *umran badawi* (nomadic, desert, or rural life) and *umran hadari* (sedentary, urban life). In the author's view of historical evolution, the first (or "primitive") stage gradually and naturally leads to the last (and more advanced) stage of social and political development.

In the *Muqaddimah*, Ibn Khaldûn explains the rise and fall of civilizations and states in medieval North Africa by resorting to the concept of *'asabîyah*, variously translated as "social solidarity," "group feeling" or "group consciousness." Tunisian scholar Mohammed Talbi defines *'asabîyah* as "at one and the same time the cohesive force of the group, the conscience that it has of its own specificity and collective aspirations, and the tension that animates it and impels it ineluctably to seek power through conquest."[42] A fairly accurate translation of the concept in modern terms would be "nationalism." As N. J. Dawood has noted, *'asabîyah* refers not only to groups related by common ancestry (clan or tribe): "Politically, the *'asabîyah* can also be shared by people not related to each other by blood ties but by long and close contact as members of a group."[43] *'Asabîyah* arises in simple societies where economies of necessity produce an ethos of community. Political institutions are rudimentary: the leadership of the most able and respected. As the society grows, subgroups appear, loyalties become divided, and the subgroup with the strongest solidarity becomes dominant. Chieftainship turns into kingship. The king consolidates his power through force. National solidarity disappears and decline begins. Decline leads ultimately to the disintegration of state and civilization if not checked by the appearance of a new group with *'asabîyah* (social solidarity). Such a new group is unlikely to rise within the state, however. Rather, a less advanced people with rising *'asabîyah* typically takes over the state and changes its manner of life—albeit temporarily. Eventually they also will generate the same processes that led to the decline of the state they conquered. Note that Ibn Khaldûn rejects the view that former nations were better endowed for achieving a high civilization than contemporary nations. For him, it is merely the decay of political organization and power of government that gives the impression that contemporary civilization is inferior to that of the past.[44]

Ibn Khaldûn's main purpose is to explain the rise and fall of the various civilizations and states that have emerged and disappeared in medieval North Africa. In essence, a tribe is able to build and maintain an empire only if it is endowed with certain social and political characteristics embodied in the concept of *'asabíyah*, which is found exclusively in societies characterized by *umran badawi*. Yet, after assuming power, the leader will progressively steer the society toward *umran hadari*, thus leading to the weakening and eventual disintegration of the state. Thus *'asabíyah* is the main source of energy and the essential driving force of the state. As such, it is a key political concept in Ibn Khaldûn's theory of political power and the state.[45]

THE NINETEENTH-CENTURY ISLAMIC THEOCRATIC STATES IN THE WESTERN SUDAN

The nineteenth century was the great century of Islamic expansion in West Africa. At the dawn of the century, the large and powerful Western Sudanic states had disintegrated and split into a multiplicity a small kingdoms and chiefdoms at war with each other not so much for the purpose of expansion as for the capture of slaves. In this context of extreme social and political fragmentation and relative anarchy, Islam regressed and indigenous African religions became once again dominant, as in the Bamana kingdoms of Segu and Kaarta. As the century progressed, the actual expansion of Islam was achieved by means of the alliance of the military and Muslim clerics. Radical Muslim clerics, reacting against the Western Sudanese accommodation of Islam and indigenous African religion, proclaimed the *jihad* (holy war) and found in the theocratic state a unique means for the attainment of power and the subjection to the state of all the diverse social, regional, and ethnic elements incorporated in their empires.

The core social and ethnic element of this Islamic revivalist movement was primarily Fulani (and secondarily Hausa), and it took the form of an alliance between a military aristocracy and a Muslim clerical class, characterized by many authors as an alliance of the sword and the book. Thus Islam became an agent of social mobilization and a powerful factor of social integration, which undermined the fragile equilibrium and coexistence of the Muslim faith with indigenous African beliefs and traditions. In spite of its derogatory description of indigenous African religion, the following statement by J. Spencer Trimingham perfectly captures the essence of this dilemma: "The transformation which took place in the relations of Islamic and pagan [*sic*] societies constituted a religious, political, and social revolution. The religious change brought about by the nineteenth-century reformers lay in the stress laid on the uniqueness of Islam and its incompatibility with worship within the old cults. The political revolution set in motion by the need to impose the religion upon all societies, Muslim as well as pagan [*sic*], broke the long established social equilibrium."[46]

In the remainder of this chapter, we shall successively (and briefly) examine the theocratic state of the Futa Jalon, 'Usman dan Fodio and the Sokoto caliphate, the Fulani Kingdom of Sheiku Ahmadu and his successors, and the Segu Tukulor Empire of al-Haji 'Umar Tall.

The Theocratic State of the Futa Jalon

Founded in 1725 by *karamoko* Ibrahim Musa, a theocratic state was consolidated during the period from 1760 to 1770 in the Futa Jalon and became firmly established there in 1776 under the rule of *almami* Ibrahim Sori. The state was organized as a confederation of nine provinces, each headed by a Muslim cleric who pledged allegiance to the *almami* (the leader of the prayer) in a feudal type of relationship. As supreme leader, the *almami* was inaugurated in the religious capital (Fugumba) according to Islamic rituals. The *almami* ruled from Timbo (the political capital) assisted by a Council of Elders. The *Futanke* system of governance functioned as a diarchy in which power was alternatively held by two prominent Fulani aristocratic families: the Alfa of Timbo and the Sori of Labe. While dominated by the Fulani, the state was truly multiethnic in nature: the dominant Fulani culture, Islam, as well as economic prosperity and a relative political stability all acted as factors favorable to a high degree of ethnic homogenization and social integration.[47]

'Usman dan Fodio and the Sokoto Caliphate

In 1804–8, 'Usman dan Fodio, a prominent Fulani Muslim cleric and theologian, conducted a successful *jihad* over a vast area including most of Central Sudan that resulted in the creation of the theocratic state of Sokoto. This vast empire incorporated various cultural and ethnic groups—mostly Hausa and Fulani—into a single Islamic community (*umma*) ruled by Islamic law (*shari'a*) and led by a caliph (or *sarkin musulmi*: commander of the faithful) deriving his power from Allah and invested with supreme religious and temporal power and authority. The task of consolidating and organizing the empire fell to 'Usman dan Fodio's son, Muhamad Bello (1817–37). The administration of the empire was highly centralized, with a central government located in the capital, Sokoto (where the caliph resided), and regional governments organized in emirates. Appointed by the caliph, the provincial emirs owed him obedience; every year, they travelled to Sokoto to pay tribute and renew their pledge of allegiance to the caliph, from whom they received specific instructions on matters of governance. The Sokoto caliphate constituted a vast space of economic prosperity, political stability, and social peace and tranquility that survived until the British eventually took control of the area at the end of the nineteenth century.[48]

The Fulani Kingdom of Sheiku Ahmadu and His Successors

In 1818, yet another Fulani Muslim cleric and theologian, Sheiku Ahmadu, invested by the authority of 'Usman dan Fodio, proclaimed the *jihad*, defeated a military coalition of the states of Segu and Masina, and established a theocratic state (*Dina*) in the Central Niger Bend with its capital in Hamdallay. Having assumed the title of *amir al-muminim* (commander of the faithful), Sheiku instituted an ascetic and austere Muslim regime strictly regulated by *shari'a* law and with strict control over the moral behavior and education of citizens. As *amir*, Sheiku ruled over a centralized theocratic state with the assistance of two advisory bodies: a religious council composed of two eminent Muslim clerics and a forty-member council-at-large with combined legislative, executive, and judicial powers. The territorial administration was divided into five units, each led by a military governor (*amiru*) assisted by a religious council, a judicial council, and a technical council. The administration of justice was highly decentralized, and each district had a government-appointed judge (*cadi*). In 1844, Sheiku Ahmadu's son, Ahmadu Sheiku, succeeded his father, and under his austere leadership, the *Dina* continued to prosper under Islamic faith and law. Under its third ruler, Ahmadu Ahmadu (1853–62), the kingdom began to disintegrate as a result of interpersonal rivalries for power, and it was eventually taken over in 1862 by another Fulani Muslim leader, al-Haji 'Umar Tall.[49]

The Segu Tukulor Empire of al-Haji 'Umar Tall

At one and the same time Muslim cleric, theologian, prophet, and statesman, al-Haji 'Umar Tall—who hailed from Fuuta Tooro—built, over a 12-year period (1852–64), a sprawling empire extending from the middle Senegal river to the Niger Bend. 'Umar was appointed caliph of the Tijaniyya for the Western Sudan. Founded in the eighteenth century, the Tijaniyya is a Muslim sect whose egalitarian philosophy and democratic features had broad popular appeal, as opposed to the more aristocratic Qadriyya. Al-Haji 'Umar created a kind of military theocracy. As caliph of the Tijaniyya and *amir al-muminim* (commander of the faithful), he was invested with supreme religious and temporal power and authority. In the administration of the empire, 'Umar strictly adhered to *shari'a* law and was assisted by a council including prominent Muslim clerics as well as some of his brothers. Provincial government was divided between a civilian governor (*pacha*) and a military governor (*bey*). In addition, a well-defended fortress (*tata*) headed by a military commander was built in each province. After his death in 1864, 'Umar was succeeded by his son Ahmadu Sheiku (1864–93), who consolidated the empire and established its capital in Segu. As central power began to disintegrate, the empire progressively split into a number of autonomous provinces under various sons and nephews of 'Umar who paid titular allegiance to Ahmadu. In 1893, the Tukulor Empire eventually succumbed to the relentless military assaults of the French.[50]

The Islamic Theocratic States and Indigenous Beliefs and Institutions in the Western Sudan

The nineteenth-century Islamic revival in the Western Sudan generally took the form of a militant, messianic movement in which a prominent Fulani Muslim cleric/theologian is invested by the highest religious authority with the duty to wage a holy war (*jihad*) against the "infidels" and establish a centralized theocratic state ruled by *shari'a* law. He then acts as supreme leader (caliph or *amir*) with the assistance of some advisory bodies (councils) and a tightly controlled provincial administration. Based on an interpretation of Islam that had broad popular appeal, this movement took the form of a social revolution leading to a truly multiethnic community (*umma*). Thus the social basis of Usman dan Fodio's movement was constituted by the Hausa peasantry revolting against years of exploitation at the hands of a corrupt aristocracy. Similarly, al-Haji 'Umar Tall was able to exploit the contradictions in the non-Muslim African kingdoms—such as the Bamana kingdoms of Segu and Kaarta—to organize a truly multiethnic army composed of Futanke, Tukulor, Bamana, Hausa, and Kanembu contingents.[51]

While the Islamic theocratic states created, during the two decades of the mid-nineteenth century, a space of economic prosperity, political stability, and social peace and tranquility throughout the Western Sudan, they also came in direct conflict with indigenous African beliefs, culture, and tradition. In essence, the novel concept of the Islamic theocratic state collided with indigenous African political systems and institutions, and the two systems could not be reconciled. This particular factor (rather than European penetration) seems to account for the theocratic states' eventual demise; as Trimingham rightly observes, they failed mainly because they were not based on African indigenous values, traditions, and institutions: "Through the nineteenth-century revolution Islam was transformed into a social and political force which ushered in a new age because its relationship to indigenous civilizations was changed . . . The new states foundered, not primarily because they coincided with increasing European penetration, but because they could not transcend the basic African organization of society . . . *These states fell to pieces because they were not based on indigenous institutions.*"[52]

CONCLUSION

Islam as a religion and way of life is one of the fundamental aspects of African civilization. During the "Islamic Age" (i.e., the period from the seventh to the eleventh century), Arabs conquered North Africa (starting with the Maghreb) and the Berbers, who adopted Islam but rejected Arab rule. The Islamization of North Africa led, in the ninth century, to the emergence of a typically Islamic form of governance, the Caliphate, as exemplified by the kingdoms of Fès, Tahert, Tlemcen, and Qayrawan. These North African states developed trade relations (exchanging salt for gold) with states in the Western Sudan. This led, in the eleventh century, to a peaceful Islamization of the ruling elite and aristocracy of the states of the Western and Central Sudan through the agency of Islamized Maninka and Soninke merchants. In addition, at that time, Muslim Berber reformist Sufist movements—such as the Almoravids and the Almohads—spread Islam from Northwest Africa to neighboring areas in the Western Sudan (Takrur and Ghana).

The period from the seventh to the sixteenth century witnessed the progressive Islamization of the states and societies of North Africa, the Western and Central Sudan, Ethiopia, Somalia, the East African coastal areas, and the Indian Ocean islands. In these last two areas, Islam spread through the agency of Arab and Persian Muslim commercial networks and led to the emergence of the Swahili culture (a mixture of Islamic religion and culture with indigenous African culture).

In West Africa, Islam spread mostly to the urban commercial and political centers—such as Jenne, Timbuktu, and Gao—among the ruling elite and aristocracy, and it led to the emergence of a clerical class (*ulama*) in these urban centers. The majority of the people—mostly peasants living in the rural areas—were barely influenced by Islam and remained faithful to their indigenous African beliefs. The success of Islam in Africa is usually attributed to its tolerance of non-Islamic religious beliefs and practices. As a result, Islam in the Western Sudan was very much a *mixed religion* that included elements of the Berber and other indigenous African religions.

This situation raises a fundamental philosophical and existential question: should Africans renounce their culture and traditions and adopt Arab culture and values instead? In other words, could *Islamization* lead to *Arabization*? The available historical evidence shows that from the eleventh to the eighteenth century, a process of *Africanization of Islam* took place. This process of mutual cross-fertilization resulted from a fusion of elements of Islamic religion, culture, and values with elements of indigenous African religion, culture, and values that produced a *mixed religion* retaining aspects of both. The historical record also shows that African leaders borrowed from Muslim society what was convenient for the administration of their kingdoms and helped them sustain their legitimacy and consolidate their power. In fact, the conversion of African leaders was essentially a matter of economic and political expediency. These leaders retained elements of indigenous values, beliefs, traditions, and decorum in order to ensure the loyalty of their citizens.

This chapter also introduced the philosophy of history of the North African scholar Ibn Khaldûn (1332–1406), widely acknowledged as the founding father of the social sciences and, specifically, of history. Ibn Khaldûn identifies two main types of societies: *umran badawi*, characterized by nomadic, rural, and desert life, and *umran hadari*, referring to sedentary, urban life. The author explains the rise and fall of civilizations and states in medieval North Africa by resorting to the concept of *'asabíyah* (i.e., group feeling, or group consciousness). According to Ibn Khaldûn, the inevitable decline and disintegration of states and civilizations allows a less advanced people with a rising *'asabíyah* to take over the state, and the same cycle repeats itself over and over again.

The last section of the chapter focuses on the Islamic theocratic states that emerged in the Western Sudan in the eighteenth and nineteenth centuries: the theocratic state of the Futa Jalon (1725–76); Usman dan Fodio and the Sokoto Caliphate (1808–37); the Fulani kingdom of Sheiku Ahmadu and his successors (1818–62); and the Segu Tukulor Empire of al-Haji 'Umar Tall (1852–93). Nineteenth-century Islamic revival in the Western Sudan took the form of a militant messianic movement in which a prominent Muslim cleric waged a holy war (*jihad*); established a centralized, theocratic state ruled by Islamic (*Shari'a*) law; and acted as an authoritarian supreme leader (caliph or amir) with a tightly controlled provincial administration. In this case, Islam acted as a powerful agent of social mobilization and social integration leading to the creation of a multiethnic community (*umma*). This social revolution led to the creation of a new political entity, the *Islamic theocratic state*, which collided with a preexisting political structure—namely, *indigenous African political systems and institutions*. As Trimingham correctly observed, the two systems could not be reconciled, and the main reason the theocratic states failed is because they were not based on indigenous values, traditions, and institutions.

FURTHER READING

Dramani-Issifou, Z., "Islam as a Social System in Africa since the Seventh Century," in *General History of Africa III*, edited by M. El Fasi and I. Hrbek (Paris: Unesco, 1988), 92–118.

Khaldûn, Ibn, *The Muqaddimah: An Introduction to History*, edited by N. J. Dawood, translated by Franz Rosenthal (Princeton, NJ: Princeton University Press/Bollingen Series, 2005 [1967]).

Levtzion, Nehemia, and Randall L. Pouwels, eds., *The History of Islam in Africa* (Athens, Oxford, and Cape Town: Ohio University Press/James Currey/David Philip, 2000).

Robinson, David, *Muslim Societies in African History* (Cambridge, UK: Cambridge University Press, 2004).

Trimingham, J. Spencer, *A History of Islam in West Africa* (London: Oxford University Press, 1970).

—⊷◈⊶—

CHAPTER 3

AFRICAN THEORIES AND IDEOLOGIES OF WESTERNIZATION, MODERNIZATION, AND LIBERAL DEMOCRACY FROM EARLY WEST AFRICAN NATIONALISM TO HUMANISM

The principles of democracy—freedom of speech . . . , freedom of assembly and association . . . , freedom of the people to choose their governments in general elections, and to change them peacefully; freedom of religion, freedom from arbitrary arrest and imprisonment without trial; the rule of law; guarantees for human rights and civil liberties—all these principles of parliamentary government are universal . . . They can be institutionalized in any culture.

—K. A. Busia, *The Challenge of Africa*, 142

INTRODUCTION

This chapter begins with an overview of the European image of Africa—informed by "social Darwinism"—developed from the sixteenth century onward describing Africa as the "Dark Continent" and Africans as "primitive" and "backward." The European ideas of the Enlightenment entailed a "humanitarian duty" to bring the "blessings of European civilization" to the "backward" areas of the world such as Africa. The chapter then proceeds with an overview of the French colonial policies of assimilation and association and the British colonial policy of "Indirect Rule." The chapter then examines the ideas of the African advocates of westernization, modernization, and liberal democracy. These include some of the early West African nationalists of the late nineteenth century and early twentieth century, mostly Western-educated members of the West African elite such as James B. Africanus Horton, Edward W. Blyden, and Joseph E. Casely Hayford. This is followed by an overview of the political ideas of two prominent mid-twentieth-century moderate African nationalists: K. A. Busia of Ghana and Kenneth Kaunda of Zambia.

IMAGINING AFRICA: EUROPEAN CONSTRUCTION OF AFRICA

From the sixteenth century onward, Europeans created a new image of Africa and Africans: an image consistent with European exploitation of African labor and resources, in general, and their central role in the trans-Atlantic slave trade (1492–1890), in particular. As agents of the European imperial and colonial project in Africa, European explorers, geographers, scientists, missionaries, and political, business, and military leaders engaged in the construction of the African as the "other." As V. Y. Mudimbe succinctly puts it, "This is the discrepancy between 'Civilization' and 'Christianity' on the one hand, 'primitiveness' and 'paganism' on the other, and the means of 'evolution' or 'conversion' from the first stage to the second."[1] In this imagery, Africa is described as the "Dark Continent" or the "Heart of Darkness," and Africans are variously represented as "primitive," "backward," "uncivilized," "pagans," and "irrational." As Kevin Dunn has shown, these colonially scripted images still shape contemporary Western understanding of Africa in general and of the Democratic Republic of the Congo (DRC) in particular.[2] European imperial policy was shaped by social Darwinism, which believed that the intellectual development of Africans was at the same level as that of animals. The real motive for the imperial-colonial project—exploitation of the colony's natural and human resources for the maximum economic profit of the metropolis—was disguised under humanitarian principles—namely, suppressing the slave trade and bringing Christianity and the benefits of Western civilization to the Africans.

THE IDEAS OF THE ENLIGHTENMENT IN FRANCE AND ENGLAND

French Colonial Ideology and Policy: Assimilation and Association

An intellectual movement that emerged in Europe (particularly France and England) in the eighteenth century, the Enlightenment's central idea was the primacy of rational thought, linked to the idea of progress as being both inevitable and universal. Implicit in Enlightenment thinking was a humanitarian duty to bring the blessings of European civilization—presumed to be superior to all others—to all areas of the world, including those still languishing in darkness. As Robert July notes, "As France and England became increasingly involved in West Africa during the nineteenth century, each brought its own ideas, prejudices, national beliefs, religious convictions, philosophic systems, political institutions, economic experiences and other viewpoints distilled from centuries of antecedent activities in Europe. These ideas, which were to have a profound effect on African thought, were essentially similar whether French or English."[3]

France prides itself on being the home of a particularly rich culture and on having a vocation to spread this culture overseas. Stimulated by the universal ideals of the French Revolution of 1789 (i.e., *Liberté, Égalité, Fraternité*: Freedom, Equality, and Brotherhood), this vocation became, in the nineteenth century, a *mission civilisatrice* (civilizing mission), intimately linked with French imperialist expansion and colonialism in Africa. Even after decolonization, France retained its claim to be the center of an international culture and pursue a policy of cultural *rayonnement* (diffusion). Underlying this quest is a belief in the innate value of the French language. But cultural pride has also been mixed with a need to spread the culture beyond France and a claim to share with Africans—via association or assimilation—the ideals of French civilization by imparting to them the essentials of that language and culture. Assimilation and association were the main doctrines that dominated French colonial thought and practice during most of France's imperial rule in Africa (1880 to 1960). The concept of "assimilation" refers to a process by which Africans were to be incorporated into the French nation, taught its language, and indoctrinated in its culture. They were to become French through an acculturation process. In its most extreme form (rarely achieved), assimilation could lead to the granting of French citizenship to colonial peoples.[4] The alternative French colonial policy of "association" recognized the separate cultures and institutions of African peoples and established protectorates over them, as they did for instance in Morocco and Tunisia. Although neither of these doctrines was ever really practiced, they both implied an intimate link between France and its colonies that survives (albeit in a modified form) to this day.[5]

British Colonial Ideology and Policy: Indirect Rule

Contrary to the French, the British were more interested in colonial expansion and economic profit than in any so-called civilizing mission in Africa. As a result, they totally rejected the French policy of assimilation and adopted instead their own version of association, renamed "Indirect Rule" and first conceived and implemented by Lord Lugard in northern Nigeria. According to Michael Crowder, "Indirect Rule was the antithesis of assimilation. Indirect rule was inspired by the belief that the European and African were culturally distinct though not necessarily unequal, and that the institutions of government most suited to the latter were those which he had devised for himself. Therefore, the European colonial powers should govern their African subjects through their own political institutions."[6]

Thus, in the indirect rule system, local government was exercised by indigenous political institutions and, in practice, emphasized the role of the chief in the governance of African peoples. Lord Lugard conceived Indirect Rule as a dynamic system of local government, progressively evolving from the traditional to the modern: "The indigenous political institutions, under the guidance of the resident European political officer, would be continually developing into more efficient units of administration, responding to and adapting themselves to the new situations created by colonial rule."[7]

The Rise of Economic and Political Liberalism and Humanitarianism in Nineteenth-Century Europe

As a result of the Industrial Revolution in Europe—particularly in Britain, France, and Germany—the (commercial and industrial) bourgeoisie became an enthusiastic advocate of the liberal ideas of such classical economists as Adam Smith and John Stuart Mill. Smith and his followers argued that free trade could best lead to increased world production and exchange; urged the abolition of colonies as an expensive impediment to economic expansion; argued for world peace and disarmament as a necessary prerequisite to an international economy of plenty; and demanded a reduction of the role of the state in the economy to the barest minimum necessary for the maintenance of law and order. Gradually translated into action, economic liberalism progressively led to political liberalism. If the state should not interfere with the natural growth of commercial and industrial activities, it followed that the best type of government was a government run in a businesslike manner by commercial and industrial interests and limiting its activities to minimum maintenance of law and order. Soon, economic and political liberalism were joined by a third strand of liberal thought: humanitarianism. An ideology that had survived unchanged from the Age of Enlightenment, humanitarianism was a belief in the innate goodness and perfectibility of man—an appeal to the heart and spirit rather than to rational thought. The ideology of humanitarianism informed the nineteenth-century European missionary movement designed to abolish the slave trade and bring to all the peoples of the world (including Africans) the blessings of Christianity as well as the benefits of the—presumably more advanced—European civilization.[8]

WESTERN LIBERALISM BASED ON AFRICAN CULTURE AND TRADITIONS AS AN IDEOLOGY OF MODERNIZATION IN THE LATE NINETEENTH CENTURY

During the last three decades of the nineteenth century, a small Western-educated West African intellectual elite felt duty-bound to reconcile Western systems of thought with African culture, values, and tradition—Western liberalism with African democracy. As such, they were engaged in an audacious and perilous experiment in political modernization. As Boele van Hensbroek aptly notes, "From a sociological point of view, the educated elite were intermediaries between the Western powers and the indigenous leaders and peoples. They were ambassadors of Christianity and modernization as well as protagonists of African interests."[9] By the end of the nineteenth century, only two pathways to political development remained open to Africans. The first—advocated by Edward W. Blyden—was to reject the utopia of a "modern"

Africa and wholeheartedly embrace African indigenous culture and values. The second—developed by James Africanus Horton, John Mensah Sarbah, and Joseph Casely Hayford—was to accept the ideology of modernization while grounding it in African culture and traditions.[10]

The "African Personality" and "African Regeneration": Edward Wilmot Blyden (1832–1912)

Born in St. Thomas (Virgin Islands) in 1832, Edward Wilmot Blyden was a politician, writer, and diplomat. He was one of the most important nineteenth-century Afro-Caribbean intellectuals and one of the key thinkers in the development of Pan-African ideas. After being refused admission to US colleges in 1850 on racial grounds, Blyden was sent to Liberia—founded by former African American slaves in 1817—by the *American Colonization Society* in 1850–51. After completing his academic studies in a broad range of disciplines, he became an educator and journalist. From 1864 to 1870, he was involved in Liberian politics in various positions, including secretary of state. Because of conflicting views on race and color, he was forced to flee to Sierra Leone in 1871. Blyden eventually returned to Liberia and held various educational and diplomatic appointments. In 1884, he returned to Sierra Leone, where he became involved in Muslim education and journalistic writing until his death in 1912.

Although Blyden's public service was significant, his intellectual contributions were more enduring. He sought to prove that Africans had a noble history and culture, and he opposed theories of white superiority. Although he was a Christian, he was critical of the racial discrimination practiced within Christian churches, challenged the suitability of Christianity for Africa, and defended such African customs as polygamy. Blyden's political thought focused around two key issues: the emergence of an "African personality" and the unity of all African peoples. To promote the first, he favored the use of African names and opposed colonialism, which he (presciently) thought would have a devastating psychological impact. Blyden advocated a modern Africa based on African—rather than European—culture, with higher education and cultural institutions reflecting the priorities and needs of the continent. This emphasis would involve reclaiming the African personality from the degradation of slavery, restoring racial pride, and rediscovering black history. To achieve the unity of African peoples, Blyden hoped for a single major African state that would champion the cause of Africans everywhere and be a focus for their advancement. His original hope was that this African nation would arise from the union of Liberia and Sierra Leone, and he spent some years promoting the repatriation of former slaves in the Americas and the Caribbean. He subsequently adopted the strange position that Western imperialism and colonialism would be transitional and would promote African unity; he even argued that the partition of the continent by the European powers was in the interest of "African Regeneration" and "for the ultimate good of the people." Blyden believed that under British rule, Africans could be educated for self-government.

In general, however, Blyden was much more concerned with cultural rather than political nationalism, and he never provided political leadership either in Africa or elsewhere. Nevertheless, he was one of the key contributors to the ideologies of Pan-Africanism and West African nationalism, and he was one of the first to articulate a notion of "African personality" and the uniqueness of the "African race." His ideas—including support for European imperialism, the "civilizing mission," and the partition of Africa—are clearly rooted in the nineteenth century and place Blyden among those most steeped in Eurocentric thinking. Yet his ideas can be seen as influencing many in the twentieth century, from Marcus Garvey to George Padmore and Kwame Nkrumah.[11]

"African Nationality" and the Fanti Confederation: James Africanus Beale Horton (1835–83)

Physician, scientist, historian, writer, and Pan-Africanist, James Africanus B. Horton has been called "the father of modern African political thought." Born in the British colony of Sierra Leone in 1835, Horton attended Fourah Bay Institute (later College) and then went on to study medicine in Great Britain, graduating from the University of Edinburgh in 1859. He then joined the army medical service and was posted to the Gold Coast (now Ghana). In his numerous writings—most notably, his *West African Countries and Peoples* (1868)—Horton developed his views on African civilization, national development, and independence. Like most nineteenth-century Western-educated Africans, Horton argued that Africa, now opened to Western society, should develop along European lines, utilizing Western education, science, and technology. Horton argued for a substantial degree of African self-reliance and independence from Europe. However, Horton saw African independence primarily in the mastery by Africans of the philosophy and techniques of a European civilization that he considered to be superior to indigenous African societies. The principle of racial equality that he defended rested on his belief in the ability of all races to absorb and utilize with equal facility the greatest achievements that civilized communities had been able to produce through the ages. In *West African Countries and Peoples*, Horton declared that his aim was to develop a "true political science" among West Africans and "prove the capacity of the African for possessing a real political Government and national independence." Horton was thus the first modern African political thinker to openly campaign for self-government for the West African colonies and champion the cause of what he referred to as "African nationality." He combated the racist notion that Africa and Africans were backward and incapable of improvement and pointed to the progress made by former slaves in Sierra Leone. Horton's ideas influenced the institutionalization of the Fanti Confederation—a federal grouping of various Gold Coast ethnic groups—which emerged in 1868 and was based on a written constitution, and they provided a basis for modern patterns of governance in West Africa.[12]

Toward a West African Union: Joseph E. Casely Hayford (1866–1930)

Born in September 1866 in Cape Coast (Gold Coast, now Ghana) within a prominent coastal elite family with European ancestry, Joseph Ephraim Casely Hayford was a writer, lawyer, politician, Pan-Africanist, and a founder of the *National Congress of British West Africa* (NCBWA), one of the first Pan-African organizations on the African continent. He was educated at Fourah Bay College (Sierra Leone) and in Britain (Cambridge and London), where he studied economics and law. Upon returning to the Gold Coast, Casely Hayford immediately entered local politics and became the lawyer for the *Aborigines' Rights Protection Society* (ARPS), taking a leading role in the dispute over the colonial government's attempt to control land. From 1916 to 1925, he served as an appointed member of the Gold Coast Legislative Council (GCLC), and from 1927 until his death (1930), he was an elected member of the GCLC.

Influenced by and building on the ideas and work of James Africanus Horton and Edward Wilmot Blyden, Casely Hayford advocated the development of a regional "West African nationality" and a broader "African nationality," encouraged "race emancipation," and proudly claimed that Africa was the "cradle of civilization." He also advocated the mobilization of people of African descent throughout the world in order to modernize African society while retaining its African character. He also strongly favored the creation of a university in West Africa that might become a center of excellence for students from the region and throughout the African diaspora. Such a university, he argued, must provide an Africanized curriculum so as to promote African culture and overcome the Eurocentrism typical of colonial rule. His proposal for a Gold Coast university was instrumental in the creation of Achimota College in 1927.

Casely Hayford's attempts to achieve the ideal of a "West African nationality" and work toward a "united West Africa" led to the creation, in March 1920, of the NCBWA, which brought together nationalists from Gambia, Nigeria, Ghana, and Sierra Leone, and of which he became first vice-president, then president. Casely Hayford's ideas of West African nationalism had a major influence on African students in Britain and were the guiding ideology of the West African Students' Union (WASU) created in London in 1925 as well as Kwame Nkrumah's West African National Secretariat created in the 1940s. While promoting a West African nationalism that demanded unity and cultural awareness among Africans, Casely Hayford only advocated constitutional political reforms within the framework of British colonialism and the British Empire. His belief that Western education and African traditions and cultural values could be combined led him to advocate reforms of the colonial system rather than self-determination or independence. To that extent, his remained an essentially elitist movement, which failed to enlist the support of either the traditional rulers or the masses in the four British West African colonies.[13]

KOFI A. BUSIA

A Biographical Note

Kofi Abrefa Busia (1914–78) was a scholar as well as a politician. As nationalist leader and prime minister of Ghana (1969–72), he helped to restore civilian government to the country following military rule. He obtained his doctorate in history from Oxford University; his pathbreaking research led to the publication in 1951 of his doctoral dissertation titled *The Position of the Chief in the Modern Political System of Ashanti.* After being appointed the first professor of African Studies at the University of Ghana-Legon in 1949, Dr. K. A. Busia entered politics in 1951 with his election to the Legislative Council; the following year, he became head of the Congress (later United) Party, the main opposition party to Kwame Nkrumah's Convention People's Party (CPP), and, as a result, resigned his university post. Discouraged by Nkrumah's repressive policies toward the opposition, Busia went in voluntary exile in Europe and became professor of sociology in the Netherlands, first at the University of Leiden, then at the Institute of Social Studies at The Hague until 1962. He then became a Fellow at St. Anthony's College, Oxford, until 1966. This marked his most productive years as a scholar, during which he was acknowledged as an outstanding, world-renowned African intellectual. His most significant works included *The Challenge of Africa* (1962) and his work of political philosophy *African in Search of Democracy* (1967). Following Nkrumah's overthrow in 1966, Busia returned to Ghana to serve on the National Liberation Council of General Joseph Ankrah, the military head of state. Busia was elected to parliament in 1969 and became prime minister in the new civilian government. Ironically, Busia resorted to the same repressive measures that he had criticized in Nkrumah's regime. As a result of this and social dissent resulting from a failing economy, Busia was overthrown by General Ignatius Acheampong in 1972 while on a visit to England, where he remained to take up his old position at Oxford University and live peacefully until his death in August 1978.[14]

Liberal Democracy in Africa

In *The Challenge of Africa*, Kofi A. Busia observes that contrary to Africa's indigenous political institutions, which were responsive to the local needs of their communities and in which ordinary people participated in political life, colonial governments were essentially authoritarian in nature: "All colonial governments can be characterized as authoritarian. For a colonial government exists in its own right, by virtue of conquest or power, and its superiority entitles it to demand obedience, which is not derived from the will or the interest of the colonial subjects its rules . . . the essential character of colonial administration is authoritarian. The master commands, the servant must obey."[15]

This explains the authoritarian (even totalitarian) nature of the political systems and institutions of the newly independent African states, including their widespread adoption of one-party systems and a strong executive (but a weak opposition): "All the new nations of Africa have inherited a legacy of authoritarian political structures from their former rulers."[16] More fundamentally, Busia argues that the core principles of liberal democracy are not essentially Western but are universal; as such, they can be institutionalized in any culture, including African culture: "The principles of democracy—freedom of speech . . . , freedom of assembly and association . . . , freedom of the people to choose their governments in general elections, and to change them peacefully; freedom of religion, freedom from arbitrary arrest and imprisonment without trial; the rule of law; guarantees for human rights and civil liberties—all these principles of parliamentary government are universal . . . They can be institutionalized in any culture."[17]

In *Africa in Search of Democracy*, Busia notes that "in traditional African communities, politics and religion were closely associated . . . behind Africa's search for modernization and for new political and social institutions lie an interpretation of the universe which is intensely and pervasively religious."[18] Busia then goes on to identify the major problem of political organization in Africa as the shift in emphasis from ethnic groups based on kinship to the nation-state.[19] He further argues that the various European colonial powers have left a legacy of Western democratic ideas and techniques in Africa and observes that "one of Africa's most intractable problems is how to integrate different tribes [sic] into a modern nation within a democratic framework."[20] Among the institutions he identified as required in a democracy are the party system, the organized opposition, the press, the rule of law, and the independent judiciary.[21] Busia concludes by observing that while democracy "has a moral language which is universal," it nevertheless "reflects the history, the culture, and the values of each country." At its most basic, "democracy is the expression of faith in man's capacity for the progressive extension of freedom and justice in society."[22]

KENNETH D. KAUNDA

A Biographical Note

Kenneth David Kaunda, father of Zambian nationalism and leader of the Frontline States against South African apartheid, was one of Africa's longest-serving heads of state and one of the few to leave office after having been defeated in a fair election. Born in 1924 at Lubwa, Kaunda was the son of David Kaunda, the first African missionary in Nyasaland in 1904; he was educated at mission schools in Northern Rhodesia (now Zambia) and later completed teacher training. In 1953, he became Secretary-General of the newly created African National Congress (ANC). His political activism caused him to be imprisoned by the British colonial authorities in 1959. Upon his release, he broke away from the ANC and formed a new party, the United National Independence Party (UNIP). Following local self-government in 1962, Kaunda and his party joined a coalition government. In 1964, UNIP swept the elections; on October 24, Northern Rhodesia gained independence as Zambia, and Kenneth Kaunda became the republic's first president. Kaunda's 27-year rule was dominated by regional political conflicts with white-dominated governments (Southern Rhodesia/Zimbabwe and South Africa), which increased pressure on a structurally weak Zambian economy heavily dependent on the export of copper. In 1972, Kaunda suspended all opposition parties and declared a one-party state, which lasted until 1991; he also extended his control over the media, labor unions, and the army. Following major disturbances and an attempted coup in 1988, Kaunda conceded a referendum on multiparty government. In 1991, UNIP lost the country's first freely contested election. Kenneth Kaunda then retired to private life and was replaced as president by his challenger Frederick Chiluba. Zambia's current (and fourth) president is Rupiah Banda, who succeeded Levy Mwanawasa in 2008; Mwanawasa himself replaced Chiluba as president in 2002.[23]

Non-violence and African Humanism

Kenneth Kaunda's world view and political ideas were informed by his deep and abiding Christian faith (resulting from his Christian upbringing); indeed, his two acknowledged role models were Jesus and Mahatma Gandhi (the greatest apostle of nonviolence), whom he saw as realists with a vision: "Kenneth's thought was early and profoundly influenced . . . by Mahatma Gandhi who illuminated for him the personality and teaching of Jesus Christ." One of his guiding principles was the Christian precept of "do to others as you would have them do to you." Kaunda was also greatly influenced by the political ideas and strategy of Kwame Nkrumah, the acknowledged "father of African nationalism" and the first president of Ghana (1957–66).[24] Throughout his struggle for the independence of Zambia (formerly known as Northern Rhodesia), Kaunda was a passionate and relentless advocate of nonviolence in general and "nonviolent positive action" in particular: "My concept of non-violence is that it is the central thing . . . For me, non-violence is the ultimate weapon . . . I was determined to combine Gandhi's policy of non-violence with Nkrumah's positive action . . . We . . . know what we want, self-government now, and we also know how to get it, through non-violent means plus positive action."[25]

Another key concept in Kaunda's political thought informed by his Christian faith was that of "humanism" (or "African humanism"). Indeed, Kaunda's Christian concept of man led him to adopt a staunchly humanitarian, non-racialist attitude: "We are humanitarians and have no time for the color of a person. We respond favorably to the Christian concept of man . . . White and black should live and work together. Not white against black and black against white . . . we have based our policy on humanitarian principles. The battle still remains the same. It is not anti-white, but anti-wrong."[26]

Another source of inspiration in Kaunda's political ideology was the American Revolution. Thus Kaunda quotes the US Declaration of Independence verbatim when he says, "We believe that 'all men are created equal and that they are endowed with certain inalienable rights, among them *Life*, *Liberty* and the *Pursuit* of *Happiness*,'"[27] and his definition of "democracy" is taken straight out of Abraham Lincoln's playbook: "We are organizing to bring into being here a government of the people, by the people and indeed for the people."[28]

Finally, Kaunda rejected capitalism and advocated a popular democracy politically as well as state capitalism economically (though he failed to elaborate further on these concepts): "This is why I find capitalism . . . completely unacceptable and why I consider state-capitalism in Zambia to be only a transition stage. For we must move towards a people's democracy in economic life as in political."[29]

According to Marina and David Ottaway, the inability to translate the ideology of humanism into concrete policies and actions is at the heart of the failure of policymaking in Zambia. Their analysis in this regard is quite pertinent:

> The heart of the Zambian malaise was that the doctrine of humanism never affected the government's actual policies and probably could not have because it bore little relationship to the conditions prevailing in the country . . . he [Kaunda] viewed humanism more as an ethical stance, a mode of personal behavior, than as a guideline for reorganizing society into socialist structures . . . it was impossible to translate humanism into concrete action in Zambia; the ideology just did not fit the society and thus could not be used to transform it in the direction humanism pointed . . . the specific interpretation Kaunda gave to socialism was just too far removed from those conditions to help change and remold them along socialist lines.[30]

CONCLUSION

This chapter began with an overview of the new image of Africa and Africans constructed by Europeans from the sixteenth century onward—an image consistent with the Europeans' central role first in the trans-Atlantic slave trade (1492–1890) and then in imperialism and colonialism. Informed by the theory of "social Darwinism," Europeans viewed Africa as the "Dark Continent" and Africans as "primitive," "backward," and "uncivilized." The ideas of the Enlightenment in France and Britain allowed the Europeans to dissimulate the real motives of their imperial and colonial projects—the ruthless and systematic exploitation of African resources and people for the maximum economic profit—under the pretense of suppressing the slave trade and "bringing the blessings of Western civilization and Christianity" to the Africans. The chapter then focused specifically on the French colonial policies of assimilation and association, predicated on a presumed "civilizing mission" (*mission civilisatrice*), as well as on the British colonial policy of "Indirect Rule," according to which local government was exercised by indigenous political institutions under the authority and guidance of the British colonial administration. The chapter also examined the rise of economic and political liberalism in nineteenth century Europe as a background to the rise of "humanitarianism": a belief in the innate goodness and perfectibility of man that informed the European missionary movement of the nineteenth century.

The next section focused on a small Western-educated West African intellectual elite that attempted to reconcile Western systems of thought with African culture, values, and traditions, or Western liberalism with African democracy. By the end of the nineteenth century, only two pathways to political development seemed opened to these bold experiments in political modernization:

1. Reject the utopia of a "modern Africa" and wholeheartedly embrace African indigenous culture and values (a position advocated by Edward W. Blyden).
2. Accept the ideology of modernization while grounding it in African culture and traditions (a view propounded by James Africanus B. Horton, John Mensah-Sarbah, and Joseph E. Casely Hayford).

The last section of the chapter examined the ideas of two prominent African advocates of liberal democracy: an academic and one-time prime minister (1969–72), Kofi Busia of Ghana, and the "Father of Zambian Nationalism" and president of Zambia for 27 years (1964–91), Kenneth Kaunda. In *The Challenge of Africa* (1962), Kofi Busia argues that all the postcolonial African states have inherited a legacy of authoritarian political systems from their former rulers. In addition, Busia believes that the principles of liberal democracy are not specifically Western but universal. As such, they apply to Africa as they would to any other region of the world. A Christian imbued with the ideology of nonviolence of Mahatma Gandhi and the political strategy of "Positive Action" of Kwame Nkrumah, Kenneth Kaunda advocated the political ideology of African humanism. Unfortunately, this ideology failed to translate into concrete, workable policies in Zambia.

FURTHER READING

Busia, Kofi A., *Africa in Search of Democracy* (New York: Frederick A. Praeger, 1967).

Busia, Kofi A., *The Challenge of Africa* (New York: Frederick A. Praeger, 1962).

July, Robert W., *The Origins of Modern African Thought: Its Development in West Africa during the Nineteenth and Twentieth Centuries* (London: Faber and Faber, 1968).

Kaunda, Kenneth D., *Zambia Shall Be Free: An Autobiography* (London: Heinemann Educational Books, 1962).

Mudimbe, V. Y., *The Invention of Africa: Gnosis, Philosophy and the Order of Knowledge* (Bloomington: Indiana University Press, 1988).

Wilson, Henry S., ed., *Origins of West African Nationalism* (New York: Macmillan/ St. Martin's Press, 1969).

CHAPTER 4

---✶✶✶---

PAN-AFRICANISM AND AFRICAN UNITY

FROM IDEAL TO PRACTICE

If we are to remain free, if we are to enjoy the full benefits of Africa's rich resources, we must unite to plan for our total defense and the full exploitation of our material and human means, in the full interests of all our peoples. "To go it alone" will limit our horizons, curtail our expectations, and threaten our liberty.

—Kwame Nkrumah, *Africa Must Unite*, xvii

INTRODUCTION

During the first 15 years of the struggle for independence in Africa (1945–60), two competing views of African cooperation and integration were promoted by two groups of African nationalist leaders. On the one hand, the gradualists (or functionalists) led by Félix Houphouët-Boigny of Côte d'Ivoire, Nnamdi Azikiwe of Nigeria, Jomo Kenyatta of Kenya, and Julius Nyerere of Tanzania advocated a gradual, step-by-step integration in the areas of transport, telecommunications, science, technology, and the economy leading up to—in a distant future—political integration. The Pan-Africanists, led by Kwame Nkrumah of Ghana—and including Ahmed Ben Bella of Algeria, Patrice Lumumba of the Congo, Ahmed Sékou Touré of Guinea, and Modibo Kéïta of Mali—proposed, following Nkrumah's blueprint as outlined in *Africa Must Unite*, immediate political and economic integration in the form of a "United States of Africa" consisting of an African Common Market, African Monetary Union, African Military High-Command, and a continent-wide Union Government.[1]

This chapter first shows how the Pan-Africanist leaders' dream of unity was deferred in favor of the gradualist-functionalist approach, embodied in a weak and loosely structured Organization of African Unity (OAU) created on May 25, 1963, in Addis Ababa (Ethiopia). Indeed, the Ghana-Guinea-Mali Union created in 1959 as the nucleus of the United States of Africa never really took off. Similarly, the French, through the *Loi-Cadre* (Framework Law) of June 1956, dismantled the large federations that they had set up in the early 1900s—*Afrique Occidentale Française* (AOF) and *Afrique Équatoriale Française* (AEF)—and, along with such faithful African allies as Félix Houphouët-Boigny of Côte d'Ivoire, deliberately and consistently worked toward the breakup of these large federations (French West Africa and French Equatorial Africa) into small, economically nonviable states incapable of independent development. The same policy of "balkanization" was systematically applied by France to the 1959 Mali Federation, an attempt to partially salvage AOF by Senegal, French Sudan (Mali), Dahomey (Benin), and Upper Volta (Burkina Faso), which ended in failure after the successive withdrawal of Dahomey and Upper Volta and the irreconcilable differences that emerged between the political elites of the remaining two constituent units, Senegal and French Sudan/Mali.[2]

This chapter then analyzes the reasons for the failure of the Pan-Africanist leaders' dream of unity: fear of tampering with the colonially inherited borders; reluctance of newly independent African leaders to abandon their newly won sovereignty in favor of a broader political entity; suspicion on the part of many African leaders that Kwame Nkrumah intended to become the superpresident of a united Africa; and divide-and-rule strategies on the part of major Western powers—led by France and the United States—meant to sabotage any attempt at African unity. It took African leaders some forty years to realize their mistake. A project for an African Common Market, leading to an African Economic Community (The *Lagos Plan of Action/Final Act of Lagos*), was launched in 1980 within the OAU. Then, on May 26, 2001, the African Union (AU) formally replaced the OAU. One of the reasons why the project for a United States of Africa failed is that it was modeled on the United States of America. Similarly, because it is a top-down project modeled on the European Union, the African Union is bound to know the same fate.

This chapter then surveys past and current proposals for a revision of the map of Africa and a reconfiguration of the African states put forward by various authors such as Cheikh Anta Diop, Marc-Louis Ropivia, Makau wa Mutua, Arthur Gakwandi, Joseph Ki-Zerbo, Daniel Osabu-Kle, Godfrey Mwakikagile, Pelle Danabo, and Mueni wa Muiu.[3] While each of these proposals has merit, they are not (except for Cheikh Anta Diop's) grounded in an overarching political framework, and they lack specificity in terms of the actual structure and functioning of the reconfigured states.

This chapter concludes with a brief examination of me and Mueni wa Muiu's proposal for state reconfiguration in Africa. Our view is that the Pan-Africanist leaders' dream of unity can only be realized through a model conceived by and for Africans themselves—namely, the *Federation of African*

States (FAS). The FAS is based on five subregional states for each main subregion of the continent—Kimit (North); Mali (West); Kongo (Central); Kush (Eastern); and Zimbabwe (Southern)—with a federal capital (Napata) and a rotating presidency, eventually leading to total political and economic integration. We argue that only with the advent of FAS will Africa's "Dream of Unity" finally become a reality.[4]

CONTENDING PERSPECTIVES ON AFRICAN UNITY: PAN-AFRICANISM VS. FUNCTIONALISM

Pan-Africanism and African Unity

Broadly conceived, Pan-Africanism is an ideal and movement designed to regroup and mobilize Africans in Africa and the diaspora against racial discrimination, foreign domination and oppression, and economic exploitation. Thus Pan-Africanism has three different dimensions: cultural, political, and economic. Culturally, it aims at reclaiming Africa's heritage, history, culture, traditions, and values and is embodied in such historical movement as *Négritude* (in France in the 1930s) and the Harlem Renaissance (in the United States in the 1920s). Politically, Pan-Africanism is linked to the African nationalist struggle for independence. Economically, Pan-Africanism is linked to the struggle against imperialism, colonialism, neocolonialism, and globalization—that is, the Western strategies of "divide and rule" that resulted in the balkanization of Africa.[5]

Following its thematic breakdown, Pan-Africanism may be divided into two successive historical phases, one cultural, the other political: Pan-Africanism as ideal and utopia, 1900–1957, and "Homecoming". The African phase, in which economic factors prevail, marks the transition from Pan-Africanism to African Unity (1957 to the present).

Pan-Africanism as Ideal and Utopia

This refers to the cultural dimension of the Pan-African ideology. At this stage, Pan-Africanism remained in the realm of ideas and was embodied in the ideal of the "Dream of Unity." It first developed during the first two decades of the twentieth century around such prominent African American and Afro-Caribbean intellectual and activist leaders as W. E. B. Du Bois, Paul Robeson, C. L. R. James, George Padmore, and Marcus Garvey. The latter founded a populist movement in 1919, the *Universal Negro Improvement Association* (UNIA); created a shipping line, the "Black Star Line"; and built on the "back-to-Africa" movement that led to the creation of Liberia, which was founded in 1817 by freed slaves from the United States and became an independent state in 1847.[6] The cultural dimension of Pan-Africanism is best exemplified by the *Négritude* movement initiated in Paris by French-educated African and Afro-Caribbean poets—such as Léopold Sédar Senghor (Senegal), Aimé Césaire (Martinique), and Léon-Gontran Damas (French Guyana)—aiming to reassert the value and contribution of African culture.[7]

Homecoming: The Political Dimension of Pan-Africanism

As P. Olisanwuche Esedebe has shown, the Manchester Pan-African Congress of October 1945 truly marked a turning point in the history of the Pan-African movement. Henceforth, the struggle for the emancipation of people of African descent focused on the homeland. At that particular juncture, the North American Pan-African movement linked up with the nationalist struggle for independence in Africa itself.[8] The roster of personalities in charge of the congress's organization testifies to this: W. E. B. Du Bois (co-chair); George Padmore and Kwame Nkrumah (co-political secretaries); Jomo Kenyatta (assistant secretary); and Peter Abrahams (publicity secretary).

As Vincent Bakpetu Thompson rightly argues, it was with the return of Kwame Nkrumah to the Gold Coast (now Ghana) in December 1947 that "Pan-Africanism moved from the realm of idealism and romanticism to that of practical politics." Indeed, "Pan-Africanism remained in the realm of ideas until Ghana became a sovereign state."[9] At this point, the Pan-Africanist ideal actually morphed into the policy objective of African Unity. With the Independence of Ghana (March 1957) and until the creation of the Organization of African Unity (OAU, May 1963), Ghana became the focal point of the struggle for African Unity, and Kwame Nkrumah became its indefatigable standard-bearer. Indeed, Nkrumah invited the elder statesman of Pan-Africanism, W. E. B. Du Bois, to come and live in Accra, where he started the *Encyclopedia Africana* and eventually died on August 27, 1963. Nkrumah also invited George Padmore to lead the *Bureau of African Affairs* within Ghana's ministry of foreign affairs, which Padmore did until his death in September 1959.

Radical Pan-Africanism: African Unity

According to this perspective—exemplified by Kwame Nkrumah but shared by many other African political leaders,[10]—political integration is a prerequisite to economic integration: "Economic unity to be effective must be accompanied by political unity. The two are inseparable."[11] Furthermore, African leaders should aim at the immediate and total integration—political, economic, as well as military—of Africa within the framework of a "Union of African States." These ideals were embodied in the African Charter adopted at the Casablanca Conference of radical African states of January 1961, as well as in the Union of African States—also known as the Ghana-Guinea-Mali Union—of 1958–59 conceived as the nucleus of a future "United States of Africa" in which each member state voluntarily agreed to give up part of its sovereignty in favor of a broader continent-wide union.[12]

In a prefatory note to the new edition of his book *Africa Must Unite*, Kwame Nkrumah states bluntly that "unless Africa is politically united under an All-African Union Government, there can be no solution to our political and economic problems," adding, "we are Africans first and last, and as Africans our best interests can only be served by uniting within an African Community."[13] This book, published to coincide with the opening of the OAU's founding conference (May 22–25, 1963), is truly a political manifesto of African unity. As a student of history, philosophy, politics, and economics, strongly influenced by the ideas of W. E. B. Du Bois, Marcus Garvey, and George Padmore, Nkrumah became a passionate advocate of the "African Personality" embodied in the slogan "Africa for the Africans" earlier popularized by Edward Wilmot Blyden. He viewed political independence as a prerequisite for economic independence. He argued that Africans must counter the neocolonial policies of the former colonial powers (such as France) based on "divide and rule" and balkanization—that is, the breakup of large entities (such as AOF) into small, unviable territories incapable of independent development. Nkrumah also rejected as essentially neocolonial the association between Africa and Europe: "Pan-Africa and not Eurafrica should be our watchword, and the guide to our policies."[14] More specifically, "The European Common Market . . . is but the economic and financial arm of *neocolonialism* and the bastion of European economic imperialism in Africa."[15] The Union Government of African States (or United States of Africa) envisaged by Nkrumah consisted of the following common processes and institutions: continental economic planning leading to the creation of an African Common Market; a common currency, a monetary zone, and a central bank of issue; a unified military and defense strategy leading to a unified Defense Command for Africa; a unified foreign policy and diplomacy; and a Continental Parliament.[16] Similarly, writing in the late 1960s on the economics of Pan-Africanism, Reginald Green and Ann Seidman observed that "no African state is economically large enough to construct a modern economy alone. Africa as a whole has the resources for industrialization, but it is split among more than forty African territories. Africa as a whole could provide markets able to support large-scale efficient industrial complexes; no single African state nor existing sub-regional economic union can do so . . . Can continental African economic unity be achieved? The answer is not only that it *can* be achieved, but that it *must* be achieved."[17]

It is interesting to note in this regard that the recently ousted Libyan leader Muammar Qaddafi proposed the exact same project (rejected by the majority of member states) at the fifth extraordinary summit of the OAU held in Qaddafi's hometown of Sirte (Libya) in September 1999, which adopted the Constitutive Act of the African Union (formally established in May 2001). After the death of Kwame Nkrumah in 1972, Muammar Qaddafi assumed the mantel of leader of the Pan-Africanist movement and became the most outspoken advocate of African Unity, consistently calling—like Nkrumah before him—for the advent of a "United States of Africa." There is strong evidence to suggest that, disillusioned by the failure of various Pan-Arab plans and initiatives, Qaddafi decided to focus his attention, energies, and resources on the African continent.[18] Qaddafi worked tirelessly for the creation of a powerful and effective African Union at successive OAU meetings in his home town of Sirte (September 1999 and March 2001). However, the relatively ineffective and powerless African Union—modeled on the European Union—that came into being in July 2001 and that Qaddafi chaired for one year (February 2009–January 2010) was markedly different from the organization envisaged by Qaddafi. The latter was outlined in the Sirte Declaration (September 9, 1999), which provided for an African Congress, a Summit Council, a Federal Executive Council, 15 Federal Executive Commissions, a Federal Supreme Court, and three Federal Financial Institutions (an African Central Bank, an African Monetary Fund, and an African Investment Bank).[19]

Ignace Kissangou's concise and spirited political manifesto—appropriately titled *One Africa, One Hope*—calls for the realization of the Pan-African ideal of African unity in order to achieve the elusive goals of peace, security, and development. Borrowing generously from Kwame Nkrumah's project, Kissangou—a research scholar in African politics at the University of Paris I—proposes the creation of a Federation of African Nation-States (or United States of Africa) with a common defense and security policy, a continent-wide army, a common currency, and such Pan-African institutions as a Security Council for African Development, an African Parliament, and an African Senate (or Representative Council of African Institutions).[20]

The Functionalist/Gradualist Approach to African Cooperation and Integration of the Moderate African Leaders

The Functionalist/Gradualist Approach

The leaders associated with this school of thought—whose undisputed leader was Félix Houphouët-Boigny of Côte d'Ivoire[21]—advocated a gradual, step-by-step approach to African integration, in accordance with the functionalist theory of integration. According to this perspective, African states should not aim—as the Pan-Africanists advocated—at immediate and total political integration; rather, they should start by cooperating in non-controversial technical and economic areas such as transport and communications, telecommunications, joint management of rivers/lakes, trade and customs, market integration, and so on. Immediately after independence in 1960, the moderate African states assembled within various fora, such as the Brazzaville Group (December 1960) and the Monrovia Group (May 1961), and they created a range of institutions such as the *Conseil de l'Entente* (Council of the Entente, April 1959) and the *Organisation Commune Africaine et Malgache* (OCAM: Common African and Malagasy Union, February 1965).

The Creation of the Organization of African Unity: A Victory for the Functionalists/Gradualists

On May 25, 1963, 32 African leaders representing a cross section of the Pan-Africanists (Casablanca Group) and Functionalists/Gradualists (Brazzaville/Monrovia Groups) met in Addis Ababa (Ethiopia) to set up a truly Pan-African organization inclusive of the North African and Indian Ocean island states. In the end, the Pan-Africanists gave in to the Gradualists/Functionalists and adopted a charter creating a weak and relatively powerless *Organization of African Unity* based on cooperation, the respect of sovereignty and territorial integrity, non-interference in internal affairs of states, and the sanctity of colonially inherited borders. Most of the policy-making power was vested in an Assembly of Heads of States and Government (AHSG), while the *Administrative* Secretary-General was conceived as a mere executant of the AHSG's decisions.[22] Thirty years after its creation, the OAU finally adopted some of the institutions envisaged in Kwame Nkrumah's Pan-African project, notably an African Common Market (by 2020) leading to an African Economic Community (by 2025). Whether these projects will actually see the light of day remains to be seen.

The thirty-seventh summit of the AHSG meeting in Lusaka, Zambia (June 2001), decided to formally transform the OAU into an African Union (AU), which became operational in May 2002. As for the Union of African States project originally conceived by Nkrumah and proposed by Libya's leader Muammar Qaddafi at the Lusaka summit, it was rejected by the African leaders in attendance as "unrealistic" and "utopian."[23] Modeled after the European Union, the AU does not essentially differ from the OAU and is basically "an old wine in a new bottle" as it continues—just as its predecessor—to be based on the hallowed principles of state sovereignty, noninterference in the internal affairs of states, and inviolability of borders.

RECONFIGURING THE AFRICAN STATES: TOWARD A NEW MAP OF AFRICA

We shall now briefly survey past and current proposals for a revision of the map of Africa and a reconfiguration of the African states put forward by various authors, notably Cheikh Anta Diop, Marc-Louis Ropivia, Makau wa Mutua, Arthur Gakwandi, Joseph Ki-Zerbo, Daniel Osabu-Kle, Godfrey Mwakikagile, Pelle Danabo, and Mueni wa Muiu.

Cheikh Anta Diop's Federal African State

In a compact book of just over one hundred pages, Cheikh Anta Diop—arguably one of Africa's greatest scientists, most original thinkers, and prolific writers—outlines the economic and cultural foundations of a Federal African State.[24] Building on earlier research documenting the essential historical, cultural, and linguistic unity of Africa,[25] Diop advocates the adoption of a single African language for official, educational, and cultural use throughout the continent.[26] Warning against the dangers of the "South Americanization"—the proliferation of small, dictatorial states afflicted by chronic instability—of Africa and calling for a break with "fake institutions"—such as the Franco-African Community, the Commonwealth, and Eur-Africa—Diop recommends (like Nkrumah) the creation of a strong African army and notes that sub-Saharan Africa's abundant natural, energy, and food resources can easily sustain a larger population than the present one.[27] According to the author, the Federal African State would extend from the Tropic of Cancer to the Cape and from the Indian Ocean to the Atlantic, thus uniting Francophone, Anglophone, and Lusophone Africa (but excluding North Africa). Sub-Saharan Africa's hydroelectric potential, he argues, is one of the greatest in the world. The Congo Basin alone (with the Inga and Kinsangani dams) could provide electricity to the whole continent. Africa's abundant solar and uranium resources, Diop observes, could sustain an elaborate solar and nuclear industry. All these resources should be harnessed toward the processing of the continent's raw materials. The author further argues that Africa's import dependence could be drastically reduced if three key industries were developed: food processing (rice), clothing (cotton), and housing (cement and concrete). In the area of transport and communication, Diop suggests that priority should be given to the construction of tarmacked roads and the development first of civil aviation, then maritime transport, and last railways.[28]

According to Diop, the constituent economic and cultural elements of a Federal African State would be a single African language, based on the essential historic, cultural, and linguistic unity of Africa; the immediate political and economic unification of Francophone, Anglophone, and Lusophone Africa; the creation of a strong Pan-African army; an elaborate industrial infrastructure (heavy industry and manufacturing) using Africa's abundant hydroelectric, solar, and uranium resources in order to process the continent's raw materials; an elaborate transport network; and a policy encouraging population growth.[29]

It is noteworthy that the two blueprints of Nkrumah and Diop are infused by the same Pan-Africanist ideal but differ in emphasis in a complementary fashion. Nkrumah provides a broad canvas and elaborate political, economic, and military institutional infrastructure, while Diop fills in the policy details in terms of language and culture, population, energy, industry, agriculture, transport, and communication. The fact that Nkrumah was first and foremost a political man, and Diop essentially an academic and scientist, probably explains their different approaches.[30]

Marc-Louis Ropivia's Geopolitics of African Regional Integration

Marc-Louis Ropivia proposes a new theoretical approach to federalism and economic and political integration in sub-Saharan Africa. Ropivia summarizes the whole problematic of African federalism and political integration in sub-Saharan Africa in six statements:

1. Being of North American origin, Pan-Africanism has only had a limited impact on the African continent. As a result, this ideology has not elicited a movement toward political unity in sub-Saharan Africa.
2. The whole of sub-Saharan Africa cannot be considered as a single cultural unit.

3. A federalism based on an association of independent states can only be built on the foundation of a prior cultural unity.

4. An ideology of the political unity of sub-Saharan Africa based on cultural unity naturally leads toward a unitary continental state, but it does not create a federal continental state.

5. Sub-Saharan Africa must be considered as an entity predominantly characterized by cultural diversity.

6. Africa's cultural diversity is, at the same time, a regional diversity that leads to federalism in the form of a multiplicity of federal regional states.[31]

This new African federalism is based on two-state integrative units called "bistate nuclei" or "federative dyads," within which the two federated units are linked to each other by a federative link. Thus this constitutes a gradual strategy to build federalism in sub-Saharan Africa, based on a two-state nucleus that is progressively expanded until it ultimately leads to a continental federal state.[32]

A federative link (or direct link) is characterized by an initial bistate nucleus based on two states sharing the same colonial inheritance and leads to the most intensive type of integration. An indirect federative link usually develops around a core ethnic group that straddles one or several borders in states with different colonial inheritances and results in a lesser degree of integration.[33] Based on this approach, the author proposes a restructuring of the African political map into eight superstates—one in North Africa, one in Central Africa, and two states in West, East, and Southern Africa.[34] Ropivia concludes by saying that while nuclear federalism might be rightly viewed as utopian, it is on the basis of utopia that the great transformational political projects of humankind have been built. Africa would thus be reborn as the phoenix rising from the ashes.[35]

Makau wa Mutua's New Map of Africa

Starting from the observation that the "consequences of the failed postcolonial state are so destructive that radical solutions must now be contemplated to avert the wholesale destruction of groups of the African people," the Kenyan human rights scholar-activist Makau wa Mutua proposed in 1994 a redrawing of the map of Africa to construct 15 viable states as opposed to the 55 mostly nonviable states existing today. The criteria for the creation of these new states include historical factors (such as precolonial political systems and demographic patterns), ethnic similarities, and alliances based on cultural homogeneity and economic viability.

Based on these criteria, Mutua's map of Africa creates new countries by abolishing some and combining others. Thus the new Republic of *Kusini* (meaning "south" in Ki-Swahili) would include South Africa, Namibia, Zimbabwe, Mozambique, Lesotho, Swaziland, and Malawi. The new *Egypt* would combine Egypt and northern Sudan. *Nubia* would bring together Kenya, Uganda, Tanzania, and southern Sudan. *Mali* (an ancient medieval

West African empire) would include Mali, Senegal, Guinea, Sierra Leone, Liberia, Gambia, Guinea-Bissau, and Cape Verde. *Somalia* would absorb Djibouti, the Ogaden province of Ethiopia, and Kenya's northeastern province. *Congo* would combine ethnically similar people of the Central African Republic, the Congo Republic, the Democratic Republic of the Congo, Rwanda, and Burundi, while *Ghana* would consist of Ghana, Côte d'Ivoire, Benin, Togo, Nigeria, Cameroon, Gabon, Equatorial Guinea, and São Tomé and Principe. *Benin* would take in Chad, Burkina Faso, and Niger. *Algeria* and *Angola* remain the same, while *Libya* absorbs Tunisia. Morocco, Western Sahara, and Mauritania become *Sahara*. The new state of *Kisiwani* (which means "island" in Ki-Swahili) brings together Madagascar, Mauritius, and the Comoros. Ethiopia and Eritrea constitute a federation.[36]

Arthur S. Gakwandi's New Political Map of Africa

Noting that "African leaders and intellectuals are desperately groping for solutions that will arrest the current drift towards the outer margins of global currents and steer the Continent towards the center of world events," Gakwandi goes on to assert "that *political restructuring* of the continent is a more important priority that needs to be addressed before economic restructuring can bring about the desired results."[37] Furthermore, Gakwandi observes that the key to solving the African predicament lies in politics rather than economics. According to him, "The center of the problem does not lie in economics but in politics. Africa's economic stagnation is a result of political instability and not the other way round. The political framework therefore has to be changed so that dynamic, confident and coherent politics are established before economic goals can be pursued meaningfully."[38]

Furthermore, Gakwandi agrees with many other African leaders and intellectuals that the colonially inherited borders are the source of the small size of the majority of African states, leading to poverty, dependency, non-development, and ethnic conflict. This analysis leads the author to propose a restructuring of the African political map based on the imaginary lines of broad cultural differentiation derived from "a broad coincidence between climatic and cultural zones." According to Gakwandi, the new political map of Africa would achieve the following objectives:

- eliminate landlocked countries, as well as border disputes
- reunite African nationalities currently divided by the colonial borders (such as the Hausa, Fulani, and Yoruba)
- provide all the new states with an adequate resource base and a critical mass of population that would form a solid basis for development
- considerably ease existing intrastate ethnic tensions
- enhance Africa's standing in the world, as well as the confidence in Africa, and provide fresh momentum to the quest for self-reliant and self-sustaining development

- reduce inter-ethnic tensions, thereby considerably reducing the number of African refugees and internally-displaced persons.[39]

Consequently, Gakwandi proposes a new political map of Africa made up of seven African superstates in each major African subregion: Sahara Republic (North Africa); Senegambia (West Africa); Central Africa and Swahili Republic (Central Africa); Ethiopia (as is, plus Eritrea); Swahili Republic (includes East Africa and part of Central Africa); Mozambia (Southern Africa); and Madagascar (as is).[40]

Joseph Ki-Zerbo's Federal African State

The late, prominent Burkinabe historian Joseph Ki-Zerbo's concept of African unity is very similar to that of Kwame Nkrumah. Like Nkrumah, Ki-Zerbo starts from the observation that "the typical size of the African micro-state is generally too small for industrialization and public services purposes," adding, "Africans must create large, viable economic units predicated upon a degree of political integration."[41] Ki-Zerbo then proposes a three-tier, pyramidal system of African citizenship—local citizenship, federal citizenship, and regional citizenship—as well as a Federal African State based on three main African languages (such as Bambara/Maninka/Dyula, Hausa, and Ki-Swahili). This state would be multiracial and multiethnic, possibly based on the reconstitution of such large and culturally homogeneous medieval African states as Mali.[42]

Daniel Osabu-Kle's United States of Africa

Reviving Kwame Nkrumah's "Dream of Unity" of the early 1960s, Osabu-Kle firmly believes in Pan-Africanism, which, according to him, should materialize in the form of a United States of Africa and should include an African High Command (AHC) "with operational readiness to intervene swiftly to foil any coup attempt in any African country" as well as a Pan-African Youth Organization (PAYO) "with branches both inside and outside Africa to unite African youth and enable interaction and exchange of views." In addition to these institutions and establishing a common transport and telecommunications infrastructure, the United States of Africa envisaged by Osabu-Kle would have a common currency, a common defense policy, and a common foreign policy.[43]

Godfrey Mwakikagile's African Federal Government

In his book *The Modern African State*, Godfrey Mwakikagile argues that the severity of the African predicament calls for nothing less than a closer union in the form of an *African confederation* or *African federal government*, starting with economic integration and leading to an *African common market* and, eventually, to a political union.[44] Concretely, Mwakikagile proposes the following plan for a Union of African States: "If the future of Africa lies in federation, that kind of federation could even be a giant federation of numerous autonomous units which have replaced the modern African state in order to build, on a continental or sub-continental scale, a common market, establish a common currency, a common defense, and may be even pursue a common foreign policy under some kind of central authority—including collective leadership on rotational basis—which Africans think is best for them."[45]

Observing that a substantial degree of informal cross-border movement of people already exists in Africa—such as the back and forth movement of the Masai across the Kenya-Tanzania border—Mwakikagile believes that "the larger supra-national units . . . would function as a single entity allowing free movement and settlement of its peoples wherever land is available in the region." Mwakikagile offers an East African Federation composed of Kenya, Uganda, Tanzania, Rwanda, Burundi, and the Democratic Republic of the Congo (DRC) as an example of regional integration leading to larger supranational units.[46]

Pelle D. Danabo's Pan-African Federal State

In his fascinating dissertation on "Africana Democracy," Pelle Darota Danabo pulls together elements of the analyses of Diop, Ropivia, Mutua, and Gakwandi into a coherent and all-inclusive ideological framework. The author starts from the observation that what unites Africans more than anything else—such as shared culture and geography—is "our shared and collective suffering and afflictions in the history of the modern world"—that is, the shared history of trans-Atlantic slavery, imperialism, colonialism, and neocolonialism.[47] Noting that Western liberal democracy is antithetical to African values and traditions, he advocates an *Africana democracy* based on African values and traditions. Defining colonization as "a project of dehumanization pursued rationally," Danabo goes on to lament the fact that the greatest obstacle to Africa's democracy and development lies in the artificiality of the colonially inherited borders that divided people sharing common ethnicity, language, cultures, and traditions.[48] The resulting balkanization of Africa into more than fifty states is the root cause of Africa's current predicament. The solution, says Danabo, resides in the creation of a "Pan-African Federal State" (or United African Federal Union) based on a common Pan-African identity and society. In addition, "both United Africa and Pan-African values ought to become the normative foundations of development, peace and democracy in Africa." Danabo further notes that "since the core concept here is redressing both the spatial and political/moral injustices committed on African peoples, both inherited and practiced at present, it matters little whether large federations or unions of states, or small self-governing communities are chosen in so far [as] the decision is not imposed and enforced upon the people who made the choice."[49] This explains why Danabo's proposed Pan-African Federal State is rather vague, lacks the specificity of the other projects reviewed in this section, and offers various options:

A United African federal union (United Africa) can be constituted from various alternate federal arrangements of all possibilities also, a federal union of competing norms of federal arrangements, for instance. These may include ethno-cultural and linguistic federalisms (a federalism founded on shared history, common language, etc.), environmental federalisms centering around African Peoples sharing common resources like rivers or port services or other like the Nile Basin federation or the Niger river basin federation or the Great Lakes region federation, etc. The possibility and probability of regional unions of federal States is another sound way to go based on founding principles and choices of peoples concerned, etc. is conceivable also. Even the superposition of different complementary arrangements where nation-states, environmental federations, regional unions and other co-function depending on the reasoned and deliberated choices made by those concerned cannot be excluded. In Africa, therefore, suggesting the possibility, even the feasibility of a second level federal structure does not constitute stretching the issue to the point of irrelevance.[50]

While each of these proposals has merit, they are not (except for Cheikh Anta Diop's and Danabo's) grounded in an overarching political framework, and they lack specificity in terms of the actual structure and functioning of the proposed reconfigured states. Beyond proposing a new political map of Africa variously based on 7, 8, or 15 states, these proposals do not specify (except Danabo's) the type of government to be set up or the way in which power would be divided between the constituent federated states and the federal government. Mueni wa Muiu's "Federation of African States," proposed in her book *Fundi wa Arika* (jointly authored with me), actually addresses these concerns.

Mueni wa Muiu's Federation of African States

In *Fundi wa Afrika*—meaning "tailor" or "builder of Africa" in Ki-Swahili—Mueni wa Muiu and I introduce a new paradigm to study the African state. According to this paradigm, the current African predicament may be explained by the systematic destruction of African states and the dispossession, exploitation, and marginalization of African people through successive historical processes: the trans-Atlantic slave trade, imperialism, colonialism, and globalization. In this book—inspired by the Pan-African projects of Kwame Nkrumah, Cheikh Anta Diop, and Godfrey Mwakikagile—we argue that a new, viable, and modern African state based on five political entities—the Federation of African States—should be built on the functional remnants of indigenous African political systems and institutions and based on African values, traditions, and culture.[51]

In the *Federation of African States* (FAS), Africa will have one constitution and a common foreign defense policy. Instead of the current 55 states, Africa will be divided into 5 superstates (see map of FAS in Figure 4.1). The new state of *Kimit* will include Algeria, Libya, Morocco, Egypt, Tunisia, and Western Sahara, plus the Arab populations of Mauritania, Northern Sudan, and Northern Chad. *Mali* will include Benin, Burkina Faso, Cape

Figure 4.1 Map of the Federation of African States (FAS)

Verde, Côte d'Ivoire, Gambia, Ghana, Guinea, Guinea-Bissau, Liberia, Mali, Niger, Nigeria, Senegal, Sierra Leone, and Togo, plus the African population of Mauritania. *Kongo* will include Congo (DRC), Congo Republic, Cameroon, Southern Chad, Central African Republic, Equatorial Guinea, Gabon, São Tomé and Principe, Uganda, Rwanda, and Burundi. *Kush* will include Southern Sudan, Ethiopia, Eritrea, Djibouti, Somalia-Somaliland, Kenya, Tanzania, Zanzibar, Seychelles, and Comoros. *Zimbabwe* will include Angola, Botswana, Namibia, Malawi, Mozambique, Madagascar, Mauritius, Lesotho, Swaziland, South Africa, Zambia, and Zimbabwe. The new federal capital city will be called Napata; it will not belong to any of the five states. Each region will have a key player, based on population and resources—for example, Kongo, Egypt, Ethiopia, Nigeria, and South Africa. FAS will be protected by a federal army made up of diverse members from the five states. All external economic relations will be conducted by the federal government. Economic and political power will be decentralized, giving people more input in the day-to-day activities of the federation.[52]

In FAS, power will start from the village councils made up of the local people. This will be followed by a regional council of elders, then a national council, and finally the federal council of presidents. Each of the five regions of FAS will be governed by five rotating presidents on the basis of a federal system. Africa will have a popular democracy—based on accountability and responsibility—that will be organized from below. Since each section of the population will have representatives at all levels of government, power will be decentralized and the people will determine their destiny based on their interests, priorities, and needs.[53]

CONCLUSION

Without political and economic unity among African states, and without a political system based on the interests of Africans and informed by indigenous institutions, there can be neither a united Africa nor an African renaissance. As the preceding discussion amply demonstrates, this calls on Africans to take control of their own development. Kwame Nkrumah correctly observed in the early 1960s, "We in Africa have untold agricultural, mineral, and water-power resources. These almost fabulous resources can be fully exploited and utilized in the interests of Africa and the African people, only if we develop them within a Union Government of African States."[54] Africa's unity is still essential for development, peace, and security, Godfrey Mwakikagile notes: "If the future of Africa lies in federation, that kind of federation could be a giant federation of numerous autonomous units which have replaced the modern African state in order to build, on a continental or sub-continental scale, a common market, establish a common currency, a common defense, and maybe even pursue a common foreign policy under some kind of central authority—including collective leadership on a rotational basis—which Africans think is best for them."[55] On the occasion of his seventy-fifth birthday, the late former Tanzanian president Julius Nyerere left these words of wisdom for the benefit of Africans: "Africa . . . is isolated. Therefore, to develop, it will have to depend upon its own resources basically, internal resources, nationally, and Africa will have to depend upon Africa. The leadership of the future will have to devise, try to carry out policies of maximum national self-reliance and maximum collective self-reliance. They have no other choice. *Hamma!* [meaning: "there is none" in Ki-Swahili]."[56] At a more general level, for Joseph Ki-Zerbo the main duty and responsibility of African intellectuals, who should act as the pioneers of the new African culture in twenty-first-century Africa, is to come up with concrete, positive proposals.[57] He concludes, "We must find within ourselves the intellectual and moral strength to initiate positive change . . . we must rely essentially on ourselves to create a new, autonomous African civilization . . . the salvation of the continent will require from the Africans . . . an extraordinary effort of innovation and reconversion. We shall have to start anew, to go beyond the surviving colonial structures."[58]

FURTHER READING

Abdul-Raheem, Tajudeen, ed., *Pan-Africanism: Politics, Economy and Social Change in the Twenty-First Century* (New York: New York University Press, 1996).

Akokpari, John, A. Ndinga-Muvumba, and Tim Murithi, eds., *The African Union and Its Institutions* (Cape Town: Center for Conflict Resolution, 2008).

Diop, Cheikh Anta, *Black Africa: The Economic and Cultural Basis for a Federated State*, revised edition, translated by Harold J. Salemson (Chicago: Lawrence Hill Books, 1987).

Esedebe, P. Olisanwuche, *Pan-Africanism: The Idea and Movement, 1776–1991*, 2nd edition (Washington, DC: Howard University Press, 1994).

Nkrumah, Kwame, *Africa Must Unite*, new edition (New York: International Publishers, 1970).

Thompson, Vincent Bakpetu, *Africa and Unity: The Evolution of Pan-Africanism* (London: Longman, 1969).

CHAPTER 5

---··—⋇◈⋇——··---

THE SOCIALIST-POPULIST
IDEOLOGY I

FROM PATRICE LUMUMBA
TO SAMORA MACHEL

The ideological deficiency, not to say the total lack of ideology, within the national liberation movements—which is basically due to ignorance of the historical reality which theses movements claim to transform—constitutes one of the greatest weaknesses of our struggle against imperialism, if not the greatest weakness of all . . . nobody has yet made a successful revolution without a revolutionary theory.

—Amilcar Cabral, *Revolution in Guinea*, 92–93

THE SOCIALIST-POPULIST AND
POPULIST-SOCIALIST IDEOLOGIES

This chapter is a survey of the political, economic, social, and cultural dimensions of the socialist-populist ideology from a distinctly socialist perspective. The concept of "populist-socialism" is borrowed from Crawford Young, who states that this group "consists of states that espouse a socialist orientation but that either do not stress or expressly reject Marxism."[1] According to Young, populist socialism is a doctrine of development that characterized the "first wave" socialist regimes of the 1960s such as Algeria, Ghana, Guinea, Guinea-Bissau, Mali, and Tanzania. The author identifies five elements that define the populist-socialist perspective: (1) radical nationalism; (2) a radical mood; (3) anti-capitalism; (4) populism and an exaltation of the peasantry; and (5) adherence to a moderate form of socialism (or social democracy) and a rejection of orthodox Marxism.[2]

In fact, these rather broad and general characteristic features equally apply to the two categories introduced in this book—namely, the socialist-populist and the populist-socialist ideologies. In the first, we refer to political leaders (and regimes) strongly—but not exclusively—influenced by the Marxist-Leninist ideology. The statesmen affiliated with this ideology were either not in power at all or else ruled for only a short period of time. Furthermore, these leaders were unable or unwilling to exercise authoritarian rule, and they truly had the best interest of their people at heart. This category includes Patrice Lumumba (Congo), Ahmed Ben Bella (Algeria), Amilcar Cabral (Guinea-Bissau), Oginga Odinga (Kenya), Agostinho Neto (Angola), Samora Machel (Mozambique), and Robert Sobukwe (South Africa). This chapter shall focus exclusively on Lumumba, Ben Bella, Cabral, and Machel.

Note that in the socialist-populist ideology, the emphasis is on *socialist*, while in the populist-socialist ideology (which will be the subject of Chapter 7), the emphasis is on *populist*. Furthermore, in all these instances, the focus of our study is on the *political ideas* and the common themes that bind them rather than the individual leaders themselves. The chapter begins with an overview of the unfinished revolution in the Congo (1960–61) under the leadership of Patrice Emery Lumumba. It continues with an analysis of the Algerian revolution and the construction of socialism in Algeria by Ahmed Ben Bella. Next comes a study of the revolutionary theory and practice of Amical Cabral in Guinea-Bissau. The chapter ends with an overview of Samora Machel's Popular-Democratic government in Mozambique. Note that (except for the Congo), all the countries studied in this chapter achieved independence as a result of a long and protracted armed struggle.

PATRICE ÉMERY LUMUMBA

A Biographical Note

Patrice Émery Lumumba led the struggle for the independence of the Congo (now the Democratic Republic of the Congo) and became that country's first prime minister. His political murder just six months after independence made him a martyr of anticolonial resistance and a symbol of the African and Pan-African struggles throughout the world. Lumumba was born in 1925 in the district of Sankuru, Central Kasai province of the then Belgian Congo. In the course of his primary and secondary education, Lumumba became familiar with the writings of Karl Marx and Jean-Paul Sartre, which shaped his political ideas. He worked eleven years for the Belgian colonial service in the Congo, primarily in the post-office. As a member of the *évolués* (educated elite), Lumumba began writing and agitating for the Congolese anticolonial movement; he wrote articles for various anticolonial publications and was also active in a number of professional organizations. Lumumba's anticolonial activities brought him to the attention of the Belgian authorities, who sent him to Belgium in 1956 on a goodwill tour. The political reforms of 1957 led to the emergence of numerous political parties in 1958, including the *Mouvement National Congolais* (MNC/Congolese National Movement)—the first truly nationalist, non-ethnic and non-regional Congolese party—which was led by Patrice Lumumba. That same year, a Brussels branch of *Présence Africaine*—a Paris-based African cultural society and journal—was established; this brought the Congolese intellectual elite (including Lumumba) in contact with African nationalist thought from the rest of the French-speaking countries and anticolonial leftist groups in Belgium.[3] In December 1958, Lumumba travelled to Accra (Ghana) to participate in the All-African Peoples Conference (AAPC) convened by Kwame Nkrumah. By April 1959, the MNC and other Congolese political parties demanded Congolese self-government by 1960. When rioting broke out in November 1959, Lumumba was held responsible, arrested, and sentenced to six months' imprisonment; he was released just in time to attend the Belgian-Congolese Round Table Conference in Brussels (Belgium) in January–February 1960.

As agreed at the conference, Congo became independent on June 30, 1960, following parliamentary elections in which the MNC obtained a majority of the votes. Patrice Lumumba became prime minister, while Joseph Kasa-Vubu (a moderate party leader close to the West) was named president of the new republic. However, within two weeks of the proclamation of independence, Lumumba was faced with both a nationwide mutiny of the army and a secessionist movement in the mining province of Katanga, both instigated by the Belgians, who intervened militarily on July 10, 1960. The events that followed may best be described as the first major crisis of decolonization in Africa. Lumumba successfully appealed to the United Nations (UN) Security Council to send a UN peacekeeping force to the Congo. However, the UN Secretary-General interpreted the UN mandate in accordance with Western—primarily Belgian and American—geo-strategic and economic interests, which, by that time, had decided that Lumumba had to be eliminated "by fair means or foul."[4] The Belgian-instigated and unconstitutional destitution of Lumumba by Kasa-Vubu on September 5, 1960, marked the beginning of a long period of constitutional, institutional, and political instability in the Congo, culminating in the assassination of Lumumba on January 17, 1961. Evidence has recently come to light that the Belgians actually planned and carried out the murder of Patrice Lumumba, with the help of their American allies and in the presence of Katangese government officials (notably Prime Minister Moïse Tshombe).[5]

The Unfinished Congolese Revolution

Patrice Lumumba's political ideas were not static; they evolved from a moderate to a radical position over the years. In a book published in 1961 (*Le Congo, terre d'avenir, est-il menacé?*), he came through as a moderate liberal advocating minor reforms—rather than a complete overhaul—of the colonial system.[6] Writing in 1956, he developed such moderate themes as "Eurafrica, racial equality, status for the elite, and the Belgo-Congolese community."[7]

Greatly influenced by the political thought of Kwame Nkrumah and other radical African nationalist and Pan-Africanist leaders participating in the December 1958 All-African People's Conference (AAPC; Accra, Ghana) such as Frantz Fanon, Gamal Abdel Nasser, and Ahmed Sékou Touré, he brought back to the Congo new political ideas and a strong commitment to African nationalism and Pan-Africanism. In his speech at the Accra conference, Lumumba revealed some of these ideas, outlined in the MNC's program of action, which included the following priorities: independence, democracy, unity, and territorial integrity:

> The fundamental aim of our movement is to free the Congolese people from the colonialist regime and earn them their independence . . . We wish to see a modern democratic state established in our country, which will grant its citizen freedom, justice, social peace, tolerance, well-being, and equality, with no discrimination whatsoever . . . In our actions . . . we are against no one, *but rather are simply against domination, injustices, and abuses, and merely want to free ourselves of the shackles of colonialism and all its consequences* . . . Along with this struggle for national liberation waged *with calm and dignity, our movement opposes, with every power at its command, the balkanization of national territory under any pretext whatsoever.*"[8]

In the realm of culture, Lumumba called for a revalorization of African culture that, appropriately mixed with the positive elements of Western culture, would give rise to a new type of African civilization: "On the cultural plane, the new African states must make a serious effort to further African culture. We have a culture of our own, unparalleled moral and artistic values, an art of living and patterns of life that are ours alone. All these African splendors must be jealously preserved and developed. We will borrow from Western civilization what is good and beautiful and reject what is not suitable for us. This amalgam of African and European civilization will give Africa a civilization of a new type, an authentic civilization corresponding to African realities."[9] In terms of political organization, Lumumba advocated broad popular movements and unified political parties operating on the basis of internal democracy, with a constructive opposition and, eventually, a democratic political system based on pluralism: "In my view, there is only one way: bringing all Africans together in popular movements or unified parties . . . A genuine democracy will be at work within these parties and each one will have the satisfaction of expressing its opinions freely . . . The existence of an intelligent, dynamic, and constructive opposition is indispensable in order to counterbalance the political and administrative action of the government in power. But his moment does not appear to have arrived yet."[10] In foreign affairs, Lumumba—just like his political mentor Nkrumah—advocated a policy of nonalignment and "positive neutralism" vis-à-vis the two main politico-ideological blocs (East and West), a policy based on the specifically African ideology of the "African Personality": "Africa will tell the West that it wants the rehabilitation of Africa now, a return to the sources, the reinstitution of moral values; the African personality must express itself; that is what our policy of positive neutralism means . . . We have no intention of letting ourselves be guided by just any ideology. We have our own ideology, a strong ideology, a noble ideology, the affirmation of the African personality."[11] It was at the Pan-African Conference that he convened in Leopoldville (now Kinshasa; August 25–31, 1960) that Lumumba outlined his Pan-African project, the ideological cornerstone of his foreign policy. Having earlier declared that "the independence of the Congo represents a decisive step toward the liberation of the entire African continent," he went on to identify the various areas of African cooperation and integration, notably military cooperation, trade agreements, and cooperation in telecommunications and scientific research, concluding with the following call to action: "African unity and solidarity are no longer mere dreams; we must now embody them in concrete decisions."[12]

As noted before, Patrice Lumumba was only in power for six short months before falling prey to his sworn enemies, who had variously portrayed him as a racist, ultra-radical, dangerous "Communist," a Soviet stooge, and even as a "mad dog!"[13] He was thus unable to implement his ambitious political agenda.

AHMED BEN BELLA

A Biographical Note

Ahmed Ben Bella was born in Marnia (on the Moroccan-Algerian border) on December 25, 1916, into a peasant family. He was educated in Marnia and then attended secondary school in Tlemcen. Upon leaving school, Ben Bella did a variety of jobs before being called up for military service by the French government in 1937. During World War II, he served with distinction in the French Army, receiving many citations for valor. After the war's end (May 1945), he returned to Algeria and became active in various Algerian political movements agitating for independence, such as the *Mouvement pour le Triomphe des Libertés Démocratiques* (MTLD/Movement for Democratic Freedoms) and its more radical offshoot, the *Organisation Spéciale* (OS/Special Organization). Ben Bella was one of nine "historic leaders" who, in November 1954, launched the Algerian war of liberation spearheaded by the *Front de Libération Nationale* (FNL/National Liberation Front) and its armed wing, the *Armée de Libération Nationale* (ANL/National Liberation Army). In October 1956, he was detained in Algiers by the French authorities and imprisoned in France for six years. In 1958, while still in detention, he was appointed vice-chairman of the *Gouvernement Provisoire de la République Algérienne* (GPRA/Provisional Government of the Algerian Republic), the Algerian government-in-exile. After the Evian Peace Accords (March 1962) formally ended the war, Ahmed Ben Bella became prime minister of the Democratic People's Republic of Algeria proclaimed in September 1962 and president of the republic in 1963; the FLN was then declared "the one and only party of progress" and socialism became the state ideology. On

June 19, 1965, Ben Bella was overthrown by a military *coup d'état* led by his minister of defense, Colonel Houari Boumedienne. Detained until October 1980, he went into exile in Switzerland, only returning to Algeria in 1990. He died at his home in Algiers on April 11, 2012, at age 96.[14]

The Algerian Revolution and Algerian Socialism

Upon assuming power in 1962, Ahmed Ben Bella proclaimed "Algerian Socialism" to be the official state ideology; thus he declared, "We want an Algerian socialism which is based on our own experience and, at the same time, also draws on that of the socialist countries."[15] While evidently influenced by Western ideologies—such as Marxism and Socialism—Ben Bella's concept of Algerian Socialism was also firmly grounded in moral values derived from a (racially and ethnically) inclusive and broadly conceived Arab culture and civilization: "I have a way of acting and thinking in life, a certain ethic, a definite heritage of culture and civilization, a specific type of humanism and certain moral values."[16] Observing that in Algeria the peasantry constitutes the core of the "revolutionary masses," Ben Bella advocated a comprehensive program of agrarian reform driven by and directly benefiting the peasantry: "We wish to promote agricultural reform from below so that the peasant masses may be involved and participate directly in its [implementation] through large-scale movements in the countryside."[17] As a result, former French agricultural estates were reorganized into large-scale self-managed units. At the same time, an *Office National de la Réforme Agraire* (ONRA) was created.[18] Politically, Ben Bella favored a single party, the FLN (National Liberation Front), which he invited the members of all the other parties and movements to join.[19] Denouncing neocolonialism—defined as the "modernization" of colonialism after independence—as "our greatest scourge" and "a new form of slavery," Ben Bella advocated neutralism as the cornerstone of Algeria's foreign policy.[20] Article 2 of the Algerian Constitution stated, "Algeria is an integral part of the Arab Maghreb, of the Arab world, and of Africa;" it practices "positive neutralism and non-engagement." Ben Bella was a committed Pan-Africanist, and Algeria became a founding member of the Organization of African Unity (OAU) on May 25, 1963. Algeria concretely manifested its support for the African liberation movements of Angola, Guinea-Bissau, Mozambique, and South Africa by providing them with military assistance, logistical support, and training facilities. The October–November 1963 border war between Algeria and Morocco was eventually resolved by an OAU mediation led by Malian president Modibo Kéïta at the Bamako Conference of October 29–30, 1963.

Ben Bella firmly believed that the Algerian state should control the "commanding heights" of the economy and thus initiated—through the decrees of March and October 1963—a policy of nationalization of the agricultural and industrial sectors. Furthermore, Ben Bella was convinced that real economic independence—characterized by full control over natural resources and a comprehensive industrialization program—could only be achieved by a close cooperation between less-developed countries, as exemplified by OPEC (Organization of Petroleum Exporting Countries). Algeria, Ben Bella declared, would take the lead in this process, first by providing natural gas to Morocco, Tunisia, and other African countries; then by setting aside a portion of its oil and gas revenues for the financing of development projects in the Maghreb and in other African countries.[21] Did the overthrow of Ben Bella in June 1965 have anything to do with this bold policy of South-South cooperation, which ran counter to the interests of the major Western transnational oil corporations then operating in Algeria? One can only speculate!

Toward the end of his brief 21-month tenure, Ben Bella became progressively estranged from his former companions—notably, Mohamed Boudiaf, Mohammed Khider, and Hocine Aït Ahmed—who all joined the opposition to his regime.[22] Furthermore, there is some evidence that Ben Bella's rule became increasingly personal, exclusive, and authoritarian. In Alistair Horne's words, "Ben Bella veered more and more towards measures of abstract socialism, more and more towards authoritarianism and the 'cult of personality.'"[23] In the end, he was the victim of the military elite on whom he increasingly relied and that continues to rule the country to this day.

AMILCAR CABRAL
A Biographical Note

Born in Bafata (Guinea-Bissau) on September 12, 1924, Amilcar Lopes Cabral was a man of many talents, at one and the same time poet, agronomist, intellectual, theoretician, revolutionary, political organizer, and diplomat. After attending school in the Cape Verde, he went on to study agronomy and hydraulic engineering at the *Instituto Superior de Agronomia* (Advanced School of Agronomy) in Lisbon. While in Portugal, he helped establish in 1951 the *Centro de Estudos Africanos* (Center for African Studies), advocating a "return to the source," a reclaiming of African culture and history, and a "re-Africanization of the mind." In Lisbon, Cabral's circle of African friends included Mario de Andrade, Agostinho Neto, Marcelino dos Santos, and Eduardo dos Santos. In 1952, Cabral returned to Portuguese Guinea as an agricultural engineer and was tasked with the colony's first agricultural census; this gave him a unique opportunity to get intimately acquainted with the land, its people, and its problems. In September 1956, he founded—with his brother Luis Cabral, Aristides Pereira, and others—a national liberation movement, the *Partido Africano da Idependencia da Guiné e Cabo Verde* (PAIGC/African Party for the Independence of Guinea and Cape Verde). After an extensive period of training and political education, the armed struggle began in January 1963. It was so successful that by 1969 the PAIGC controlled two-thirds of the territory. Unfortunately, Cabral did not live to see Guinea-Bissau's independence; he was assassinated in Conakry (Guinea) by Portuguese agents on January 20, 1973. Following a military coup d'état in Lisbon that ended the Portuguese dictatorship, Guinea-Bissau became independent on September 10, 1974, with Luis Cabral (Amilcar's brother) as its first president.[24]

Revolutionary Theory and Practice in Guinea-Bissau

For Amilcar Cabral, theory and practice were inextricably linked; like two sides of the same coin, one does not go without the other. Furthermore, he argued that an ideology—or revolutionary theory—was essential for any national liberation movement to succeed and that ideology is precisely what was most lacking in these movements: "The ideological deficiency, not to say the total lack of ideology, within the national liberation movements . . . constitutes one of the greatest weaknesses of our struggle against imperialism, if not the greatest weakness of all . . . nobody has yet made a successful revolution without a revolutionary theory."[25] In addition, Cabral points out that each national liberation and social revolution has its own specific characteristics grounded in its particular historical situation and circumstances: "National liberation and social revolution are not exportable commodities; they are . . . the outcome of local and national elaboration, more or less influenced by external factors . . . but essentially determined and formed by the historical reality of each people."[26] Commenting on the nature of the PAIGC, Basil Davidson emphasizes this crucial point: "The PAIGC is a revolutionary movement based on an analysis of social reality *in Guiné*: revolutionary precisely and above all because its guiding lines are drawn from totally indigenous circumstances."[27] Cabral argues (like Frantz Fanon) that because of the violence inherent in colonial and neocolonial rule, national liberation movements must necessarily resort to violence: "The essential instrument of imperialist domination is violence . . . there is not, and cannot be national liberation without the use of liberating violence by the nationalist forces, to answer the criminal violence of the agents of imperialism."[28]

Central to Cabral's concept of national liberation is the notion of "return to the source"—namely, the right of a people to reclaim their culture and history: "The national liberation of a people is the regaining of the historical personality of that people, its return to history through the destruction of the imperialist domination to which it was subjected."[29] Basil Davidson puts it succinctly: "Hence the concept of national liberation was to be defined not so much as the right of a people to rule itself, but as the right of a people to regain its own history."[30] Pushing the argument one step further, Cabral argued that because cultural oppression is a key element of imperialist domination, national liberation is essentially an act of cultural liberation on the part of the people: "If imperialist domination has the vital need to practice cultural oppression, national liberation is necessarily an act of culture . . . we may consider the national liberation movement as the organized political expression of the culture of the people who are undertaking the struggle."[31]

At independence, the African states and leaders face a stark ideological choice—either capitalism or socialism: "There are only two possible paths for an independent nation: to return to imperialist domination (neo-colonialism, capitalism, state capitalism), or to take the way of socialism."[32] Cabral's vision of the ideal future society implied the liberation of people from oppression, exploitation, and poverty, leading to the creation of a "new man" and a "new society." As Lars Rudebeck succinctly puts it, "The long-term, overriding goal of the PAIGC has always been the socialist ideal of ending—once and for all—'the exploitation of man by man' . . . From this perspective, socialism is synonymous with human emancipation and liberation from exploitation."[33] Similarly, Patrick Chabal observes that while Cabral's "analysis of history, development and society are predicated on a Marxist framework, . . . he found little inspiration in Marxism for his work as an African nationalist and was thus forced to step outside accepted social and political theories."[34] Chabal argues that Cabral was, above all, a nationalist, a realist, a pragmatist, and a humanist: "Cabral was first and foremost a nationalist. Nationalism, not communism, was his cause. But he was also a humanist, a socialist and above all, a pragmatist. His political values were largely based on moral commitments . . . The other key aspect of his personality was his deep commitment to humanist ideals and his direct concern for human beings, especially the oppressed and the down-trodden."[35] Politically, Cabral favored direct democracy through decentralized regional assemblies, and he viewed the village councils as a grassroots base of society. The model of development envisaged by Cabral, sometimes referred to as "developmental nationalism," was based on self-reliance, meeting the people's basic needs, and a decentralized, people-centered, and bottom-up type of decision making.[36] Unfortunately, Cabral did not live to implement his vision of the ideal polity and society. However, he left these words of wisdom as his intellectual testament to the people of Guinea-Bissau and Africa: "Always bear in mind that the people are not fighting for ideas . . . They are fighting to win material benefits, to live better and in peace, to see their lives go forward, to guarantee the future of their children . . . Create schools and spread education in all liberated areas . . . Hide nothing from the masses of our people. Tell no lies. Expose lies whenever they are told. Mask no difficulties, mistakes, failures. Claim no easy victory."[37]

SAMORA M. MACHEL

A Biographical Note

Born in the Chokwe district of Gaza province on September 29, 1933, Samora Moïses Machel was one of the main leaders of the liberation struggle in Mozambique (with Eduardo Mondlane) and a foremost African revolutionary thinker and strategist. After nursing training, Machel joined the Front for the Liberation of Mozambique (FRELIMO) at its creation in June 1962 as well as the armed struggle against Portuguese colonialism initiated in September 1964. Machel took overall command of the guerilla forces in 1966; he became secretary of defense and, in May 1970, president of FRELIMO following the assassination of Eduardo Mondlane in February 1969.

After the collapse of dictatorship in Portugal, FRELIMO signed the Lusaka Accord of September 1974 that led, on June 25, 1975, to the formal independence of Mozambique from Portugal, with Samora Machel as president. With an economy in ruins, the top priority of his government was the provision of basic services, notably education and health care.

The advent of the white minority regime of Ian Smith in neighboring Southern Rhodesia (now Zimbabwe) (1965–80) significantly handicapped Mozambique's development. Smith (and South Africa) supported a reactionary movement, the Mozambique National Resistance Movement (RENAMO). After the advent of majority rule in Zimbabwe, Machel drafted an ambitious ten-year plan and took part in the creation of the Southern African Development Co-ordination Conference (SADCC) to reduce economic dependence on South Africa. Machel began moving away from doctrinaire Marxism toward a more mixed economy. As RENAMO's insurgency increased, Mozambique—which also provided sanctuary to the African National Congress (ANC)—descended into civil war, and the economy further deteriorated. This forced Machel to negotiate and sign the Nkomati Accord with South Africa, by which both countries agreed to expel ANC and RENAMO fighters from their territories. Returning from a Front-Line States summit in Zambia on October 19, 1986, Samora Machel was killed in a plane crash just inside the South African border. It has since been revealed that a South African radar manipulation actually led to the fatal crash.[38]

The Popular-Democratic Revolution in Mozambique

The political ideas of Samora Machel and Amilcar Cabral are strikingly similar. This is due to the fact that both leaders—plus the leader of Angola's liberation movement, Agostinho Neto—faced the same enemy: an extremely backward, reactionary, dictatorial, and exploitative Portuguese regime that depended on its colonies for its economic survival. As noted before, students from all the Portuguese colonies studying in Lisbon in the early 1950s socialized (and exchanged ideas) within such institutions as the Center for African Studies; they also participated in—and were deeply influenced by—the Portuguese anticolonial movement spearheaded by the Communist Party.

As was the case in the other Portuguese colonies (Guinea Bissau, Cape Verde, and Angola), the dialectical relationship between theory and practice was a key element of the liberation struggle in Mozambique: "Without revolutionary theory there is no revolutionary practice."[39] The point is made most emphatically by Machel in the following statement: "Ideology is always the result of a people's concrete revolutionary struggle; for this ideology to become real, it must be accepted and internalized by the broad masses; this is when theory is re-born and becomes embodied in the process of the daily struggle. This is the only way in which ideology is transformed into an irresistible material force which allows the people to overthrow the old order and to build the new society."[40] In fact, Machel attributed FRELIMO's success to "the priority of ideology." Once national unity within the liberation movement has been achieved, Machel argued, ideology becomes essential in the planning of the new society: "Once these forces [for national liberation] are mobilized around the platform it is imperative to define their unity at the ideological level, to give them a clear and common perspective."[41] According to Machel, one of the key elements of this ideology is an inclusive, people-based nationalism transcending race, ethnicity, region, and religion: "No one can claim that they are representatives of a race, ethnic group, region or religious belief. They represent the working people . . . No one fought for a region, race, tribe or religion. We all fought and are still fighting for the same nation, for the single ideal of liberation of our land and our people."[42] The *people*, argues Machel, are front and center in the liberation struggle, and because in independent Mozambique sovereignty belongs to the *people*, it follows that the leaders should be in their service. Thus article 9 of FRE-LIMO's program hammered out at its First Congress (September 23–28, 1962) promised "to form a government of the people, by the people, and for the people in which sovereignty of the nation will reside in the will of the people."[43] Machel further elaborates on this important point: "Power belongs to the people. It has been won by the people and it must be exercised and defended by the people . . . Because power belongs to the people, those who exercise it are the servants of the people."[44]

As Marina and David Ottaway have aptly observed, "A socialist revolution, in Frelimo's view, could not take place immediately in Mozambique, but had to be preceded by two preliminary stages: a 'national democratic revolution' and a 'popular democratic revolution.' The first having been achieved with independence, Frelimo was now launching the popular democratic revolution devoted to the 'intensification of class struggle,' the creation of a 'New Man,' and the development of the economy under state control."[45] Indeed, the type of political system to be established by FRELIMO at independence may best be characterized as "popular-democratic," based on consensual, collective decision making and aimed at creating a "New Man": "We will thus establish true democracy throughout the country . . . FRELIMO's People's Democratic Government is also distinguished . . . by its collective working style, joint discussion and analysis of problems, mutual cooperation . . . We are engaged in a Revolution whose advance depends on the creation of the new man, with a new mentality. We are engaged in a Revolution aimed at the establishment of People's Democratic Power."[46] Machel makes a distinction between three aspects of democracy: political, military, and economic: "Political democracy is based on collective discussion, on a collective solution of our problems . . . Military democracy is ensured by the participation of everyone in absorbing our combat experience . . . Economic democracy is an integral part of our fight to destroy the system of exploitation of man."[47]

With regard to political organization, Machel emphasizes the primacy of politics over all other sectors; concretely, this means that it is the party that must guide government action: "Politics must guide government action . . . it is FRELIMO's political line . . . that must guide government action, FRE-LIMO that must orientate the government and the masses."[48] According to Machel, there must be *internal democracy* within the party, based on the following principles: free discussion, collective decision making and responsibility, submission of the minority to the majority, and criticism and self-criticism.[49] Machel also emphasizes the point that the party's decisions must be genuinely democratic—that is, they must reflect the people's interests as well as involve the people in the decision-making process: "Our decisions must always be democratic in both content and form. Democratic in content means that they must reflect the real interests of the broad masses. Democratic in form means that the broad masses must take part in reaching a decision, feeling that it is theirs and not something imposed from above."[50] Machel advocates a self-reliant strategy of development in which priority is given to the agricultural sector, and industrialization is based on agriculture: "What can be done immediately by relying on one's own efforts should be analyzed in every productive unit, village, neighborhood, and family cell . . . Agriculture will therefore be the base of our development and industry its galvanizing factor. Industrial development must be based on the processing of our natural resources, which will make it possible to diversify and increase the value of exports."[51]

It is important to point out here that the particular historical circumstances of the liberation struggle in Mozambique had a major influence on the nature and *modus operandi* of FRELIMO as the embodiment of the interests, priorities, and needs of the peasant masses. Indeed, the front did not try to run the liberated zones from the top down; instead, it encouraged the peasants to organize themselves and elect their own leaders, relying on persuasion rather than coercion. Toward the end of the liberation struggle, the liberated zones covered one-fifth of the national territory, with a population of about 800,000. In these conditions, FRELIMO inevitably relied heavily on the peasants to run their own affairs, favoring a type of direct democracy. The key local unit created during the war was the *aldeia communal* (or communal village). Thus the experience of the Mozambican people during the war of liberation naturally led to FRELIMO's reliance on the communal villages to promote both participation and collectivization at independence. In a striking example of "grassroots" democracy at work, 894 "people's assemblies" were established at the local, district, municipal, provincial, and national levels in the elections of 1977 (September to December). In a rare example of direct democracy in Africa, the names of the candidates in this election were subject to public scrutiny at open meetings where villagers were invited to speak up and comment on the qualifications of the candidates.[52]

Finally, Machel held that particular attention should be given in an independent Mozambique to culture, education, training, primary health care, and the liberation of women, with particular focus on basic education and the promotion of literacy among the peasant masses.[53]

CONCLUSION

This chapter surveyed the political, social, and cultural dimensions of the socialist-populist ideology from a distinctly socialist perspective. The common characteristics of the leaders associated with this ideology are (1) their short tenure of office; (2) their preference for democratic governance; and (3) their populism, meaning that they have the best interest of their people at heart. A factor common to their countries is the fact that three of them (Algeria, Guinea-Bissau, and Mozambique) achieved independence as a result of an armed struggle.

Of all the leaders surveyed in this chapter, Patrice Lumumba was the one who ruled for the shortest time (just over six months), hence the subtitle "The Unfinished Congolese Revolution." This fact explains why his vision of a socialist society based on pluralism, a broad popular movement, internal democracy, and a Pan-African foreign policy never materialized. While Ahmed Ben Bella ruled a bit longer (two and a half years), it was not long enough to effect a substantial and lasting transformation of Algerian society. Ben Bella advocated a form of socialism based on Arab culture and civilization and on state control of the economy. He initiated agrarian reform and conducted a nonaligned, Pan-African foreign policy.

Amilcar Cabral and Samora Machel led the liberation struggle against Portuguese colonial rule in their respective countries, Guinea-Bissau and Mozambique. Their common colonial experience explains why their political ideologies are so similar and emphasize the same themes:

1. *Ideology* being essential to the building of the new society
2. The need to link *theory* and *practice*
3. The primacy of the *political*
4. The need to *return to the source*, to retain African culture and history, and to create a *"new man"*
5. Acknowledging *the people* as the main actors and beneficiaries of the socialist revolution
6. Implementing direct, popular democracy through the agency of decentralized regional assemblies and village councils
7. Implementing a *self-reliant*, people-centered strategy of development

Unfortunately, the premature and untimely death of both Amilcar Cabral and Samora Machel did not enable them to fully implement the policies that they had begun to test on an experimental basis in the liberated areas of their respective countries.

FURTHER READING

Africa Information Service, ed., *Return to the Source: Selected Speeches by Amilcar Cabral* (New York: Monthly Review Press, 1973).

Cabral, Amilcar, *Revolution in Guinea: Selected Texts by Amilcar Cabral*, edited and translated by Richard Handyside (New York: Monthly Review Press, 1972).

Davidson, Basil, *The Liberation of Guiné: Aspects of an African Revolution*, foreword by Amilcar Cabral (Baltimore, MD: Penguin Books, 1969).

Merle, Marcel, *Ahmed Ben Bella* (New York: Walker, 1967).

Munslow, Barry, ed., *Samora Machel: An African Revolutionary* (London: Zed Books, 1985).

Van Lierde, Jean, ed., *Lumumba Speaks: The Speeches & Writings of Patrice Lumumba, 1958–1961*, translated by Helen R. Lane, introduction by Jean-Paul Sartre (Boston: Little, Brown and Co., 1972).

CHAPTER 6

———⋆◄❂►⋆———

THE SOCIALIST-POPULIST
IDEOLOGY II

FROM KWAME NKRUMAH
TO JULIUS NYERERE

*The basis of colonial territorial dependence is economic, but the basis of
the solution of the problem is political. Hence political independence is an
indispensable step towards securing economic emancipation.*

—Kwame Nkrumah, *Towards Colonial Freedom*, xv

INTRODUCTION

This chapter continues the survey—started in Chapter 5—of the political,
economic, social, and cultural dimensions of the socialist-populist ideology
from a distinctly socialist perspective. It shall focus on the statesmen (and
regimes) who, in spite of their socialist rhetoric, have used the socialist-
populist ideology as an instrument of control and coercion and sometimes—as in the case of Guinea's Sékou Touré—even as an instrument of
terror. These political systems are characterized by relatively authoritarian
(sometimes totalitarian) regimes, a top-down system of administration, as
well as state control over the economy. Gamal Abdel Nasser (Egypt), Kwame
Nkrumah (Ghana), Ahmed Sékou Touré (Guinea), Modibo Kéïta (Mali),
and Julius Nyerere (Tanzania) all fall in this category. It is important to note
in this regard that there is a significant difference of degree between these
leaders in terms of the authoritarian vs. democratic nature of their regimes.
Thus the most autocratic and authoritarian (even totalitarian) tendencies
were exhibited by Sékou Touré and Kwame Nkrumah (more pronounced
in the former than in the latter), while Modibo Kéïta and Julius K. Nyerere
were somewhat more liberal, open, and democratic in their exercise of power
(Nyerere more so than Kéïta).

As we have noted in the previous chapter, in the socialist-populist ideology the emphasis is on *socialist*, while in the populist-socialist ideology (which will be the subject of Chapter 7) the emphasis is on *populist*. Furthermore, in all these instances, the focus of our study is on the *political ideas* and the common themes that bind them rather than the individual leaders themselves. This chapter begins with a study of the "Father of African Nationalism," Kwame Nkrumah of Ghana, whose influential political ideas are encapsulated in the concept of the "African Personality." The chapter then surveys the political ideas and policies of two key proponents of "African Socialism" in Francophone Africa: Ahmed Sékou Touré of Guinea and Modibo Kéïta of Mali. The chapter concludes with a survey of the political ideology and policies of another prominent advocate of "African Socialism," *Mwalimu* Julius K. Nyerere of Tanzania.

Problems of ideology and political organization were foremost in the minds of most African leaders in the immediate pre- and postindependence period. These leaders were of the opinion that such problems should be tackled before any attempt to solve economic problems could be envisaged. Nkrumah makes the point succinctly: "The basis of colonial territorial dependence is *economic*, but the basis of the solution of the problem is *political*. Hence *political independence* is an indispensable step towards securing economic emancipation."[1] Such is also the meaning of Kwame Nkrumah's famous motto: "Seek ye first the political kingdom, and everything shall be added unto it." For these leaders, the economic policy should result from a consistent political ideology, and not the reverse. The two most prominent proponents of this view in West Africa were Ghana's Kwame Nkrumah and Guinea's Ahmed Sékou Touré.

KWAME NKRUMAH

A Biographical Note

Francis Nwia Kofi Kwame Nkrumah—Pan-Africanist, one of the founders of the Organization of African Unity, and the first leader of independent Ghana—was born in September 1909 (day unknown) in Nkroful, Nzima region, in southwestern Gold Coast. He was educated first at local missionary schools, then at Achimota College, graduating as a teacher in 1930. In 1935, Nkrumah travelled to the United States to study at Lincoln University. He then pursued graduate studies at the University of Pennsylvania. From 1943 to 1945, he taught at Lincoln and served as president of the African Students Association of the United States and Canada. During his ten-year stay in the United States, Nkrumah became familiar with the writings of such African American scholar-activists as W. E. B. Du Bois and Marcus Garvey, who inspired his ideas about Pan-Africanism; he also socialized with (and learned political organization from) prominent Caribbean activists such as C. L. R. James and George Padmore. In 1945, Nkrumah went to London, presumably to study at the London School of Economics and Political

Science (LSE). There, he became active in (and vice-president of) the West African Students' Union (WASU). Nkrumah also played a prominent role in the organization of the Fifth Pan-African Congress in Manchester (October 15–19, 1945), acting as co-treasurer (with George Padmore). This also gave Nkrumah an opportunity to get acquainted with other African nationalist leaders such as Peter Abrahams (South Africa), Obafemi Awolowo (Nigeria), Hastings K. Banda (Malawi), and Jomo Kenyatta (Kenya). W. E. B. Du Bois and C. L. R. James were also in attendance. Following the congress, Nkrumah was one of the founders and general-secretary of the West African National Secretariat aiming at a "United West African Independence."

In 1947, Nkrumah left Britain and returned to the Gold Coast to become secretary-general of the newly-created, anti-colonial United Gold Coast Convention (UGCC). In 1948, following his arrest and detention as a result of labor unrest, Nkrumah left the UGCC over political differences, and in June 1949, he founded his own radical nationalist political party, the Convention People's Party (CPP), which demanded "full Self-Government now!" In 1950, the CPP campaign of "positive action" led to strikes and demonstrations throughout the colony. The colonial authorities declared a state of emergency, and Nkrumah was, once again, arrested and detained. Released from prison in 1951, Nkrumah became leader of government business the same year and prime minister from 1952. The CPP won comfortable majorities in the general elections of 1951, 1954, and 1956. Nkrumah led the country to "internal self-government" and, eventually, to formal independence in March 1957. Nkrumah became Ghana's first president and was re-elected unopposed in 1965 He was overthrown by a military coup d'état on February 24, 1966, while on a trip abroad and went into exile in Guinea, where Sekou Toure made him honorary co-president. After some years of ill health, Nkrumah died of cancer in Bucharest (Romania) on April 27, 1972. In 1994, he received an official re-burial in a special mausoleum in Accra.[2]

African Socialism and CONSCIENCISM

Nkrumah's definition of *ideology* differs somewhat from the conventional one, according to which an ideology is a body of writing of one individual, or a small group of individuals, directed only at radical change in a society. For Nkrumah, "an ideology, even when it is revolutionary, does not merely express the wish that a present social order should be abolished. It seeks also to defend and maintain the new social order which it introduces."[3] He also views ideology and practice as being inextricably (even dialectically) linked: "Practice without thought is blind; thought without practice is empty."[4]

The intellectual eclecticism of Kwame Nkrumah is evident from the following remarks by Thomas Hodgkin, a British scholar who was also a friend and political adviser of the late president: "He had . . . the kind of intellect at the same time organizing and practical, which enabled him to search and turn to practical use, bits of theories that came his way and seemed likely to fit the context of the Gold Coast—collecting ideas and storing them against the future as a squirrel collects and store nuts. The essential eclecticism of this approach is worth stressing."[5] It is necessary to refer to Nkrumah's *Autobiography* to trace the evolution of his political thought. From his political awakening to his overthrow, the constant and most prominent feature in Nkrumah's character was his staunch, unremitting, and truly passionate *nationalism*. The formulation of his strong resentment against colonialism dates from as far back as his years as a student in America: "Independence for the Gold Coast was my aim. It was a colony and I have always regarded colonialism as the policy by which a foreign power binds territories to herself by political ties with the primary object of promoting her own economic advantage."[6] Nkrumah observes that nationalism constitutes only one stage in the liberation struggle, whose ultimate goal is the achievement of Pan-Africanism and Socialism: "The nationalist phase is a necessary step in the liberation struggle, but must never be regarded as the final solution to the problem raised by the economic and political exploitation of our peoples."[7]

While in London, Nkrumah devoted much of his time and energy to the study and practice of socialism and Pan-Africanism. He mentions the political writers who inspired him in the shaping of his own political thought as being "Hegel, Karl Marx, Engels, Lenin and Mazzini. The writings of these men did much to influence me in my revolutionary ideas and activities, and Karl Marx and Lenin particularly impressed me as I felt sure that their philosophy was capable of solving these problems."[8] The question of whether Nkrumah was a convinced Marxist has perplexed Ghana scholars for some time. In fact, Nkrumah views Marxism more as a tool to be adapted to specific local conditions than as an end in itself. Hence his emphasis on the *practical* side rather than on the theoretical aspects of Marxism: "My aim was to learn the technique of organization . . . I know that whatever the program for the solution of the colonial question might be, success would depend upon the organization adopted. I concentrated on finding a formula by which the whole colonial question and the problem of imperialism could be solved."[9] This formula was Marxism-Leninism. Later, Nkrumah would remind the cadres of the party, "Let us not forget that Marxism is not a dogma but a guide to action."[10] It is probably the Marxist analysis of imperialism—and particularly Lenin's characterization of imperialism as "the highest stage of capitalism"— that Nkrumah found most convincing as he reflected on imperialism's impact on Africa: "The most searching and penetrating analysis of economic imperialism has been given by Marx and Lenin."[11] It is interesting to note in this regard that Nkrumah deliberately paraphrased Lenin in the subtitle of his book *Neo-Colonialism: The Last Stage of Imperialism*, published in 1965.[12]

Criticizing the "muddled thinking" about African socialism, Nkrumah observed that "there is only one true socialism and that is *scientific socialism*, the principles of which are abiding and universal." He went on to summarize socialism as "(1) Common ownership of the means of production, distribution and exchange . . . (2) Planned methods of production by the state, based on modern industry and agriculture. (3) Political power in the hands of the people . . . in keeping with the humanist and egalitarian spirit which characterized African traditional society . . . (4) Application of scientific methods in all spheres of thought and production."[13] Another important aspect of Nkrumah's political thought that developed during these days was his strong Pan-Africanism. He himself admits that "of all the literature that I studied, the book that did more than any other to fire my enthusiasm was *Philosophy and Opinions of Marcus Garvey* published in 1923."[14] Since this dimension of Nkrumah's political thought has been abundantly documented in Chapter 4, it is not necessary to elaborate on it further at this point. Suffice it to note here Nkrumah's deep conviction that the independence of Ghana would be incomplete and meaningless unless it is linked with the liberation of the whole African continent. For him, African unity implied that (1) imperialism and foreign oppression should be eradicated in all their forms, (2) neo-colonialism should be recognized and eliminated, and (3) the new African nation must develop within a continental framework.[15]

There are strong indications in Nkrumah's thought of the influence of Christian ethics that were impressed on him while a student of theology at Lincoln Seminary in the United States. Nkrumah is at great pains to demonstrate that his philosophy of "Consciencism"—defined as "a philosophy and ideology for decolonization"—and religion are not necessarily inconsistent: "Philosophical consciencism, even though deeply rooted in materialism, is not necessarily atheistic."[16] In his *Autobiography*, he describes himself as "a non-denominational Christian and a Marxist socialist," and, he adds, "I have not found any contradiction between the two."[17]

In his book *Consciencism*, Nkrumah identifies the three main segments of African society, animated by competing ideologies, as being the traditional, the Western, and the Islamic. As a result, Nkrumah argues, a new ideology reflecting the unity of society, based on indigenous humanist African principles and catering to the needs of all, needs to emerge. Such an ideology he names *philosophical consciencism*:

> There are three broad features to be distinguished here. African society has one segment which comprises our traditional way of life; it has a second segment which is filled by the presence of the Islamic tradition in Africa; it has a final segment which represents the infiltration of the Christian tradition and culture of Western Europe into Africa . . . These different segments are animated by competing ideologies . . . A new emergent ideology is therefore required, . . . an ideology which will not abandon the original humanist principles of Africa . . . Such a philosophical statement I propose to name *philosophical consciencism*, for it will give the theoretical basis for an ideology whose aim shall be to contain the African experience of Islamic and Euro-Christian presence as well as the experience of the traditional African society, and, by gestation, employ them for the harmonious growth and development of that society.[18]

This approach has, more recently, been popularized in African studies by Ali A. Mazrui through his concept of "*Triple Heritage*," introduced in his television series and companion volumes titled *The Africans*, and refers to the fact that "three civilizations have helped to shape contemporary Africa: Africa's rich indigenous inheritance, Islamic culture, and the impact of Western traditions and lifestyles."[19]

In his struggle for Ghana's independence, Nkrumah found an important source of inspiration in the method of "non-violence" used by Mahatma Gandhi in his own struggle for India's independence. When Gandhi died, Nkrumah acknowledged that "we too mourned his death, for he had inspired us deeply with his political thought, notably with his adherence to non-violent resistance."[20] It is from Gandhi's concept of "non-violent resistance" that Nkrumah derived his own "Positive Action," which he evolved when organizing the Convention People's Party (CPP) in the struggle against British colonial rule. What he meant by "Positive Action" was "employing legitimate agitation, newspaper and political educational campaigns and the application of strikes, boycotts and non-cooperation based on the principle of non-violence."[21]

Nkrumah's conception of the party and the state is informed by the—distinctly Leninist—view of the preeminence of politics over economics, both in the liberation struggle and in the building up of the socialist state. Such is the meaning of the CPP early slogan (paraphrasing the Bible) "Seek ye first the political kingdom, and everything shall be added unto it." The CPP operates according to the Leninist principle of "Democratic Centralism," which Nkrumah defines as follows: "All are free to express their views. But once a majority decision is taken, we expect such a decision to be loyally executed, even by those who might have opposed that decision. This we consider and proclaim to be the truest form of Democratic Centralism—decisions freely arrived at and loyally executed. This applies from the lowest to the highest level. None is privileged and no one shall escape disciplinary action."[22] Nkrumah views the state as the main instrument of the building up of socialism in Ghana, eventually becoming "the state of all the people.": "In Marxism the State is the instrument of class dictatorship. While admitting the essential truth of this view, 'Consciencism' holds that the State is the great regulator of human behavior."[23]

In the final analysis, Nkrumah's essential political philosophy, variously labeled as "Consciencism" or "Nkrumaism," may best be characterized as "African socialism"—namely, socialism adapted to African indigenous culture and society seen as essentially classless, communal, and egalitarian:

> I would define *Nkrumaism* as a non-atheistic socialist philosophy which seeks to apply the current socialist ideas to the solution of our problems . . . by adapting these ideas to the realities of our everyday life. It is basically socialism adapted to suit the conditions and circumstances of Africa . . . The African traditional social system is basically communalistic, i.e. socialistic—a society in which the welfare of the individual is bound up with the welfare of all the people in the community. For this reason *Nkrumaism* is a socialist idea and way of life that is completely at home in Africa.[24]

Ultimately, Nkrumah's whole political philosophy revolves around the central concept of *the people*. Indeed, he views African socialism as a means of not only liberating the people from the shackles of imperialism but also—politically, economically, socially, and culturally—empowering the people after independence: "The liberation of a people institutes principles which enjoin the recognition and destruction of imperialistic domination, whether it is political, economic, social or cultural . . . The true welfare of a people does not admit of compromise . . . Independence once won, . . . it is not really possible to rule against the wish and interest of the people . . . The people are the backbone of positive action . . . The people are the reality of national greatness."[25]

AHMED SÉKOU TOURÉ
A Biographical Note

Ahmed Sékou Touré—generally referred to as Sékou Touré—was arguably one of the most controversial African leaders of the postcolonial era. Revered by some as a hero of independence and as one of the "Fathers of African Nationalism and Pan-Africanism" alongside Kwame Nkrumah—to whom he was extremely close, both personally and ideologically—he was despised by others as a brutal and ruthless autocrat and tyrant who mercilessly threw thousands of Guineans in prison and systematically eliminated any Guinean intellectual or politician whom he perceived as a threat to his rule. Sékou Touré was also one of the longest serving African presidents, having been in power for 26 years (1958–84)

Born in Farannah (northern Guinea) on January 9, 1922, in what was then French West Africa into a family of poor peasant farmers, Sékou Touré claimed to descend from the late-nineteenth-century West African Muslim reformer and empire-builder Almamy Samory Touré (a claim never convincingly proven). Educated first in local schools, he went in 1936 on to attend secondary school in Conakry (*École Georges Poiret*), from which he was expelled in 1937 for organizing a student food strike. Having completed his secondary education through correspondence courses, he joined the colonial post and telecommunications administration in 1941. In 1945, he founded the Post and Telecommunications Workers' Union (SPTT, the first trade union in French Guinea), and he became its first general-secretary in 1946. The SPTT was affiliated with the French *Confédération Générale des Travailleurs* (CGT/General Workers' Union), at that time associated with the French Communist Party (PCF). In March 1946, Sékou Touré attended the CGT Congress in Paris; in October of the same year, he became a founding member of the *Rassemblement Démocratique Africain* (RDA/African Democratic Union), an anticolonial movement created in Bamako that included representatives from all the French West African colonies. In 1948, Touré became secretary-general of the Coordinating Committee of the CGT in French West Africa and in 1952 secretary-general of the *Parti Démocratique de Guinée* (PDG/Democratic Party of Guinea), the territorial branch of the RDA. In 1953, he organized a successful anticolonial general strike. In January 1956, he was elected deputy for Guinea in the French National Assembly in Paris, and in November of that year he became mayor of Conakry. Following the enactment of the French *Loi-Cadre* of 1956, which granted internal autonomy to each constituent territory of French West Africa, and as a result of the elections of March 1957, Sékou Touré was elected vice-president of Guinea. That same year, he was also elected vice-president of the RDA. The year 1958 was quite eventful in the political history of Guinea. In what is arguably one of the best-documented events in the history of French decolonization, an apparent misunderstanding between the visiting French president Charles de Gaulle and his Guinean host Sékou Touré (August 25–26) led to Guinea's lone "No" vote in the September 28 Referendum, resulting in Guinea's early independence (October 2) and the breakup of Franco-Guinean relations. It was on August 25 that Sékou Touré famously declared, "We prefer poverty as free men to riches as slaves," to which de Gaulle retorted, "If Guinea wants independence, let her take it, with all the consequences!" After which he pronounced these ominous parting words: "*Adieu, la Guinée!*"[26]

Sékou Touré was on friendly terms with Ghana's Kwame Nkrumah, whom he greatly admired and whose political philosophy he shared. It thus came as no surprise that when Nkrumah was overthrown by a military coup in February 1966, Touré readily gave him asylum and made him honorary co-president of Guinea. A convinced Pan-Africanist, Sékou Touré engineered the Ghana-Guinea-Mali Union in May 1959 and was one of the "Founding Fathers" of the Organization of African Unity (OAU) in May 1963. Over the years, his regime became increasingly authoritarian and repressive. By February 1978, it was estimated that about a thousand people were still in prison simply for opposing the regime; all were released in 1984. In addition, hundreds of prominent Guinean intellectuals and cadres were jailed, tortured, and executed, including former OAU Secretary-General Diallo Telli in 1976. By the early 1980s, Sékou Touré had moved away from African socialism, initiated a *rapprochement* with the world Islamic movement, and was attempting to attract foreign private investment, even visiting the United States and France in 1982. Sékou Touré eventually died of heart failure in an American hospital (Cleveland, Ohio) on March 26, 1984.[27]

Building the Popular-Revolutionary Republic in Guinea

There is no doubt that Sékou Touré's years as a member of the French communist-oriented CGT strongly influenced his political thought. He also spent some time at a trade union seminar in Prague (former Czechoslovakia). These are strong indications that Sékou Touré's Marxist-Leninist education was more thorough than that of Kwame Nkrumah. Sékou Touré himself admits readily that "it would be absurd to deny that I have read a great number of Mao Tse-tung's writings, as well as the writings of all the great Marxist philosophers."[28] Famous for his fiery and lengthy oratory, Sékou Touré has left us an abundant corpus of works, including all his speeches and other writings collected in 28 volumes in French (25 volumes in English) as well as some more theoretical works.[29]

A number of scholars—such as Lapido Adamolekun and Yves Bénot—have observed that during the first decade of Guinea's independence (1958–67), Sékou Touré not only refused to launch the country on a clear path to socialism but also deliberately downplayed the role of ideology in the construction of the new society. In his view, Guinea was initiating a revolution that was specifically African, outside of any ideological frame of reference and that adamantly refused to choose between capitalism and socialism: "Whenever we are asked to define ourselves and to choose, we reply that . . . we define ourselves in reference to Africa and we choose Africa. We are told that we must necessarily choose between capitalism and socialism, but I regret to say that . . . we are practically incapable to define what capitalism is, what socialism is."[30] In an interview with French journalist Fernand Gigon, Touré is even more explicit: "It is almost certain that we would have failed if we had stuck blindly to an abstract philosophy . . . We are not interested in philosophy. We have concrete needs"[31] He went on to assert that concern with "theories which are strange to us" had little to do with the crucial tasks facing the country: "If we confine ourselves to purely ideological speculations, we shall not achieve anything"[32] For Touré, the main function of ideology is to mobilize the masses for the political and economic development of Guinea.

It was only at the Eighth National Congress of the PDG (1967) that Sékou Touré formally launched Guinea on the path to socialism: "The fundamental option of the Democratic Party of Guinea is to construct a socialist society . . . We must be clear: we are committed to socialism. That is an irreversible fact."[33] Sékou Touré's concept of socialism clearly derives from the orthodox definition of scientific socialism: "Socialism . . . is expressed by the effective exercise of political, economic and cultural power by the working people."[34] However, Touré also articulates a socialist ideology adapted to African realities, stating his preference for the term *communaucratic* instead of *African Socialism*: "Africa is essentially 'communaucratic.' Collective life and social solidarity give her habits a humanistic foundation . . . an African cannot imagine organizing his life outside that of his social group—family, village, or clan. The voice of African people is not individualistic."[35]

Like Nkrumah, Touré is eclectic in his choice of ideology in general and on his conception of Marxism in particular, viewing the latter more as a means to be adapted to specific local conditions than as an end in itself. Hence the emphasis on the practical side rather than on the theoretical aspects of Marxism: "In Marxism, the principles of organization, of democracy, of control, etc. everything which is concrete and concerns the organic life of given movements, perfectly find the means of becoming adapted to the prevailing conditions of Africa . . . I say that philosophy does not concern us. We have concrete needs."[36] Touré firmly believes in the supremacy of politics over the economy, just as Nkrumah does: "We shall . . . have the economy of our

politics and not the politics of our economy."[37] In an official party docu-
ment, he elaborates further on this point: "In Guinea's revolutionary context, economic and social action is the materialization of the *political line*, the
concrete expression of *political options*, the implementation of the creative
principle of the PDG's *political philosophy.*"[38]

Touré was profoundly influenced by the Marxist-Leninist ideology in his
definition of the roles of the state and the party in the creation of institutions
designed to translate socialist ideas into practice. The following statement
clearly illustrates the Leninist doctrine of the preeminence of the party over
the state: "We intend that the reason of State, the State interest, should be
determined in a manner consistent with the interests and aspirations of the
People, whose power, initiatives and actions are mediated by the Democratic
Party of Guinea (PDG) . . . The Party assumes the leading role in the life
of the nation: the political, judicial, administrative, economic and technical
powers are in the hands of the PDG."[39] For Touré, the Democratic Party of
Guinea is the definer of the general interest, the custodian of the popular will,
and the incarnation of the collective thought of the whole Guinean people:
"The Party constitutes the thought of the people of Guinea at its highest
level and in its most complete form. The thought of the Party indicates the
orientation of our actions; the thought of the Party specifies the principles
which ought to direct our behavior, our collective and individual attitude."[40]

Evidently, Touré's whole political philosophy—as that of Nkrumah—
revolved around the central concept of *the people*: "Our Plan will succeed
because it has the People as its main focus, because it will be conceived by
the People and realized for the People."[41] As a mass party, the PDG is the
party of "the entire people of Guinea": "Revolution can only be the act of
the people . . . No, the PDG is not a communist party; it is not a class party,
it is the party of all the people of Guinea . . . it is a popular party whose program of action is based exclusively on the national interest of the Republic
of Guinea."[42] As a result, the PDG (like Nkrumah's CPP) operated according to the principle of "Democratic Centralism," which allowed for a fairly
high degree of popular participation in the political decision-making process.
At the local level, local revolutionary authorities (*Pouvoirs Révolutionnaires
Locaux*/PRL) were responsible for the management of social and economic
development projects down to the village level. The Guinean socialist development strategy was based on a mixed economy in which the emphasis was
on the creation of a dominant public sector with a relatively sizeable—mostly
foreign—private sector.

The political thought of Sékou Touré has been concisely summed up by
Immanuel Wallerstein: "The political thought of Sékou Touré combines
the communaucratic impulse of Rousseau, the Leninist theory of the party
structure with the Hobbesian theory of sovereignty."[43] Claude Rivière offers
a more comprehensive and accurate summary of Touré's political thought:
"The final statement of this [PDG] ideology was above all the brainchild
of the Guinean leader who had been trained in three schools of thought—
those of Africa, the West, and Marxist socialism. The basic aim of Sékou

Touré's socialism or non-capitalist approach . . . is to alter the relationship between human beings. This is to be done by decolonizing their viewpoints and attitudes, and by creating a new man freed from a system of capitalistic exploitation and participating with all his strength in the development of his nation. Here nationalism transcends socialism."[44] In the final analysis, the failure of socialism in Guinea may be attributed to the extremely personalized rule of Sékou Touré, the prototype of the charismatic leader in Africa, variously referred to as Guinea's "Great Elephant" (*Sily*), "Supreme Guide of the Revolution," or even "Messiah." Indeed, from the mid-1950s until his death in 1984, Touré was the sole pivot of Guinea's politics, and the Guinean state, nation, and single party were all identified with the person of Touré himself. According to David and Marina Ottaway, perhaps his greatest failure was to create a *personalized* (rather than an *institutionalized*) political party: "Touré has worked harder and longer than any other African leader to build a party that would become the dominant political institution of the land and wield more effective, day-to-day power than the state. The end result has been a party that serves primarily as a direct extension of Touré himself rather than as a self-perpetuating body serving to institutionalize the revolution."[45] Toward the end of his regime (late 1970s–early 1980s), Sékou Touré moved progressively away from African socialism, encouraged the development of the private sector in the economy, and began to emphasize the "socialist" and "revolutionary" content of Islam. In the final analysis, Sékou Touré's obsessive and single-minded concern for power and his determination to survive as supreme leader of Guinea's unique "Party-State" prevailed over any other ideological or political considerations and led to his eventual political demise shortly before his death in March 1984.[46]

MODIBO KÉÏTA

A Biographical Note

First president of Mali, politician, and Pan-Africanist, Modibo Kéïta was born in Bamako (in what was then the French Sudan) on June 4, 1915. After attending primary and secondary school in Sudan, he went on for teacher training at *École William Ponty* in Dakar. In 1945, he (along with Mamadou Konaté) founded the *Bloc Soudanais* (BS). In 1946, the BS merged with the *Rassemblement Démocratique Africain* (RDA/African Democratic Union), an interterritorial, radical nationalist party then affiliated with the French Communist Party. In 1948, he was elected to the Territorial Assembly of the French Sudan; from 1956 to 1958, he served as deputy in and vice-president of the French National Assembly and also held a number of ministerial posts in the French government. From 1957 to 1959, he was a counselor in the French West African Federation. On January 17, 1959, he became president of the Mali Federation (including Senegal and the French Sudan) until it split apart on August 20, 1960.

On September 20, 1960, Kéïta became head of state and president of the newly-created Republic of Mali, a name chosen in reference to the glorious Mali Empire of medieval Africa. Under his presidency, Mali embarked on a path to socialism, both politically and economically. However, by 1967, the Malian economy was in crisis, forcing the Keita regime to sign a monetary agreement with France on February 15, 1967. On August 22, 1967, Kéïta's launching of a "Cultural Revolution" signaled a radicalization of the regime; more power was entrusted to a *Comité National de Defense de la Revolution* (CNDR/National Committee for the Defense of Revolution), as well as to the armed segment of the party, the Popular Militia. The militia's abuses of power apparently alienated a large segment of the populace and was the justification for the military coup d'état of November 19, 1968, which over-threw the Kéïta regime and inaugurated a military rule that would last 23 years. Modibo Kéïta died while in detention on May 16, 1977, apparently as a result of a lethal injection administered on direct orders from top officials of the government of Moussa Traoré.

Modibo Kéïta was—physically, politically, and symbolically—a giant among African statesmen. About 6 feet 3 inches tall, of an imposing build, and usually dressed in a flowing white *boubou* (gown) and white hat, he tow-ered head and shoulders above his colleagues at meetings. Former French president Charles de Gaulle was reported to have said of Modibo Kéïta: "He is the only African head of state with whom I can speak eye-to-eye." A convinced and dedicated Pan-Africanist, he was a prominent member of the radical Casablanca Group of States. He was also instrumental in the creation of the Ghana-Guinea-Mali Union, conceived as the nucleus of a "Union of African States," and one of the cofounders of the Organization of African Unity (OAU, May 1963). He successfully acted as OAU mediator in the 1963 Algerian-Morocco border war.[47]

Socialism in Mali[48]

Following the breakup of the short-lived Federation of Mali and the indepen-dence of Mali as a separate state on August 20, 1960, the Extraordinary Con-gress of the country's single party, the *Union Soudanaise*-RDA (US-RDA; September 22, 1960) enthusiastically decided to set the country on a social-ist path to development. From then on, all the energies of the leaders were directed toward the building up of "socialism in one country," economically as well as politically, with a prevalent concern for ideology. Note that the socialist era of independent Mali was fairly brief and lasted only for eight years, from September 1960 to November 1968.

From the outset, the top priority of the US-RDA's political leadership was to build, in the shortest time possible, a new society aimed at the politi-cal, economic, social, and cultural empowerment of Mali's popular masses. They firmly believed that a type of socialism adapted to the specific condi-tions of Mali would be the best ideology to achieve this goal. Seydou Badian Kouyaté—ideologue of the US-RDA, leader of the party's left-wing faction, and one-time minister of development—identifies three main characteristic features of Malian socialism: (1) a socialism based on agricultural workers and peasants rather than on a nonexistent proletariat; (2) a vibrant private sector encouraged to contribute to national development; and (3) respect of the Malian spiritual and religious values.[49] This last point deserves further scrutiny. Socialism, the Malian leaders argued, cannot be adopted wholesale; it must, of necessity, be adapted to the specific sociocultural context of Mali. Kouyaté is quite explicit on this point: "For us in Mali, the problem is clear. While our ultimate objective is *scientific socialism*, we have always believed that *our context is quite specific* . . . Under no circumstances shall we imitate what prevails and what has been done elsewhere; we must deal with our own material and moral realities . . . we do not pretend to invent socialism in the twentieth century: we simply wish *to adapt it to the conditions of our country*."[50] Modibo Kéïta himself elaborates on this important point as follows: "Africa has its own values, its own history. Africa can solve its own problems within the African context, using African methods . . . *We* thus *look at scientific socialism critically* . . . we try to extract from it values capable of infusing Malian realities . . . *We in Mali have never accepted blindly ready-made ideas*, whatever their origin."[51] Thus Malian socialism is grounded not only in African values but also, more broadly, in universal human values: "Socialism cannot be reduced to purely economic or social concerns. Its goal is man itself in its material, moral, spiritual and cultural dimensions. We think that the African man . . . must be open to all kinds of experiments."[52]

In organizational terms, the socialist option meant that the US-RDA functioned according to the Leninist principle of "Democratic Centralism," which institutionalizes communication between the leadership and the rank-and-file of the party, with ultimate decision-making power resting with the highest executive organ of the party, the National Political Bureau (*Bureau Politique National*/BPN). Other important organizational principles were the "primacy of the political" and collective decision making. According to the first, the party, being the emanation of the popular will, takes precedence over the administration. The second emphasizes the fact that decision making should be, as much as possible, the outcome of collective deliberation rather than expressing the will of a few.

As is the case in other socialist-populist regimes, *the people* were considered to be the ultimate beneficiary and the main agent of socialist development in Mali. Hence, observes Kouyaté, "the Party is the expression of the political organization of the people . . . It is to be found wherever the people lives, struggles and reflects on the problems of daily life and of economic and social progress."[53] This explains the nature of the US-RDA, which is essentially a decentralized mass party, with local branches at all levels of the country and society acting as the prime institutions of local self-government.[54]

Socialist planning was considered necessary to achieve the primary goal of improving the living conditions of the majority of the people, which, in Mali, were the peasants. Taking into account Mali's socioeconomic conditions, the top priority of socialist planning was the development of agriculture through the agency of an elaborate network of rural cooperatives, down to the village level.[55] The second priority related to cultural development and called for a complete overhaul of Mali's educational system consistent with Mali's rich cultural heritage and time-honored indigenous African values, both of which were to be the keystone of the new system of education.[56]

JULIUS KAMBARAGE NYERERE

A Biographical Note

Julius Kambarage Nyerere—*Baba Ya Taifa* ("Father of the Nation") and first president of Tanzania, a founder of the Organization of African Unity (OAU), and chairman of the South Commission—was one of the wisest and most respected leaders in Africa, as well as one of the most influential African intellectuals of his generation. Born in 1922 in Butiama (in northwestern Tanganyika, then a British colony), son of Chief Nyerere Burite of the Wazanaki, Julius Nyerere obtained a teacher's certificate from Makerere College (Kampala, Uganda) and, from 1946 to 1949, taught at a Catholic school in Tabora (Tanganyika). He then went on for further studies abroad, graduating with an MA in history and economics from the University of Edinburgh in 1952, making him the first Tanganyikan to gain a university degree. Reading widely and influenced by Fabian socialism, he evolved most of his political philosophy while at Edinburgh.

In 1954, Nyerere founded the territory's first nationalist party, the Tanganyika African National Union (TANU), whose initial aim was the improvement of the living conditions of the African people. TANU was popular, and its membership reached 200,000 by 1957. Gradual reforms in the colony led to the organization in 1958 of the first elections to the legislative council, in which TANU candidates (including Nyerere) won all 15 seats. Relentless TANU activism led to further reforms, leading up to limited self-government following the 1960 elections in which TANU swept the polls. Nyerere, who had been appointed chief minister, now petitioned the United Nations and engaged in negotiations with Britain over independence, which was eventually granted on December 9, 1961, with Nyerere as prime minister. He set about instituting a socialist form of government structured around a one-party state. In early 1962, Nyerere resigned his post and toured the country extensively to build up TANU membership. By December 1962, Tanganyika became a republic, and Nyerere returned to office as president. Political and ethnic conflict in the island nation of Zanzibar (off the Tanganyikan coast) resulted in a bloody coup d'état there in 1963 and in an army mutiny in mainland Tanganyika in 1964. After calling on British troops and restoring order, Nyerere announced the merger of Tanganyika and Zanzibar into a new state, the United Republic of Tanzania, which officially came into being on April 27, 1964. In 1977, Nyerere merged TANU and Zanzibar's Afro-Shirazi Party into a single national party, *Chama Cha Mapinduzi* (CCM).

With national unity restored, Nyerere moved to promote African social-ism. In February 1967, he proclaimed the "Arusha Declaration," which became the guide for Tanzania's policy of socialism and self-reliance, encap-sulated in the concept of *Ujamaa* (meaning "community" or "familyhood" in Ki-Swahili). In 1970, a voluntary villagization program organizing peasant farmers into collective farms was launched. Following strong peasant resis-tance, forced villagization was initiated in 1975. By that time, 80 percent of the population was organized into 7,700 villages. This eventually resulted in a sharp drop in agricultural production and in an increased dependence of the country on foreign aid. In 1971, Nyerere nationalized key sectors of the economy. However, some successes were registered in the area of social development: infant mortality was reduced by 50 percent and adult literary increased to 90 percent.

Tanzania's foreign policy focused on two main issues: support for the lib-eration movements in Southern Africa and destabilization of the dictatorial regime of Idi Amin in Uganda. In 1970, Tanzania militarily invaded Uganda, removed Amin from power, and replaced him with former president Milton Obote. This military campaign, however, had a profoundly negative effect on the Tanzanian economy. In 1984, Nyerere voluntarily stepped down from Tanzania's presidency in favor of Ali Hassan Mwinyi, although he remained chair of the CCM until 1990. By that time, Nyerere had become one of Africa's most respected and revered elder statesmen, being affectionately referred to by his honorific title of *Mwalimu* ("The Teacher" in Ki-Swahili). He did acknowledge that some of his policies (notably *Ujamaa*) had failed and that a multiparty system should be considered. Nyerere also became actively engaged in various peace and conflict-resolution initiatives in Africa (particularly in Burundi). In 1987, he became one of the founders (and later chairman) of the South Commission, which seeks to bridge the gap between rich and poor countries. Julius Nyerere died of leukemia in a London hospital on October 14, 1999.[57]

Ujamaa in Tanzania[58]

It could rightly be argued that by systematically providing ideas and symbolic frameworks through which people could understand the society in which they lived and imagine the society of the future, Julius Nyerere was one of the most "ideological" of the African leaders, on a par with Kwame Nkrumah. Furthermore—and contrary to the assertions of Henry Bienen—Nyerere did not hesitated to create a blueprint for a new society and translate his ideas into programs for action.[59] Thus, in his preface to *Ujamaa: Essays on Social-ism*, Nyerere laments the "lack of ideology" as well as "the absence of a gen-erally accepted and easily understood statement of philosophy and policy" in Tanzania since early 1962. The adoption of the "Arusha Declaration" of February 3, 1967, was meant to address this concern and fill this gap.[60]

The concept of *Ujamaa*—a specific type of African socialism, different and distinct from both capitalism and socialism—is at the core of the political thought of Julius Nyerere: "'Ujamaa' . . . or 'Familyhood,' describes our socialism. It is *opposed to capitalism*, which seeks to build a happy society on the basis of the exploitation of man by man; and it is equally *opposed to* doctrinaire *socialism which* seeks to build a happy society on a philosophy of inevitable conflict between man and man."[61] On this crucial point of doctrine, the views of Nyerere differ significantly from those of Ghana's Kwame Nkrumah and Mali's Modibo Kéïta, both of whom proclaimed the adherence of their respective states and parties to an orthodox brand of Marxism-Leninism labeled *scientific socialism* (what Nyerere calls *doctrinaire socialism*).

Where Julius Nyerere also disagrees with both Nkrumah and Kéïta is when he argues that African indigenous societies were essentially socialist in nature. As he put it himself, "Traditional African society was in practice organized on a basis which was in accordance with socialist principles."[62] For one thing, "in traditional African society *everybody* was a worker." Furthermore, "one of the most socialistic achievements of our society was the sense of security it gave to its members, and the universal hospitality on which they could rely," and "every member of society . . . contributed his fair share of effort toward the production of its wealth."[63] In addition, Nyerere rejects the capitalist notion of individual land ownership, which, he argues, is diametrically opposed to African indigenous traditions according to which land customarily belongs to the community, whose leader may allow people to use it on a "need to" basis: "To us in Africa, land was always recognized as belonging to the community . . . the African's right to land was simply the right to use it; he had no other right to it." Observing that "the foundation, and the objective, of African Socialism is the extended family" and that "Modern African Socialism can draw from its traditional heritage of the recognition of 'society' as an extension of the basic family unit," he concludes, "We must . . . regain our former attitude of mind—our traditional African socialism—and apply it to the new societies we are building today."[64]

For Julius Nyerere, socialism was, above all, "*an attitude of mind*" characterized by a non-doctrinaire political perspective: "Socialism—like democracy—is an *attitude of mind*. In a socialist society it is the socialist attitude of mind, and not the rigid adherence to a standard political pattern, which is needed to ensure that the people care for each other's welfare . . . In the individual as in the society, it is an *attitude of mind which* distinguishes the socialist from the non-socialist."[65] In the final analysis, for Nyerere true socialism is a universal, humanistic concept that relates not only to the Tanzanian man or the African man but to humanity as a whole: "Socialism is international; its ideas and beliefs relate to man in society, not just to Tanzanian man in Tanzania, or African man in Africa."[66] In "Ujamaa: The Basis of Socialism," he elaborates further on this point as follows: "Our recognition of the family to which we all belong must be extended yet further—beyond the tribe, the community, the nation, or even the continent—to embrace the whole society of mankind."[67] Ultimately, *man*—and, by extension, the concept of *human equality*—is at the center of political, economic, and social development in a socialist society: "First, and most central of all, is that under socialism *Man* is the purpose of all social activity. The service of man, the furtherance of his human development, is in fact the purpose of society itself . . . the purpose of all social, economic and political activity must be *man* . . . The basis of socialism is a belief in the oneness of man and the common historical destiny of mankind. Its basis, in other words, is *human equality* . . . The justification of socialism is *man*."[68]

As noted earlier, the "Arusha Declaration" of February 1967 translated, for the first time, the ideology of *Ujamaa* into a concrete program of action and, as such, constituted a blueprint for the new society to be built in Tanzania. In essence, the "Arusha Declaration" outlines a strategy of development based on self-reliance and aimed at satisfying the basic needs of the majority of the Tanzanian people: "To a socialist, the first priority of production must be the manufacture and distribution of such goods as will allow every member of the society to have sufficient food, clothing and shelter, to sustain a decent life."[69] Put differently, the principal aim of the party is "to see that the Government mobilizes all the resources of this country towards the elimination of poverty, ignorance and disease." To achieve this goal, "the state must have effective control over the principal means of production," and "it is the responsibility of the state to intervene actively in the economic life of the nation."[70] Furthermore, because Tanzania has a predominantly rural economy, *agriculture*—through the increased production of food and cash crops—constitutes the top priority in this strategy of development, while industrialization is based on "import substitution." This strategy of development also demands *hard work* on the part of the Tanzanian people, who must understand and implement the policy of *self-reliance*, which implies that "they must become self-sufficient in food, serviceable clothes and good housing" and that they "avoid depending upon other countries for assistance."[71] The implementation of this strategy of development required the creation of new economic, social, and political institutions, such as cooperative societies and *ujamaa* villages. It also entailed a radical restructuring of the system of education, with particular focus on adult education and literacy, universal primary and secondary education, and the promotion of African values and languages, notably the introduction of Ki-Swahili as the main medium of education at all levels.[72]

As some observers have noted—and has Nyerere himself later acknowledged—TANU's attempt at implementing a participatory form of socialist development in Tanzania was a dismal failure and resulted in the progressive deterioration of the rural economy as well as in the extended impoverishment of the peasant masses. P. L. E. Idahosa provides a concise and fairly accurate summary of the failure of Nyerere's economic policies: "Nyerere's policies . . . resulted in many features that are the opposite of what *ujamaa* was intended to achieve: forced villagization, the absence of participation coupled with alienation from the state, bureaucratization, increased class differentiations, low agricultural production and industry acquisition of most of the state's development resources."[73] Nyerere's life has been one of dedicated commitment, austerity, hard work, humility, and integrity. But even such a commitment to the ideals of justice, equity, and socioeconomic development; a leadership free from the taint of scandal or any hunger for power; and a readiness to admit and retreat from error was, alas, not enough to ensure that Tanzania would continue along the road mapped out at the beginning of his career.

CONCLUSION

This chapter continued the survey of the political, economic, social, and cultural dimensions of the socialist-populist ideology from a distinctly socialist perspective initiated in Chapter 5. This chapter focused specifically on the statesmen who, in spite of their socialist rhetoric, used the socialist-populist ideology—in various degrees—primarily as an instrument of control and coercion (sometimes even as an instrument of terror, as in the case of Sékou Touré): Kwame Nkrumah of Ghana, Ahmed Sékou Touré of Guinea, Modibo Kéïta of Mali, and Julius K. Nyerere of Tanzania. It is important to note in this regard that there is a significant difference of degree between these leaders in terms of the authoritarian vs. democratic nature of their regimes. Thus the most autocratic and authoritarian (even totalitarian) tendencies were exhibited by Sékou Touré and Kwame Nkrumah (more pronounced in the former than in the latter), while Modibo Kéïta and Julius K. Nyerere were somewhat more liberal, open, and democratic in their exercise of power (Nyerere more so than Kéïta). In addition to the nature of their political systems, the other common characteristics of these regimes are priority given to ideology and political organization over economic emancipation, a top-down system of administration, and state control over the economy.

There is a significant degree of convergence in the way in which Kwame Nkrumah, Sékou Touré, and Modibo Kéïta conceived of African socialism. One should remember that these three leaders were extremely close while in power. In May 1959, they jointly created a "Union of African States" as the nucleus of a "United States of Africa." Furthermore, after his overthrow by a military coup in February 1966, Kwame Nkrumah was given political asylum by Sékou Touré, who granted him the honorary title of "co-president" of Guinea. These three leaders' conception of African socialism had the following common characteristics:

- Ideology and practice are inextricably linked.
- *Politics* has supremacy over the economy.
- *Socialism* is not a sacred dogma but a *guide to action*.
- *African socialism* is a socialism building on and adapted to African indigenous values, culture, traditions, and society.
- *The people* are the main agents and ultimate beneficiaries of socialist development.
- African socialism aims at creating "*a new man.*"
- The single party operates according to the Marxist-Leninist principle of *Democratic Centralism*, which institutionalizes communication between

the leadership and the rank-and-file of the party, with ultimate decision-making power resting with the highest executive organ of the party.

- *Collective decision making* is based on collective deliberation and *consensus.*
- The state has control over the economy.
- *Pan-African* foreign policy is aimed at creating a *Union of African States* as a first step toward the eventual establishment of a *United States of Africa.*

In addition to this common view of African socialism, Kwame Nkrumah proposed an original philosophy and ideology for an independent Africa based on indigenous humanist African principles, which he called *"Philosophical Consciencism."* This philosophy integrates the three main segments of African society (traditional, Western, and Islamic) and was later popularized in African studies through Ali Mazrui's concept of the *"Triple Heritage."*

Julius Nyerere's concept of African Socialism (*Ujamaa,* or "Familyhood") differs somewhat from that of Nkrumah, Touré, and Kéïta in a number of respects; the essential characteristics of *Ujamaa* could be summarized as follows:

- Socialism is a *universal,* humanistic concept. *Man* is at the center of political, economic, and social development in a socialist society.
- Socialism is an "attitude of mind" characterized by a non-doctrinaire political perspective.
- *Ujamaa* differs from both *capitalism* and socialism, and it rejects *"doctrinaire socialism."*
- *African indigenous societies,* based on the "extended family," were essentially socialist in nature.
- *Ujamaa* is a *self-reliant* strategy of development based on *agriculture* and implemented through cooperative societies and *ujamaa* (communal) *villages.*

What Nkrumah, Touré, Kéïta, and Nyerere did have in common was a deep and abiding faith in the power of African socialism to radically and durably transform their societies in a way that would satisfy the basic economic and social needs of their peoples, thereby significantly improving their quality of life.

FURTHER READING

Birmingham, David, *Kwame Nkrumah: The Father of African Nationalism,* revised edition (Athens: Ohio University Press, 1998).

Diarrah, Cheick Oumar, *Le Mali de Modibo Kéïta* (Paris: L'Harmattan, 1986).

Legum, Colin, and Geoffrey Mmari, eds., *Mwalimu: The Influence of Nyerere* (London: James Currey, 1995).

Nkrumah, Kwame, *Revolutionary Path* (New York: International Publishers, 1973).

Nyerere, Julius K., *Ujamaa: Essays on Socialism* (New York: Oxford University Press, 1968).

Touré, Ahmed Sékou, *Africa on the Move* (London: Panaf Books, 2010).

CHAPTER 7

———❦———

THE POPULIST-SOCIALIST IDEOLOGY

FROM FRANTZ FANON TO STEVE BIKO

We are nothing on earth if we are not, first of all, slaves of a cause, the cause of the people, the cause of justice, the cause of liberty.

—Frantz Fanon, Letter to Roger Tayeb (November 1961), quoted in Clement Mbom, *Frantz Fanon*, 154

This chapter is an overview of the political, economic, social, and cultural dimensions of the populist-socialist ideology from a distinctly *populist* perspective, from the early 1960s to the present. As previously stated, the focus of the study is on the *political ideas* and the common themes that bind them rather than the individual leaders themselves.

The intellectuals/statesmen reviewed in this chapter were both theoreticians and practitioners who genuinely sought to improve the living conditions of their people by attempting to implement—often unsuccessfully or with mixed results—policies of political, economic, social, and cultural transformation. Sections 1 and 4 deal with those scholars/activists who remained essentially at the level of ideas, with very limited or no policy experience at all: Frantz Fanon (Algeria) and Steve Biko (South Africa). In section 2, we shall examine those intellectuals/statesmen who, because of particular historical circumstances, were in power for only a few years and thus were unable to see their policies of political and socioeconomic transformation bear fruit: Thomas Sankara (Burkina Faso) and Jerry J. Rawlings (Ghana), although the section deals only with the former. The third section of this chapter shall examine one populist leader who (until his elimination by NATO forces) had been in power for a very long time (42 years): Muammar Qaddafi of Libya.

As noted in Chapter 5, the concept of "populist-socialism" is borrowed from Crawford Young, who states that this group "consists of states that espouse a socialist orientation but that either do not stress or expressly reject

Marxism."[1] According to Young, populist socialism is a doctrine of development that characterized the "first wave" socialist regimes of the 1960s such as Algeria, Ghana, Guinea, Guinea-Bissau, Mali, and Tanzania. The author identifies five elements that define the populist-socialist perspective: (1) radical nationalism; (2) a radical mood; (3) anticapitalism; (4) populism and an exaltation of the peasantry; and (5) adherence to a moderate form of socialism (or social democracy) and a rejection of orthodox Marxism.[2]

FRANTZ FANON

A Biographical Note

Martiniquais and French, psychiatrist by training, political philosopher and political activist by choice, and journalist by trade, Frantz Fanon ended his life as an Algerian revolutionary. Fanon was, indeed, a man of many identities, many talents, and many trades; in this sense, he truly embodied the French ideal of "*un honnête homme du 20ème siècle*" (a well-rounded twentieth-century man). Born in Martinique (a French overseas territory in the Caribbean) on July 20, 1925, he grew up as a *Martiniquais*. He went on to metropolitan France first as a soldier in World War II then as a medical student at the University of Lyon. Finally, he moved to Algeria and Tunisia, working as a psychiatrist at the Blida-Joinville Hospital and later as a propagandist for Algeria's National Liberation Front (FLN) in Tunis during the bloody war of independence against the French (1954–62). In 1959, Fanon was briefly a diplomat representing the FLN in Ghana. He died of leukemia in a suburban Washington, DC, hospital on December 6, 1961, at the age of 36, barely seven months before the formal independence of Algeria (July 3, 1962) for which he had fought so hard.

Frantz Fanon was an unusually bright shooting star in the firmament of Africa's contemporary history. As the author of numerous books and articles—of which *The Wretched of the Earth* remains the most dense, powerful, and illuminating—Fanon better than anyone else represents the ideal synthesis between thought and practice and best typifies the *engagé* (i.e., politically involved) intellectual: "What matters is not death, but to know . . . whether we have achieved the maximum for the ideas we have made our own . . . We are nothing on earth if we are not, first of all, slaves of a cause, the cause of the people, the cause of justice, the cause of liberty."[3] Indeed, he exhibited a rare combination of exceptional psychological and sociopolitical analytical abilities, together with a deep, total, and unconditional commitment to the liberation struggle of the Algerian people.[4]

The Algerian Revolution

Frantz Fanon has been viewed in turn as psychiatrist, psychoanalyst, philosopher, political analyst, journalist-propagandist, and cultural critic. Such exceptional eclecticism and multidisciplinarity emerge clearly from the abundant corpus of scholarship on Fanon. What could be called the "first generation" of Fanonian studies (from the late 1960s to the mid-1980s) includes three major biographies and intellectual portraits;[5] in addition, it includes a number of pathbreaking studies on Fanon's social and political thought.[6] The "second generation" of Fanonian studies, emerging at the dawn of the twenty-first century, includes a number of works that revisit and reinterpret Fanon's life, times, and thought from a variety of postmodernist and postcolonial perspectives.[7] This chapter relies essentially on the first generation of Fanonian studies, focusing specifically on Fanon's social and political thought.

Fanon had a limited knowledge of African societies; he relied mostly on his impressions and intuition to provide "penetrating insights into the social dynamics of political conflict in postcolonial Africa."[8] In his various writings, Fanon insists on the fact that any liberation movement (or government) should have a specific doctrine, clearly defined goals and objectives, and some kind of blueprint: "Things must be explained to [the people]; the people must see where they are going, and how they are to get there . . . a program is necessary for a government which really wants to free the people politically and socially . . . in fact, there must be an idea of man and of the future of humanity."[9] Similarly, in *Toward the African Revolution*, Fanon observes, "For my part, the deeper I enter into the cultures and the political circles the surer I am that the great danger that threatens Africa is the absence of ideology."[10]

Fanon eloquently calls for a new and original African political thought, which, according to him, should be developed outside of Europe's beaten tracks: "We today can do everything so long as we do not imitate Europe, so long as we are not obsessed by the desire to catch up with Europe . . . Let us decide not to imitate Europe; let us combine our muscles and our brains in a new direction . . . If we wish to live up to our peoples' expectations, we must seek the solution elsewhere than in Europe . . . we must turn over a new leaf, we must work out new concepts, and try to set afoot a new man."[11] Fanon's ideal society is a society freed from all forms of constraints, repressions, and alienations and from all types of domination (colonialism, imperialism, and economic and cultural neocolonialism). It is essentially a free, egalitarian, nonrepressive, and nonauthoritarian society—in other words, a *socialist* society.[12] As Fanon himself puts it, "the choice of a socialist regime, a regime which is completely geared towards the people as a whole and based on the principle that man is the most precious of all possessions will allow us to go forward more quickly and more harmoniously."[13]

Central to Fanon's political thought is the notion that *the people* are the main actor and should be the main beneficiary of the revolution. According to him, the people (i.e., the rural and urban masses) are basically dynamic and open to new ideas and suggestions, provided these are made with a view to improve their condition: "Everything can be explained to the people, on the single condition that you really want them to understand . . . The more the people understand, the more watchful they become, and the more they come to realize that eventually everything depends on them."[14]

Fanon's populist approach implies a particular conception of democracy: "The national government, if it wants to be national, ought to govern by the people and for the people, for the outcasts and by the outcasts."[15] Fanon's populist conception of democracy is based on three basic elements: accountability, decentralization, and political education. With regard to accountability, Fanon observes that "no leader, however valuable he may be, can substitute himself for the popular will."[16] On the policy of decentralization, Fanon has this to say: "Nationalizing the commercial sector means organizing wholesale and retail cooperatives on a democratic basis; it also means decentralizing these cooperatives by getting the mass of the people interested in the management of public affairs . . . In an underdeveloped country, experience shows that the important thing is not that three hundred people adopt a plan and decide to implement it but that the whole people plan and decide, even if it takes them twice or three times as long."[17] Political education is a central concern for Fanon. As he eloquently puts it,

> Ultimately everything depends on the education of the masses, on the raising of the level of thought, and on what we are prompt to call "political education" . . . Now, political education means opening their minds, awakening them, and allowing the birth of their intelligence . . . To educate the masses politically . . . means . . . to try, relentlessly and passionately, to teach the masses that everything depends on them, that if we stagnate it is their responsibility, and that if we go forward it is due to them too, that there is no such thing as a demiurge . . . but that the demiurge is the people themselves and the magic hands are finally only the hands of the people.[18]

According to Fanon, the single party in postcolonial Africa has become an instrument of power, privilege, coercion, and personal advancement in the hands of the national bourgeoisie. As he views it, the ideal political party should be "an instrument in the hands of the people"; it should also be "the direct expression of the masses . . . the energetic spokesman and the incorruptible defender of the masses" and "an organism through which the people exercise their authority and express their will." For that purpose, it should be "decentralized in the extreme" and have "no administrative powers" so as to avoid any "confusion and duality of powers."[19]

Fanon calls attention to the fundamental significance of cultural domination through the global process of the neocolonial exploitation of Africa by the Western powers. He thus remarks that "the colonialist bourgeoisie, when it realizes that it is impossible for it to maintain its domination over the colonial countries, decides to carry out a rearguard action with respect to culture, values, technology etc."[20] To the extent that its very existence has been denied by the colonial powers, in the newly independent African countries "culture is necessarily linked to the emergence of a national consciousness . . . The birth of national consciousness in Africa is coterminous with the development of an African consciousness." Indeed, "it is national consciousness which is the most elaborate form of culture." The existence of a national culture, a national cultural life, and national cultural innovations and transformations is conceivable only in countries that are totally liberated from all forms of colonial and neocolonial domination; in that sense, "decolonization is truly the creation of a new man."[21]

In the postcolonial African society envisaged by Fanon, women and young people are to play a prominent role. According to him, "women will have exactly the same place as men, not in the clauses of the Constitution, but in the life of every day: in the factory, at school and in the national assembly."[22] As Fanon sees it, in developing countries the youth is generally an idle youth that needs to be kept busy, first through education, then by being engaged in appropriate productive activities: "The African youth ought . . . to be sent . . . into the fields and into the schools."[23] Finally, Fanon thinks that sport should not merely be a "pastime" or a "distraction" but should be fully "integrated into the national life"—that is, "in the nation-building process."[24]

In Fanon's political thought, the concept of "neo-colonialism" is linked with that of "false decolonization." According to Fanon, "false decolonization" refers to a process whereby political power is transferred from the colonial authorities in the metropolis to the national bourgeoisie in the former colonies, while economic power remains firmly entrenched in the former colonists. Thus political and juridical independence—or "flag independence"—does not necessarily lead to economic independence. Conversely, a "true decolonization" according to Fanon implies that African countries eventually achieve economic independence through a process of autonomous, self-centered, and self-reliant development, which could come about only within the framework of regional or subregional groupings. This process of African regional integration is predicated on a "popular"—as opposed to "state-centric"—conception of African unity: "African unity can only be achieved through a bottom-up, people-driven process, and under the leadership of the people, that is to say in opposition to the interests of the bourgeoisie."[25] Fanon (like Nkrumah) called on all the independent African states to create without delay a "United States of Africa": "African Unity is a principle on the basis of which it is proposed to achieve the United States of Africa without going through the chauvinistic-nationalist phase characterized by endless conflicts, wars and deaths."[26]

One of the "second generation" authors of Fanonian studies, P. L. E. Idahosa, opens up promising vistas on the future of democracy and development in Africa. This author clearly shows that in his quest for an alternative path to capitalist development, Fanon saw the need for a new ideology and new institutions as the basis for political and socioeconomic transformation and participatory, people-centered democracy. For Idahosa, Fanon's major contribution is to have opened to African people an alternative path to Western liberal democracy and development.[27] The powerful and thought-provoking ideas included in the concluding sentences of Les damnés de la terre are quite illuminating in this regard:

We can do anything today provided we do not blindly imitate Europe, provided we are not obsessed by the desire to catch up with Europe . . . Let us decide to not imitate Europe, and let us focus our thoughts and energies in a new direction. Let us invent the whole man that Europe has been incapable of bringing to life . . . The Third World must start a new history of man . . . If we are to satisfy the demands and needs of our peoples, we must look elsewhere than in Europe . . . For Europe, for ourselves and for humanity . . . we must shed our skin, invent new concepts, and create a new man.[28]

In essence, Fanon is telling African people, leaders, and scholars that for popular democracy and development to succeed in Africa, they must stop blindly following the West: they must stop aping Western culture, traditions, ideas, and institutions; they must think "outside of the box"; and, above all, they must be bold and innovative and develop their own ideas, concepts, and institutions based on African culture, values, and traditions. This alternative path to Western liberal democracy and capitalist development is precisely the line of thinking of an emerging African scholarship exemplified by four African political scientists—Daniel Osabu-Kle, Claude Ake, Godfrey Mwakikagile, and Mueni wa Muiu—whose political ideas will be examined in Chapter 8.

THOMAS SANKARA

A Biographical Note

Instigator, ideologue, and leader of the August 4, 1983, revolution in Burkina Faso (formerly known as Upper-Volta), Thomas Sankara, who was killed on October 15, 1987, in a bloody coup d'état at age 38, was also an unusually bright shooting star in the firmament of Africa's contemporary history. Sankara (like Fanon before him) represented a perfect blend of thought and "praxis" as a committed intellectual endowed with a keen intellect and exceptional analytical abilities, together with a deep, total, and abiding commitment to the struggle of the Burkinabè people. Indeed, there are striking similarities between Fanon's and Sankara's personal trajectories and political thought, which have been analyzed by the present author elsewhere.[29]

Thomas Sankara was born on December 21, 1949, in Yako (central Upper-Volta) in a Silmimoose (people of mixed Fulani and Moose ancestry) family. His father, Joseph Sankara, was an ex-serviceman in the French colonial army and an auxiliary in the *gendarmerie*—a French colonial paramilitary unit. The family thus moved frequently, as required by Joseph's successive posting in different parts of the territory. After completing his primary education at Bobo-Dioulasso (history being his favorite subject), Thomas Sankara entered—unbeknownst to his father—the military academy of Kadiogo in Ouagadougou. While there, he witnessed the first military coup d'état in Upper Volta led by Lieutenant-Colonel Sangoulé Lamizana (January 3, 1966). In 1970, at age twenty, Sankara went on for further military studies at the military academy of Antsirabe (Madagascar), from which he graduated as a junior officer in 1973. During that period, he read profusely on history and military strategy, thus acquiring the concepts and analytical tools that he would later use in his reinterpretation of Burkinabe political history. He later confided to a Malagasy journalist that he had read the complete works of Lenin, his favorite being *The State and Revolution.*[30] While attending the military academy of Rabat (Morocco), Sankara became acutely aware of the huge gap that existed between the obscenely wealthy ruling elite and the desperately poor Moroccan popular masses.

Back in Upper Volta, he became politically active in various leftist opposition parties and movements and was appointed secretary of state for information (1982) and later prime minister in the military government of Jean-Baptiste Ouedraogo. In the latter capacity, he attended the Non-Aligned Summit Meeting of New Delhi, India (January 1983). Following a French intervention, Sankara was detained on May 17, 1983. Pre-empting a rightist coup, his three comrades-in-arms and friends Blaise Compaoré, Jean-Baptiste Lingani, and Henri Zongo organized a leftist countercoup on August 4, 1983, resulting in the overthrow of the Ouedraogo regime, the release of Sankara from detention, and their assumption of power as National Council of the Revolution (*Conseil national de la Révolution*/CNR), presided over by Captain Thomas Sankara (then only 35 years old), who, *de facto*, became head of state and minister of home affairs and security. On October 2, 1983, he pronounced his famous "political orientation" speech that launched the country firmly on a populist-socialist path of political and socio-economic development. The transition to a new regime was best exemplified by the country's formal change of name from Upper Volta to Burkina Faso—meaning "the land of the upright men" in two national languages—on August 4, 1984. The same day, the first five-year popular development plan was launched.

The CNR regime enjoyed strong popular support from various leftist factions, movements, and organizations, both within the army and among the civilian population. In addition, various extreme leftist political parties were integrated into the CNR. On May 17, 1986, the original members of the CNR issued a joint declaration stating that all existing political parties should be dissolved in favor of a common vanguard political organization. As a result, factional conflict developed within the CNR coalition between the Marxist and other leftist element on the one hand, and the military on the other hand. In this process, Sankara and his faction became increasingly isolated, both within the CNR and in the army. Disagreements over the nature of the proposed single party and over who should be responsible for Sankara's personal security eventually led to the bloody coup d'état of October 15, 1987, engineered by his friend and companion-in-arms Blaise Compaoré. This led to the violent deaths of Captain Thomas Sankara (at age 38) and 12 of his close associates and staff members and the subsequent seizure of power by Compaoré and his faction.[31]

Thomas Sankara's biographer Bruno Jaffré, who does not hide his "sympathy, profound respect and admiration for this great man," describes Sankara as a "sensitive, sociable and profoundly human" individual as well as simple, approachable, humorous, and nonconformist; he also notes that "the Burkinabè people remember him as a just, morally upright and sincere leader who genuinely had the best interest of his people at heart."[32]

The Populist Revolution in Burkina Faso[33]

Any revolution has its ideologue and its leader. In the case of Burkina Faso, both are conveniently merged in the person of Captain Thomas Sankara. A young, articulate, and charismatic junior army officer of peasant origin with a good general and professional training, Sankara typified a new type of African military officer who had not been associated with French colonial ventures and who was fiercely nationalist and particularly sensitive and sympathetic to the needs and aspirations of the African masses.

First of all, the leader of the Burkinabè revolution acknowledged the inescapable need for some kind of ideology: "There is no politics without ideology. For us, ideologies provide a beacon, tools of analysis which enable us to better understand our social reality."[34] In spite of an avowed fascination for Marxism-Leninism, Sankara vehemently denies that the Burkinabè revolution was inspired by or patterned after any past or present foreign ideology, experience, or model. Furthermore, he deplores the constant tendency, on the part of Western observers, to categorize Third World leaders according to ideological criteria: "There is a typically Eurocentric attitude which consists in attributing ideological mentors to the leaders of the Third World . . . Why try at all cost to put us into ideological boxes, to categorize us?"[35] Much in the same vein, he declared before the 1984 United Nations General Assembly meeting that "the salvation of our peoples and our development require a total break with the worn-out models which all kinds of quacks have tried to force on us over the last twenty years."[36] Asked after which model the Burkinabè revolution was patterned, Sankara replied, "It is the revolution of Burkinabè, the people of Burkina . . . our revolution is the result of our specific experiences and history. It cannot be exported, just as we cannot copy other models."[37] However, he went on to admit that "we retain whatever is dynamic and creative in foreign experiences."[38]

Heeding Fanon's advice that "we must invent new concepts, and try to create a new man,"[39] Sankara acknowledges that a certain degree of madness is involved in such a bold and original experiment in social engineering as the Burkinabè revolution: "You cannot carry out fundamental change without a certain amount of madness. In this case, it comes from non-conformity, the courage to turn your back on the old formulas, the courage to invent the future . . . Yes, *we must dare to invent the future*."[40]

Although certain elements in his political thought are clearly influenced by Marxism-Leninism, Sankara saw himself as neither a "Marxist" nor a "Communist" as he was often been portrayed in the Western press. He was first and foremost an ardent nationalist and convinced Pan-Africanist, who had the restoration of the dignity of the African and the well-being and progress of the African continent at heart. The Burkinabè leadership openly rejected the "Socialist" label that was often applied to the country: "Nowhere is it stated that we claim to build Socialism in Burkina today . . . We are building a democratic, modern society . . . according to its economic content, our Revolution is a bourgeois revolution. It does not aim at the elimination of private property or private economic initiative and entrepreneurship."[41]

According to its leader, therefore, the Burkinabè revolution was essentially democratic and popular; it was seen as a transition toward a higher stage of development in the Burkinabè society: "After all, all modern republics, whether of capitalist or socialist orientation, have had to undergo, as a first stage, such a revolution."[42] Central to Sankara's political thought is the notion that *the people* are the main actor and should be the main beneficiary of the revolution. Thus he unequivocally stated in 1983 that "the goal of this revolution is to give the people power . . . The revolution has as its primary objective the transfer of power out of the hands of our national bourgeoisie allied with imperialism into the hands of the popular classes that make up the people."[43] As the only legal and legitimate repository of political power, *the people* should be invested with this power if it is to assume its responsibilities and control its destiny. In this perspective, democracy means that the people should be in a position to actually control the revolution's leadership. More specifically, "democracy means the freedom of expression of a conscious majority, well informed of the issues and of their internal and external implications, capable of verifying the fairness of electoral processes and in a position to influence their outcome."[44]

Sankara thus saw himself and the ruling group as the people's servants, as mere enforcers of the people's dictates: "I consider myself as someone who has a duty to respect the wishes and demands of the people. I will do as I am told by the people."[45] Asked whether he was acting as a proxy of Qaddafi's Libya in Africa, Sankara replied, "I am nobody's agent. Well, yes, in fact I am someone's agent: I am the agent of the people of Burkina."[46] "What would happen," asked another journalist, "if the Burkinabè people refused to follow your directives?" "If they don't follow me, I am out," was his reply.[47] What, one might legitimately ask, did Sankara exactly mean by "the people?" Again, the leader of the Burkinabè revolution provided a clear and precise answer to this important question. According to him, "the people" were constituted by a coalition of popular classes—including the working class, the petty bourgeoisie, the peasantry, and the lumpen-proletariat—who hitherto had been persistently ignored and marginalized politically and shamelessly and utterly exploited economically by successive colonial and neocolonial regimes.[48]

Starting from the observation that Burkinabè women were subjected to various types of domination (traditional, colonial, male, etc.), Sankara declared that "the transformation of Burkinabè women's mentality which will enable them to fully participate in the national development process alongside men is one of the revolution's priority objectives." Indeed, by giving women increased responsibilities, the revolution meant to unleash the creative potential within them. In the new Burkinabè society, women would thus be "involved at all levels of conception, decision and implementation in the national development organizational structure." The ultimate goal of this process was to "build a free and prosperous society in which women and men will be equal in every respect."[49]

The institutional instruments of the Burkinabè revolution's popular power were the National Revolutionary Council (CNR) and the Revolutionary Defense Committees (CDRs). The CNR was entrusted with the power of conception, direction, and control at the national level in the political, economic, and social fields. As for the CDRs, they were "the representatives of revolutionary power in the villages, the urban neighborhoods, and the workplaces"; they also constituted "the authentic organization of the people for wielding revolutionary power. They are the instrument the people have forged in order to take genuine command of their destiny and thereby extend their control into all areas of society."[50]

On the economic level, the assumption of popular power implied a development strategy geared toward the satisfaction of the basic economic and social needs of the people. In this perspective, the CNR aimed at establishing "an independent, self-sufficient and planned national economy at the service of a democratic and popular society." This entailed a radical socioeconomic transformation, including a transformation of the structures of production and distribution and comprehensive reforms in the areas of agriculture (land reform), administration, education, and social services (housing, health, and sanitation).[51] Furthermore, the rural masses were encouraged to actively and permanently participate in all the stages of the development projects through the agency of the newly created "Village management committees" (*Comités villageois de gestion*).[52]

Following the revolution, the Burkinabè educational system was completely restructured according to three basic objectives: democratization, relevance to production, and development of an authentic national culture. Concretely, this meant universal and free education, universal literacy, integration of productive activities (handicraft, cattle breeding, gardening, etc.) in the school's curriculum, and promotion of the national cultural heritage, particularly through the introduction of national languages as media of instruction.[53]

At the international level, the Burkinabè revolution proclaimed itself firmly opposed to any form of imperialist and neocolonialist domination and exploitation as well as all kinds of hegemony. Sankara tried to conduct a genuinely non-aligned foreign policy, politically independent but actively anti-imperialist. In its struggle for political and economic independence, justice, and dignity, Burkina Faso considered other anti-imperialist African countries as "objective allies."[54] While subscribing to the Pan-African ideal, Sankara's conception of African unity—like that of Fanon—is based on the conviction that such unity will ultimately be brought about by the *peoples*, not by the governments: "I believe in African unity, and I believe that it will come about . . . It will be realized according to the people's wishes . . . Unity at the top, among a few leaders, will not be enough."[55]

Thomas Sankara was not content with just enunciating a comprehensive and coherent political doctrine; he also tried—with limited success—to put his thoughts into practice. To that extent, he observed one of the key principles of Marxism-Leninism—namely, unity of theory and "praxis." As the ideologue of the Burkinabè revolution, he genuinely attempted to initiate a process of change within the Burkinabè society. Unfortunately, time was not on his side, and his life was cut short before he could bring this plan to fruition. Asked by a Swiss journalist what image he would like to leave of himself in the event of a sudden death, Sankara replied, "I would simply hope that my contribution had helped to convince the most disbelieving that there is an overwhelming force, called *'the people'* and that we must fight for and with these people. I would like to leave behind me the conviction that . . . we deserve a certain and durable victory . . . Maybe in our lifetime we will appear as utopian trailblazers, . . . as pioneers . . . But perhaps we are blazing the trail along which, tomorrow, others will surge blithely forward, without even thinking."[56]

MUAMMAR QADDAFI[57]

A Biographical Note[58]

One of the longest-ruling (42 years) and most controversial world leaders, the "Brother Leader" of the Libyan Arab Jamahiriya (1977–2011)—and an indefatigable champion of Pan-Arabism, Pan-Africanism, and African Unity—Muammar Qaddafi was forcibly removed from power (and eventually killed) as a result of a Western military intervention on October 20, 2011. Muammar Qaddafi was born in a peasant family in Sirte in September 1942. After attending the Sebha preparatory school in Fezzan (1956–61), he went on first to study law at the University of Libya, then to the Military Academy in Benghazi (1963–65). In 1965, he underwent further military training at the British Army Staff College in the United Kingdom, returning to Libya in 1966 as a commissioned officer in the signal corps. No doubt inspired by Egyptian president Gamal Abdel Nasser—whom he viewed as a role model—Qaddafi and a small group of officers seized power from King Idris I in a coup d'état on September 1, 1969. In 1977, Qaddafi stepped down as Chairman of the Revolutionary Command Council of Libya and retreated to the role of symbolic head of state. At that time, he replaced the Libyan Constitution of 1951 with new laws based on the political ideology of the "Third Universal Theory," as enunciated in his *Green Book*. Henceforth, Qaddafi was named "Brother Leader" of the Popular and Socialist Libyan Arab Jamahiriya (the new official name he gave Libya). Qaddafi came to be perceived as a "terrorist" and "rogue leader" by the United States and its European allies, even being referred to as "the mad dog of the Middle East" by US president Ronald Reagan in 1986. Among other acts of international terrorism, Qaddafi's regime was held responsible for the 1988 bombing of a Pan-Am airliner over Lockerbie (Scotland) resulting in 270 deaths. In 1999, Qaddafi initiated a *rapprochement* with the West, resulting in Libya being welcomed back into the international community in December 2003. In what was perhaps a fatal strategic mistake, Qaddafi allowed inspectors from the International Atomic Energy Agency (IAEA) to confiscate and remove tons of nuclear materials, and he authorized the destruction of 3,300 chemical warheads.[59]

After the death of Kwame Nkrumah in 1972, Muammar Qaddafi assumed the mantel of leader of the Pan-Africanist movement and became the most outspoken advocate of African unity, consistently calling—like Nkrumah before him—for the advent of a "United States of Africa." As documented in the next section, Qaddafi actually took a number of concrete initiatives in favor of African unity. Eventually, NATO (led by the United States, France, and the United Kingdom) militarily intervened in Libya based on UN Security Council Resolution 1973 of March 17, 2011. Under the pretense of establishing a "no-fly zone" to "protect the civilian population" of Libya, the NATO intervention resulted in violent regime change in the country. Following the fall of Sirte and the murder of Qaddafi at the hands of the self-styled "National Liberation Army" on October 20, 2011, a weak, divided, and ineffective "National Transition Council" took power in Libya.

The Third Universal Theory

As Edmond Jouve rightly observes, "It was easier for Colonel Qaddafi to discard nuclear weapons than to renounce the weapon of ideology."[60] As noted previously, in 1977 Qaddafi replaced the Libyan Constitution of 1951 with new laws based on the political ideology of the "Third Universal Theory," as enunciated in his *Green Book*. Stated briefly, the Third Universal Theory—offering an alternative to the dominant ideologies of liberal democracy/capitalism and Marxism—aims at initiating a process of revolutionary social change involving all aspects of life within the framework of a universal vision based on natural law.[61] Muammar Qaddafi offers this succinct description of the Third Universal Theory: "The Third Universal Theory is a prelude to the total freedom of the popular masses from the shackles of injustice, from despotism, from political domination and economic exploitation, ultimately leading to a society for all mankind. In this society, everyone shall be free; everyone shall have equal power, wealth and weapons so that freedom shall totally and definitively prevail."[62] In three brief, accessible, and handy volumes, *The Green Book* deals successively with "The Solution to the Problem of Democracy: People's Power" (volume I); "The Solution to the Economic Problem: Socialism" (volume II); and "The Social Basis of the Third Universal Theory" (volume III).[63]

Volume one of *The Green Book* offers a solution to the problem of democracy—namely, "people power" as the political foundation of the Third Universal Theory. This volume begins with a scathing critique of liberal theories of governance and denounces national assemblies (or parliaments), party coalitions, and referendums as fake democratic institutions and methods; these result in dictatorship—that is, the exclusion of the people from politics—as well as the confiscation of popular sovereignty and popular power by successive and conflicting governmental agencies, be they individual, class, sect, tribe, parliament, or party.[64] Qaddafi is quite explicit on this point: "Representative democracy is nonsensical, a contradiction in terms, a sham. 'Democracy' means 'people power,' not 'popular representation.' As soon as there is representation, there is no democracy."[65]

The definitive solution to this problem and the ideal type of government proposed by *The Green Book* is *direct democracy*—namely, absolute and pure *people power*, not mediated by any institution or agency, because "there is no substitute to people power." In other words, "democracy means control of the people by the people."[66] The institutional expression of people power is the popular assemblies as well as the people's committees. In other words, "there is no democracy without popular assemblies and people's committees everywhere."[67] Under this system, governance is entrusted to a three-thousand-member General People's Congress (GPC), which is responsible for implementing Brother Leader's legislative guidelines. At a secondary level, the GPC directs the activities of some three thousand committees, each headed by a leader who is a GPC member. These committees in turn are responsible to the GPC concerning various developmental matters such as health, budget and finance, and education.[68]

Qaddafi concludes, "Such is true democracy in theory, but in reality, only the most powerful rule."[69] Asked by three Western journalists if this statement applied to Libya, Qaddafi replied, "Since in Libya the people is the most powerful, it is the people that governs . . . As long as the people is the most powerful, it shall govern . . . However, this statement relates to the current reality: the most powerful rule because popular democracy exists nowhere in the world except here in Libya."[70]

In volume two of *The Green Book*, Muammar Qaddafi proposes "Socialism" as the solution to the economic problem. As with politics, Qaddafi begins with a detailed critique of the capitalist system, based on the exploitation of laborers, the pilfering of the world's natural resources, and the maximization of profits for private gain. Thus the whole purpose and rationale of economic activity must be redirected to the satisfaction of the basic socio-economic and moral needs of the people. As Qaddafi puts it, "the objective of the new socialist society is to establish a happy society, deriving its happiness from being free. Such a society is realized only through the fulfillment of the individual's spiritual and material needs, and this can be achieved by liberating these needs from the control and manipulation of others."[71] According to Qaddafi, this process involves a return to the "natural laws" of the development of societies, characterized by an "original socialism based on an equal distribution of the factors of production, as well as on an equitable distribution of nature's harvest among individuals."[72] The final stage of the new economy will be characterized by the elimination of profit and of any currency. Ultimately, "the aim of a socialist society is the happiness of man. This happiness cannot be realized except in conditions of spiritual and material freedom."[73]

Volume three of *The Green Book* analyses the social basis of the Third Universal Theory. In a major departure from Marxist theory, Qaddafi argues that the social factor—that is, the national factor, the social glue that ensures the cohesion of every social group, from family, to tribe, to nation—constitutes the prime mover and main factor of progress in the history of mankind.[74] In other words, the present phase of world history is characterized by the ongoing nationalist struggle led by the national liberation movements: "This means that the nationalist (or social) struggle constitutes the prime mover and fundamental dynamics of history; it is not only more powerful than any other factor, it is its source and foundation. Indeed, this nationalist struggle constitutes the essence of life and of humankind themselves."[75] Beyond the usual constituent elements—common territory and history—Qaddafi defines the nation as being characterized by a community feeling and a common destiny.[76] Consequently, "the Nation-State is the only permanent and enduring political construct because it coincides with the natural fabric of society."[77] With regard to gender relations, Qaddafi firmly believes in the fundamental equality of men and women and that "discrimination based on gender is absolutely unjust and unjustifiable." This being said, Qaddafi acknowledges that the physical and biological differences between the sexes determine a gender-specific division of labor.[78] Furthermore, Qaddafi is of the opinion that the time for the preeminence and rule of the African ("the Black race") in the world has finally come, even if it is not yet effective.[79] Finally, Qaddafi advocates a new type of education, an education not constrained by a specific curriculum and required subjects like the current standardized and compulsory education. Rather, the new educational system should be flexible and allow the students to spontaneously and freely choose the subjects of their choice.[80]

As noted previously, after the death of Kwame Nkrumah in 1972, Muammar Qaddafi assumed the mantle of leader of the Pan-Africanist movement and became the most outspoken advocate of African unity, consistently calling—like Nkrumah before him—for the advent of a "United States of Africa." There is strong evidence to suggest that, disillusioned by the failure of various Pan-Arab plans and initiatives, Qaddafi decided to focus his attention, energies, and resources on the African continent.[81] After acting as chairman of the Organization of African Unity (OAU; February 2009–January 2010), he worked tirelessly for the creation of a powerful and effective African Union at successive OAU meetings in his hometown of Sirte (September 1999 and March 2001).[82] However, the relatively ineffective and powerless African Union—modeled on the European Union—that came into being in July 2001 was markedly different from the organization envisaged by Qaddafi. The latter was outlined in the OAU's *Sirte Declaration* (September 9, 1999), which provided for an African Congress, a Summit Council, a Federal Executive Council, 15 Federal Executive Commissions, a Federal Supreme Court, and three Federal Financial Institutions (an African Central Bank, an African Monetary Fund, and an African Investment Bank).[83]

Putting his money where his mouth was, Qaddafi actually took a number of positive steps and concrete initiatives in favor of African unity. Thus one of his grand schemes involved linking the Great Artificial River to Lake Chad; this would have linked the Bangui and Chari rivers (in the Central African Republic) and fed into a vast hydraulic network servicing North Africa and the rest of the continent. This plan involved linking the Bangui and Chari rivers over a distance of one thousand to two thousand kilometers as well as building a thousand kilometer road linking Libya to Lake Chad and Niger.[84] In general, Qaddafi's Libya had been consistently providing financial aid and private direct investment to other African countries for the building of mosques as well as for transport and tourism infrastructure. The cordial relations between Qaddafi's Libya and Sankara's Burkina Faso have been well documented.[85] Similarly, following a state visit of Kenya's President Mwai Kibaki in June 2007, the leaders of the two countries signed a bilateral agreement according to which Kenya was to receive oil from Libya at preferential rates. According to this agreement, Libya was to upgrade Kenya's petroleum refinery and supply 60 percent of the 1.6 million tons of crude oil that Kenya needs to make the refinery commercially viable. This was realized through an investment of the Libya Arab African Investment Company in Libya Oil Kenya Ltd and its *Oilibya* network of service stations.[86]

But by far the boldest and most far-reaching plan conceived by Qaddafi—which probably caused his demise—had to do with African monetary union. According to some sources, he began to call, at two secret international conferences (1996 and 2000) for a return to the "gold standard" as a substitute for the US dollar as an international currency, a plan mooted by former French President Charles de Gaulle in the early sixties. Specifically, Qaddafi's plan called for making the gold dinar (the Libyan currency) into a single currency—based on its vast oil resources—for the whole African continent. Evidently, such a plan constituted a serious threat to the international monetary system, specifically to the role of the US dollar as the international currency of choice. Not surprisingly, the United States and the European Union reacted extremely negatively to such an initiative.[87] Does this explain the US-led NATO military intervention that resulted in the death of Muammar Qaddafi and his regime on October 20, 2011? Only time will tell.

Asked by Edmond Jouve in November 2002 what he considered to be his enduring legacy for future generations, Qaddafi replied, "That I have implemented *direct democracy* in my country. That my people rule themselves without government, without deputies, without representatives. *Direct democracy*: that is the key to *The Green Book*."[88]

BANTU STEPHEN BIKO

A Biographical Note

On September 12, 1977, Bantu Stephen Biko was the twenty-first person to die in a South African prison within a 12-month period. He was thirty years old. Founder and ideologue of the Black Consciousness Movement and a martyr of the liberation struggle in South Africa, Steve Biko, according to one biographer, "had a vitality that drew people to him, not only for his counsel, but his exuberance, not only for his extraordinary clarity of thought but his love of life, his political insight, his capacity to listen, his capacity to learn, his ability to keep placing himself within a circle of people and not up-front—a practice contradicted by his undeniable 'presence.' His gift of leadership . . . ."[89] Calling him a "martyr of hope" and a "selfless revolutionary," Aelred Stubbs has this to say about Biko's gift of leadership: "There was my friendship with this amazing man, whose gift of leadership consisted pre-eminently in discerning the capacities of those whose trust he had gained, and in enabling them to realize them to the full."[90] Yet another author describes him as "un-dogmatic but highly disciplined in his thinking, possessed with a rare insight into human and political situations."[91]

Bantu Stephen Biko was born on December 18, 1946, in King William's Town (Eastern Cape). His father, Mzingaye Biko (a government-employed clerk), died when Steve was four. After attending primary and secondary school locally, Stephen furthered his education at the liberal Catholic St. Francis College at Mariannhill in Natal. After graduating in 1965, he entered the "non-European" section of the University of Natal Medical School at Wentworth, Durban, in 1966. Active at first in NUSAS (National Union of South African Students), he broke with it in 1968 to form SASO (South African Students' Organization), of which he was elected president in July 1969 and publicity secretary in July 1970. From 1971, Stephen became increasingly involved in political activities and helped found the Black People's Convention (BPC) in July 1972; at that time, he dropped out of Wentworth. He immediately began to work for Black Community Programs (BCP) in Durban, but in March 1973 he was banned by the authorities, together with seven SASO leaders. Restricted to his home town of King William's Town, he founded the Eastern Cape Branch of the BCP and worked as branch executive until prohibited from doing so in late 1975. In January 1977, he was appointed honorary president of the BPC. On August 18, 1977, Steve was again detained under section 6 of the Terrorism Act. He died in detention on September 12; the cause of death was determined to be brain damage. The horrible details of Biko's death stunned the world. South African journalist Donald Wood's book *Biko* (1978) and Richard Attenborough's film *Cry Freedom* (1987) based on that book contributed to bring Biko's life, times, and ideas to the attention of a worldwide audience.[92]

Black Consciousness

Born in the specific politico-historical context of the apartheid regime—extreme racial segregation based on white privilege and the marginalization and exploitation of the African majority—in South Africa in the late 1960s to early 1970s, the philosophy of Black Consciousness incorporates three distinct elements of political thought: (1) Orthodox African nationalism (or "Africanism") as developed in South Africa in the 1940s by Anton Muziwakhe Lembede and A. P. Mda; (2) anticolonial theories of African nationalism, as they developed in Africa from the Fanonian concepts of the psychological liberation and mental decolonization of the African colonial subject; and (3) radical socialism and Marxism. According to C. R. D. Halisi, Steve Biko saw Black Consciousness as a synthesis of the political philosophy of the three main black nationalist liberation movements in South Africa: the African National Congress, the Pan-Africanist Congress, and the Non-European Unity Movement. "From the elements of these distinct parts of the nationalist tradition, Biko proposed to reconstruct its successor."[93]

At its core, the concept of Black Consciousness is both *psychological* and *cultural*. In essence, it refers to the psychological liberation and cultural emancipation of the African man from centuries of political domination, economic exploitation, and socio-cultural marginalization at the hands of the white man in South Africa. In this process, psychological liberation and cultural emancipation are preconditions for the political emancipation and, at a later stage, the economic empowerment—of the African. Thus, as Gail Gerhart cogently remarked, Black Consciousness is not an ideology of revolution and violent social change; rather, it is an inward-looking ideology of the present aimed at "decolonizing the mind": "The aim of Black Consciousness as an ideology was not to trigger a spontaneous Fanonesque eruption of the masses into violent action, but rather to rebuild and recondition the mind of the oppressed in such a way that eventually they would be ready forcefully to demand what was rightfully theirs."[94] In Steve Biko's own words, "The first step therefore is to make the black man come to himself; to pump back life into his empty shell; to infuse him with pride and dignity, to remind him of his complicity in the crime of allowing himself to be misused and therefore letting evil reign supreme in the country of his birth. This is what we mean by an inward-looking process. This is the definition of 'Black Consciousness.'"[95] This process of psychological liberation is rendered necessary by the fact that the apartheid regime policies had apparently succeeded in instilling "dependency, identity-confusion, fear, and a resigned apathy about the future"[96] in the African man's psyche. In other words, these policies, according to Biko, had resulted in the complete "de-humanization" of the African man, who was nothing but an empty shell: "But the type of black man we have today has lost his manhood. Reduced to an obliging shell, he looks with awe at the white power structure and accepts what he regards as the 'inevitable position' . . . All in all the black man has become a shell, a shadow of man, completely defeated, drowning in his own misery, a slave and ox bearing the yoke of oppression with sheepish timidity."[97] The SASO Manifesto adopted in July 1971 declared that Black Consciousness was "an attitude of mind, a way of life" in which the black man saw himself "as self-defined and not as defined by others." It required, above all, "group pride and the determination of the black to rise and attain the envisaged self," as well as "group cohesion and solidarity" so that blacks would recognize that "the most potent weapon in the hands of the oppressor is the *mind* of the oppressed," so that they could be made aware of their collective economic and political power."[98]

As a first step, this process of mental decolonization required the African to cast off his complexes of dependency and deference toward whites. As Lindy Wilson cogently remarked, among other things "Black Consciousness . . . debunked long-standing myths whites had woven about Africa generally and South Africa in particular, myths present in school and university textbooks: the inherent inferiority of blacks, their skin-deep savagery, the simplistic quality of their faith and beliefs, the inferiority of Africa's oral tradition as opposed to written history, the 'primitive' nature of its culture, and so forth."[99] The second step in this process required the Africans to create for themselves a new identity and a new pride. In Biko's own words, "Black Consciousness . . . seeks to infuse the black community with a new-found pride in themselves, their efforts, their value systems, their culture, their religion and their outlook to life . . . Further implications of Black Consciousness are to do with correcting false images of ourselves in terms of Culture, Education, Religion, Economics."[100] In particular, Africans needed to revive and rehabilitate African values, customs, religion, and traditions and, simultaneously, reject the systematically negative and deliberately false interpretations of these by the white establishment. As the founders of SASO saw it, "the emphasis had to be on the current aspects of culture, and on the anticipation of a future free society in which social, cultural and economic priorities would be re-arranged to make South Africa part of Africa once more, instead of what it currently was—an extension of Europe into Africa."[101]

The ideology of Black Consciousness also emphasized the concept of "self-reliance," borrowed from Julius Nyerere's 1967 *Arusha Declaration*. According to Barney Pityana, "The message is simple. *Black man you are on your own*. Like Nyerere we must minimize reliance on external aid."[102]

As Halisi has noted, "Biko adroitly situated his version of Black Consciousness philosophy within a humanist framework . . . which allowed the development of a theological counterpart," the Black Theology movement, "the religious complement of Black Consciousness philosophy."[103] Similarly, Gail Gerhart observes that "seminary students were among the earliest and most ardent proponents of Black Consciousness and its particular application within the church under the rubric of black theology."[104] Indeed, realizing its mistake, the government moved in 1974–75 to destroy one of the leading centers of Black Consciousness thinking, the Federal Theological Seminary of Southern Africa in Alice, founded and initially managed by Fr. Aelred Stubbs, CR, a close friend and avowed disciple of Steve Biko.[105] Aelred Stubbs himself offers the following definition of "Black Theology" as well as an explanation of why he thought Biko found this philosophy attractive: "At the heart of 'Black Theology' is the perception that Jesus belonged historically in a situation of oppression, that he was a member of an oppressed people in an oppressive society, and that he came to set his people free . . . I suggest that Steve found 'Black Theology' attractive as offering this paradigm of spiritual praxis in the contemplation and imitation of the Black Christ."[106]

Initially started as a broad-based popular movement for the psychological liberation and cultural emancipation of the African man, Black Consciousness became a more focused political project when it became institutionalized through the agency of the South African Students' Organization (SASO), founded by Steve Biko and his comrades at the Turfloop Conference of July 1969 and thereafter spearheaded by African, Colored, and Indian/Asian students throughout South Africa.[107] Steve Biko and his comrades had been driven to create SASO because they became more and more dissatisfied with the multiracial and liberal National Union of South African Students (NUSAS), "an outspokenly anti-government organization with a membership drawn heavily from white English-speaking universities."[108] His personal experience as an active member of NUSAS (from 1967 to 1969) led Biko to a scathing critique of the liberals who "claim a 'monopoly on intelligence and moral judgment' . . . who say that they have black souls wrapped up in white skins" and who "arrogantly presume that the country's problems require *integration* as a means as well as an end: 'hence the multiracial political organizations and parties and the non-racial student organizations.'" Actually, what the liberals had in mind was a fake "integration": "The integration they talk about is . . . artificial . . . the integration so achieved is a one-way course, with the whites doing all the talking and the blacks the listening."[109] Biko warns the African against the dangers of such fake integration: "The myth of integration as propounded under the banner of liberal ideology must be cracked and killed because it makes people believe that something is being done when in actual fact the artificial integrated circle are a soporific on the blacks and provide a vague satisfaction for the guilty-stricken whites."[110] In addition to SASO, Biko also launched in 1972 a nationwide network of community-based organizations such as the Black Community Programs (BCP) and the Zimele Trust Fund (focusing on primary health care, founded in 1975) in which he was personally actively involved, while restricted by government banning orders to the King William's Town area, until his death. In June 1972, Biko and his comrades launched the Black People's Convention (BPC) as an "adult," non-student wing of the Black Consciousness movement, with Biko as its first president and later (January 1977) honorary president.

As SASO progressively refined the Black Consciousness ideology of self-definition, self-determination, and self-reliance, it became increasingly evident that the use of the term "non-white" to describe the African, Colored, and Indian/Asian communities in South Africa "was totally inconsistent with efforts to promote an aggressively positive self-image among African." Thus, by the mid-1970s, SASO switched from using "non-white" to "black" in reference to these communities. According to Gerhart, "the term 'Black Consciousness' was promoted openly, use of 'non-white' was denounced, and at its July 1970 annual conference, SASO formally amended its own constitution to substitute 'black' for 'non-white'."[111] In this context, "black" became a generic and inclusive term describing the African, Colored, and Indian/Asian communities in South Africa. As Halisi succinctly puts it, "The BCM [Black Consciousness Movement] made *black* nationalism superior to ethnic—African, Indian, or Colored—nationalisms . . . Colored and Indian communities were invited to unite with the African majority."[112] Put differently,

"Being black is not a matter of pigmentation—being black is a reflection of a mental attitude."[113] The question "who is black?" was addressed squarely in a SASO editorial: "The term . . . must be seen in its right context. No new category is being created but a 're-Christening' is taking place. We are merely refusing to be regarded as non-persons and claim the right to be called positively . . . It helps us to recognize the fact that we have one common enemy . . . Placed in context, therefore, the 'black consciousness' attitude seeks to define one's enemy more clearly and to broaden the base from which we are operating. It is a deliberate attempt by all of us to counteract the 'divide and rule' attitude of the evil-doers."[114] This fundamental conceptual redefinition was part of a broader process of polarization or, more precisely, of final confrontation between two polar opposites locked in a life-and-death struggle over control of the land and its people, between the colonizer (the citizens) and the colonized (the subjects), or (in the South African context) between the whites (the oppressors) and the blacks (the oppressed). Such a process of extreme polarization has been brilliantly analyzed and documented by O. Mannoni in his study of the relationship between the Malagasy people and the French colonialists, by Albert Memmi's vivid portraits of the colonizer and the colonized, and by Frantz Fanon's depiction of the self-destructive social dynamics at work between the French colonizers and the Algerian popular masses.[115] Thus, for Albert Memmi, "in order to live, the colonized must eliminate colonization. But if he wants to become a man, he must get rid of the colonized within himself . . . In other words, he [the colonized] must cease to define himself through colonial concepts . . . Provided he will no longer be this oppressed individual burdened with a host of complexes, he will become *other* . . . Having recovered all the facets of his personality, the former colonized would have finally become a normal man and, at long last, a free man."[116] This process of polarization potentially leading to radical political and social change in South Africa is well described by Gail Gerhart: "Most compelling of all the arguments for unity was the consensus, articulated so well by Biko and perhaps bolstered by the writings of Fanon, that polarization per se in the race conflict would be a strategy conducive to change. Polarization—the simplification of the conflict from a series of many skirmishes into one battle perceived as a total confrontation between black and white—required not just the initial redefinition of all whites, including liberals, as oppressors, but also required the conceptual regrouping of all non-whites into the single category of 'black.'"[117] What, ultimately, is the enduring legacy of Steve Biko? Lindy Wilson notes that "Biko's perception and energy freed people psychologically to take their destiny into their own hands."[118] Mongane Wally Serote observed that "Black Consciousness transformed the word 'black' and made it synonymous with the word 'freedom' . . . The Black Consciousness Philosophy and its slogans claimed the past for black people, a country and the right of its people to its wealth and land."[119] Biko's comrades-in-struggle confirm that "Black Consciousness broke the silence imposed by the violence of apartheid in the late sixties by enabling blacks to articulate their aspirations and to engage in forging a democratic future."[120] According to Halisi, Biko "understood Black Consciousness philosophy in terms consistent with his own personal sense of mission—a combination of theoretical honesty and devotion to the cause of liberation."[121] Friend and comrade-in-arms of Steve Biko, Fr. Aelred Stubbs, CR, explains why he called his personal memoir of Biko "Martyr of Hope": "The phrase 'selfless revolutionary' seems to me the clue to what Steve himself meant to die for . . . Steve died to give an unbreakable substance to the hope he had already implanted in our breasts, the hope of freedom in South Africa. That is what he lived for; in fact one can truly say that is what he *lived*. He was himself a living embodiment of the hope he proclaimed by word and deed. That is why I call this little personal memoir 'Martyr of Hope.'"[122]

CONCLUSION

This chapter consisted of an overview of the political, economic, social, and cultural dimensions of the populist-socialist ideology from a distinctly *populist* perspective, from the early 1960s to the present. The intellectuals/statesmen reviewed in this chapter were both theoreticians and practitioners who genuinely sought to improve the living conditions of their people by attempting to implement policies of political, economic, social, and cultural transformation. In sections 1 and 4, we examined two scholar/activists who remained essentially at the level of ideas, with limited or no policy experience at all: Frantz Fanon (Algeria) and Steve Biko (South Africa). Section 2 focused on intellectuals/statesmen who, because of particular historical circumstances, were in power for only a few years and thus were unable to see their policies of political and socioeconomic transformation bear fruit: Thomas Sankara (Burkina Faso) and Jerry John Rawlings (Ghana), although the section deals only with the former. Section 3 deals with a populist leader who was in power for a very long time (42 years): Muammar Qaddafi. By "populist-socialist," we refer to states that adhere to socialism but do not stress (or even reject) Marxism.

Although they had very different personal, educational, and professional backgrounds and political destinies—and as we have demonstrated elsewhere—the political ideas of Frantz Fanon and Thomas Sankara are strikingly similar. The common features of Fanon and Sankara's political thought may be summarized as follows:

- An *ideology* is essential to any African liberation movement and postcolonial government.
- Africans must reject the dominant Western ideologies and must conceive their own political thought based on their own values, culture, traditions, and history.
- *Cultural liberation* and *mental decolonization* should lead to the emergence of a specifically *African consciousness* based on African values, culture, and traditions.
- Decolonization should lead to the creation of "a *new man*."

- *The people* are the main actor and should be the main beneficiary of the revolution.
- African governments must adopt a *populist* conception of *democracy* based on accountability, decentralization, popular participation, and political education.
- The *political party* should be an instrument in the hands of *the people*, expressing the people's power and controlled by the people.
- The African state should pursue a *self-reliant* strategy of *development* geared toward the satisfaction of the basic economic and social needs of the popular masses.
- *Neo-colonialism* constitutes a major threat to the independence and very existence of African states.
- *African unity* must be based on the *peoples* rather than on the governments and the elites.[123]

The third section of this chapter focused on Libya's "Brother Leader" Muammar Qaddafi's Third Universal Theory, as exposed in the three volumes of *The Green Book*. Volume one (*The Solution to the Problem of Democracy*) begins with a thorough critique of liberal democracy and advocates "people power" in the form of a direct democracy with popular assemblies and people's committees. Volume two (*The Solution of the Economic Problem*) starts with a detailed critique of capitalism and advocates an "original" socialism based on an equal distribution of the factors of production as well as on an equitable distribution of nature's harvest among individuals. Volume 3 (*The Social Basis of the Third Universal Theory*) argues that the national factor is the prime mover and main factor of progress in the history of mankind. Muammar Qaddafi—who was killed following a Western military intervention on October 20, 2011—was the leader of the Pan-Africanist movement and one of the most outspoken advocates of African unity; he hosted the two meetings that led to the creation of the African Union in March 2001.

Finally, section 4 of this chapter surveyed Steve Biko's ideology of Black Consciousness, an ideology of psychological liberation and cultural emancipation of the African man in South Africa. A major dimension of this ideology was its redefinition of "non-whites" as "blacks" to designate the African, Colored, and Indian/Asian communities in the country. Thus the term *black* became a reflection of a mental attitude and came to mean "freedom."

The main lesson to be drawn from this survey of the political thought of Frantz Fanon, Thomas Sankara, Muammar Qaddafi, and Steve Biko is if popular democracy and development are to succeed in Africa, African people must stop blindly following the West, must think "outside the box," and must be bold and innovative. In other words, it is essential that Africans develop their own ideas, concepts, and institutions on the basis of African values, culture, and traditions. This alternative path to Western liberal democracy and capitalist development is precisely the line of thinking of an emerging African scholarship exemplified by Daniel Osabu-Kle, Claude Ake, Godfrey

Mwakikagile, and Mueni wa Muiu, whose political ideas will be examined in the next chapter.

FURTHER READING

Al Gathafi, Muammar, *The Green Book: The Solution to the Problem of Democracy; The Solution to the Economic Problem; The Social Basis of the Third Universal Theory* (Reading, UK: Ithaca Press, 2005).

Biko, Steve, *I Write What I Like: A Selection of His Writings*, edited by Aelred Stubbs, preface by Desmond Tutu (Randburg, South Africa: Ravan Press, 1996).

Fanon, Frantz, *The Wretched of the Earth*, translated by Constance Farrington, preface by Jean-Paul Sartre (New York: Grove Press, 1968).

Qaddafi, Muammar, with Edmond Jouve, *My Vision* (London: John Blake Publishing, 2005).

Hansen, Emmanuel, *Frantz Fanon: Social and Political Thought* (Columbus: Ohio State University Press, 1977).

Martin, Guy, "Fanon's Continuing Relevance: A Comparative Study of the Political Thought of Frantz Fanon and Thomas Sankara," *Journal of Asian & African Affairs* 5, no. 1 (Fall 1993): 65–85.

Sankara, Thomas, *Thomas Sankara Speaks: The Burkina Faso Revolution, 1983–87* (New York: Pathfinder, 1988).

CHAPTER 8

————◦◦◦————

THE AFRICANIST-POPULIST IDEOLOGY

POPULAR DEMOCRACY AND DEVELOPMENT IN AFRICA

Africa . . . is isolated. Therefore to develop, it will have to depend upon its own resources basically, internal resources, nationally, and Africa will have to depend upon Africa. The leadership of the future will have to devise, try to carry out policies of maximum national self-reliance and maximum collective self-reliance. They have no other choice. Hamna! [There is none!]

—Julius K. Nyerere, "Reflections," quoted in
John S. Saul, *The Next Liberation Struggle*, 159

INTRODUCTION

As we saw in Chapter 7, Frantz Fanon's warning to African people, leaders, and scholars was that for popular democracy and development to succeed in Africa, they must stop blindly following the West: they must stop aping Western culture, traditions, ideas, and institutions; they must think "outside of the box"; and, above all, they must be bold and innovative and develop their own ideas, concepts, and institutions based on African values, culture, and traditions. This alternative path to Western liberal democracy and capitalist development is precisely the line of thinking of an emerging African scholarship, exemplified by the four African scholars whose political ideas are examined in this chapter.

More specifically, this chapter reviews the ideas and values for a new, free, and self-reliant Africa put forth by African scholars who have the best interest of the African people at heart and thus advocate a popular type of democracy and development. However, unlike the populist-socialist scholars, the Africanist-populist scholars refuse to operate within the parameters of Western ideologies—whether of the socialist, Marxist-Leninist, or liberal-democratic persuasion—and call on Africans to get rid of their economic, technological, and cultural dependency syndrome. These scholars are also convinced that the solution to African problems lie within Africans themselves. Thus they refuse to remain passive victims of a perceived or pre-ordained fate and call on all Africans to become the initiators and agents of their own development, with the ultimate goal of creating a "new African."

It is interesting to note that all these individuals are first and foremost academics, deal strictly with ideas, and have not been directly involved in politics (although the majority are political scientists). The four Africanist-populist scholars that will be the focus of this chapter are Ghanaian political scientist Daniel T. Osabu-Kle; Nigerian political scientist Claude Ake (1939–96); Tanzanian scholar-journalist Godfrey Mwakikagile; and Kenyan political scientist Mueni wa Muiu. Note that all these scholars are dedicated Pan-Africanists, and many would shun the reference to their nationality and much prefer to be simply called "Africans." Again, our focus here is on the ideas (and what binds them) rather than on the individuals.

DANIEL TETTEH OSABU-KLE

A Biographical Note

Daniel T. Osabu-Kle was born in Ghana in 1942. He is currently an associate professor of political science—with a joint appointment in the Department of Political Science and the Institute of African Studies—at Carleton University in Ottawa, Ontario (Canada). His teaching and research areas include development politics and administration as well as African politics. He was educated in Pakistan and India and completed his graduate studies at Carleton University. He is the founder and chief executive officer of two Ghana-based nongovernmental organizations: Flodan International, involved in humanitarian work, and Flodan International Academy (FIA), dedicated to providing quality primary and secondary education to low-income families in Ghana.

Compatible Cultural Democracy

Not unlike Thomas Sankara's Revolutionary Democracy, Muammar Qaddafi's Third Universal Theory, and Steve Biko's Black Consciousness, Daniel Osabu-Kle's analysis starts from the observation that forty years after independence, Africa remains in a permanent state of political, economic, social, and cultural crisis, due in large measure to the fact that the Western type of liberal democracy actively promoted by Western countries and agencies (notably the international financial institutions) has dismally failed to take root in Africa. Thus the central thesis put forward by Osabu-Kle in *Compatible Cultural Democracy* is that "only a democracy compatible with the African cultural environment is capable of achieving the political conditions for successful development in Africa." More specifically, "This compatible cultural democracy is the key to Africa's political, economic, and social development . . . What compatible cultural democracy calls for in Africa is the authoritative allocation of African values to the African people by Africans within the context of African culture and African history, leading to the projection of the African personality and respect within the entire world community."[1] Put differently, "What Africa needs . . . is a democratic practice that is compatible with indigenous culture and not the blind emulation of any foreign political culture. This compatible cultural democracy is the key to Africa's political, economic, and social development. A modernized form of Africa's own indigenous consensual and democratic culture would provide the necessary political conditions for successful economic growth."[2] Thus compatible cultural democracy is not based on any foreign ideology—be it socialism, Marxism, capitalism, or liberalism—but is grounded in *Africanism*, "the ideological, economic and political practice of Africans on African soil, in accordance with African culture, and by Africans emancipated from colonial mentality and cleansed of foreign excrescence."[3] In other words, Africans should not be forced to choose between two Western ideologies: liberal democracy or socialism; they "will only be able to solve their problems the African way."[4]

Furthermore, Africans must modify and adapt indigenous African political systems and institutions to fit the circumstances and requirements of modern political life. Contrary to what prevails in contemporary African politics, indigenous African political culture was characterized by free discussions, consultations, and consensual decision making at all levels of government. Furthermore, in indigenous African societies, the democratic principle of accountability of the rulers to the ruled was broadly applied. The essentially democratic nature of indigenous African political systems is well captured by Osabu-Kle: "African political systems in pre-colonial times were essentially democratic, with all the trappings of government with the consent of the governed and a balance between centralized power and decentralized power to prevent the misuse of authority by any one person. They were systems with checks and balances, and accountability . . . The structure of the political organization ensured that at any level of government a chief and his council ruled with the consent of those below and above him, and the head of state and his council ruled with the consent of the people as a whole."[5] Thus, argues Osabu-Kle, what is required in Africa today is an appropriately modified and adapted indigenous political system. This system should take the form of a consociational arrangement that is inclusive, responsive to the different aspirations within society, and decentralized enough to enable local participation in indigenous languages. Furthermore, the indigenous principle of decentralized political organization is indispensable to national development, and women should participate in the political and economic decisions that affect their lives. Finally, the education system must be reformed.[6]

Osabu-Kle seeks to verify the validity of his main hypothesis by introducing six very detailed country case studies (which constitute the bulk of the book): Ghana, Nigeria, Kenya, Somalia, Rwanda, and the Democratic Republic of the Congo (DRC).[7]

The author outlines the main characteristics of a modified indigenous political system as follows:

1. A decentralized, consensual, and consociational system with the participation of interest groups, ethnic groups, clans, and professional associations directly in the decision-making process
2. A democratic process that offers equal opportunity for men and women to participate at all levels of the political process
3. A democratic system without political parties
4. A relatively stable, responsible, and decentralized state with a periodic circulation of elites
5. Relatively small but efficient regular armed forces and police organizations
6. A relatively small and efficient central state bureaucracy
7. A largely privatized but mixed economy
8. A political system that recognizes the essentially dynamic nature of culture
9. A state in which the participation of voluntary organizations is encouraged with the understanding that communal democracy expressed through voluntary organizations is an integral part of Africa's cultural democracy[8]

Another key argument of *Compatible Cultural Democracy* is that the success of development in Africa is predicated on the emergence of a new African elite able and willing to establish a culturally compatible political system: "The central problem is . . . the inability of the African elite to set in place the culturally compatible political conditions necessary for successful development."[9] Osabu-Kle further argues that this new elite would put in place a consensual (or consociational) type of democracy as an essential prerequisite to development in Africa: "Only an encompassing coalition established in accordance with Africa's own consensual democratic culture and capable of containing the stresses and strains from both the internal and external environments would be capable of defining, implementing, and sustaining coherent and effective national development policies."[10] As previously argued by Amilcar Cabral, Frantz Fanon, Steve Biko, and Ngugi wa Thiong'o, for the "African personality" to be restored, a process of mental decolonization must first take place. This is necessary because "most Africans have come to suffer from a deeply embedded form of mental slavery, a colonization of the mind in which everything African is considered inferior to everything foreign . . . Realization of compatible cultural democracy has to begin from the sphere of the mind to rid the African first of mental slavery."[11] Compatible cultural democracy also involves the fostering of a genuinely "African" (as opposed to ethnic or nationalist) mind-set: "Injection of African values and African nationalism, which recognizes Africans as one people with one destiny, must be emphasized."[12]

This requires an entirely "new education system capable of psychological and ideological transformation of . . . the mentally enslaved African into the liberated and proud African with an African-centered mind." In order to make the Africans proud of their countries and of Africa as a whole, "African studies and Afrocentric values," but, more specifically, "the study of African history, culture, literature, and geography must be emphasized in the home, schools, colleges, and universities of Africa."[13] This process of "ideological re-education of African society to create *the new African*—or, more accurately, to convert the present-day African into *a new African*—who can contribute effectively to the realization of nationalist objectives" and "who places the unity and common destiny of the nation as a whole above his or her narrow self-interests"[14] should take the form of *mass education programs*. Such programs must be "organized on a voluntary basis and offered in the local languages first" and designed "to integrate education with productivity and culture."[15] The creation of a "new African" called for by Osabu-Kle echoes Fanon's advice to "set afoot a new man," as well as Steve Biko's call for the psychological liberation and cultural emancipation of the African man (see Chapter 7).

A modified indigenous political system—or compatible cultural democracy—should, according to Osabu-Kle, take the form of *jaku* democracy—namely, a type of democracy that is compatible with the African cultural environment and that enables the elite to forge a broad coalition capable of absorbing the contradictions inherent in the development process. As Osabu-Kle rightly observes, *jaku* democracy "requires some modification of Africa's indigenous democratic practices to satisfy the present-day needs of Africans. This system—one capable of authoritative allocation of African values to Africans by Africans—is what I mean by compatible cultural democracy for Africa, or Africanism . . . *jaku* democracy would therefore be the type of culturally compatible democracy suitable for Africans."[16] Osabu-Kle justifies the use of the term *jaku*—a Ga word for the "common family of Africans" in Africa and in the diaspora but also an adjective meaning "African"—as follows: "Calling the system *jaku* democracy will send the signal to the African mind that the continent's peoples have their own type of democracy, one they can be proud of, and this knowledge will contribute to an emancipation from mental slavery."[17]

Reviving Kwame Nkrumah's "Dream of Unity" of the early 1960s, Osabu-Kle firmly believes in Pan-Africanism, which, according to him, should materialize in the form of a United States of Africa and include an African High Command (AHC) "with operational readiness to intervene swiftly to foil any coup attempt in any African country" as well as a Pan-African Youth Organization (PAYO) "with branches both inside and outside Africa to unite African youth and enable interaction and exchange of views." In addition to these institutions and to establishing a common transport and telecommunications infrastructure, the United States of Africa envisaged by Osabu-Kle should have a common currency, a common defense policy, and a common foreign policy.[18] Eventually, concludes Osabu-Kle, "Afrocentrism shall replace

Eurocentrism in Africa and *jaku* democracy shall be established not only to achieve the political prerequisites for successful development in African countries but also to realize the African dream of a United States of Africa."[19]

CLAUDE AKE

A Biographical Note

On November 7, 1996, an ADC Airlines plane outbound from Port Harcourt (Nigeria) crashed shortly before landing at Lagos Airport, killing all 141 passengers (and crew members) on board, including Claude Ake. The sudden and untimely death of Claude Ake, arguably one of the most brilliant, original, and prolific of the new generation of African political scientists who emerged to prominence in the 1970s, shocked the African and Africanist social sciences communities.

Claude Ake was born on February 18, 1939, at Omoku in the Rivers State area of southeastern Nigeria. He was educated at Kings College, Lagos, and went on to study economics at the University of Ibadan, Nigeria. He then proceeded to Columbia University (New York), where he obtained a PhD in political science in 1966. While firmly grounded in his Ogoni traditional society, Claude Ake was one of the first scholars to openly challenge the conventional wisdom of modernization theory, which was then the undisputed paradigm in African studies, and propose instead a bold and innovative political economy approach for a better understanding of Africa's chronic economic, political, and social crisis.

Claude Ake's teaching career spanned thirty years and two continents: Columbia University (1966–68); Carleton University, Canada (1969–77); and the University of Dar es Salaam, Tanzania (1972–74). From 1977 to 1983, he served as founding Dean of the School of Social Sciences, University of Port Harcourt. Claude Ake was active in various Pan-African social science organizations, notably the African Association of Political Science (AAPS; Director of Research, 1975–76) and the Council for the Development of Social Science Research in Africa (CODESRIA), becoming president of the latter's executive committee (1985–88).

Claude Ake acted as consultant for (and served on the board of) a number of international agencies, notably the United Nations Development Program (UNDP), the UN Economic Commission for Africa (UNECA), the UN World Commission on Culture, the International Social Science Council, and the World Bank. In 1989–90, he was visiting professor at Columbia University, and in 1990–91, he was a research fellow at The Brookings Institution in Washington, DC. In 1992, Claude Ake returned to Port Harcourt to start his own Centre for Advanced Social Science (CASS)—a policy advocacy and research think tank—of which he became director. On November 16, 1995, Ake resigned his position as member of the Steering Committee of the Niger Delta Environmental Survey (NDES) and issued a press statement, much to the displeasure of the ruling Nigerian military junta of General Sani Abacha, who placed him under state surveillance from that time until his death. In 1996, he was visiting professor at Yale University.

Ake's move back to Nigeria to start CASS exemplifies his utmost professional integrity and profound moral rectitude, as well as his total and selfless commitment to the advancement of social science in Africa. Ake considered it his sacred duty to work in Africa to the development of the third generation of African (specifically Nigerian) academics. What made Claude Ake truly exceptional—in a way reminiscent of Amilcar Cabral, Frantz Fanon, and Thomas Sankara—was his unique blend of theory and practice applied to the political empowerment and socio-economic uplifting of the African people. This recent homage of a Nigerian political scientist perfectly captures this dimension of the personality of Claude Ake: "In describing Ake as an *organic intellectual*, we have in mind a conception of Ake, who as a *revolutionary-theorist* and *scholar-activist* was committed to the service of humanity through his dedication to *institution-building*, *knowledge production* and *transnational advocacy* in advancing the material empowerment of the African people . . . Ake personified—perhaps more than any other scholar of his generation throughout Africa—the combination of brilliant scholarship and revolutionary commitment."[20]

From Marxism to Africanism

One has to agree with Jeremiah Arowosegbe when he states that "Claude Ake . . . is one of Africa's foremost political philosophers who worked extensively in the area of political theory and made original and uniquely perceptible contributions to the political economy of democracy and development on the continent."[21] Where we disagree with this author, however, is when he sees Ake's intellectual evolution as being from liberalism to a more radical form of scholarship grounded first in Marxism, then in Africanism.[22] While there is no substantial evidence to support the claim that Ake ever was a liberal (unless his first book, *A Theory of Political Integration*, may be labeled as such),[23] there is ample evidence that his political thought evolved from a Marxist to a radical African (or Africanist) paradigm, as the title of this section suggests.

According to Katabaro Miti and Thandika Mkandawire, Ake's paradigm shift from moderate African nationalism to orthodox Marxism occurred when he was a professor in the Department of Political Science at the University of Dar es Salaam (Tanzania), which, at that time, had an unusual concentration of Marxist scholars who frequently engaged in lively academic debates. Most notable among such scholars were Hamza Alavi, Colin Leys, Mahmood Mamdani, Dani W. Nabudere, John Saul, Issa Shivji, Walter Rodney, and Justin Rweyemamu.[24] Already in *Social Science as Imperialism* (1979), Ake argues that the bulk of Western social science scholarship on the Third World—best exemplified by the modernization paradigm—amounts to imperialism; he shows that this scholarship amounts to a manipulation of Third World peoples and contributes to the perpetuation of underdevelopment and dependency.[25] However, the two books of Ake that best exemplify his Marxist period are *Revolutionary Pressures in Africa* (1978) and *A Political Economy of Africa* (1981). In the first book, Ake argues that capitalism is on its way out in Africa because the African bourgeoisie has been unable to liberate the productive forces of the continent; as a result, Africa is moving into a new historical phase, that of a socialist revolution. In the second book, Ake analyzes the characteristic features of contemporary Africa, how they have come to be, and how they might change in future.[26]

The late Archie Mafeje was wrong when he characterized Ake's next paradigm shift as being a shift from radicalism to "mild liberalism," but he was right when he argued that Ake's paradigm shift was influenced mainly by the ideas of radical African nationalism.[27] We prefer to call Ake's new paradigm "Africanism"; in this new paradigm, his main focus of analysis became democracy and development in Africa.

Democracy and Development in Africa

Claude Ake introduced and developed his new paradigm on democracy and development in Africa in his last two books: *Democracy and Development in Africa* (1996) and *The Feasibility of Democracy in Africa* (2000; published posthumously); these constitute, as it were, his intellectual testament.[28]

Claude Ake's ideology of development and democracy starts with a thorough and systematic critique of liberal democracy that evokes the scathing critique of liberal theories of governance contained in volume one of Muammar Qaddafi's *Green Book* (see Chapter 7). Ake begins by observing that the European bourgeoisie and the American founding fathers both rejected the idea of democracy as popular power focusing on the collectivity and replaced it with *liberal democracy*, which focuses on the individual "whose claims are ultimately placed above those of the collectivity." In effect, liberal democracy substitutes legal sovereignty for popular sovereignty: "It [liberal democracy] replaces government by the people with government by the consent of the people. Instead of sovereignty of the people it offers the sovereignty of law."[29] Similarly, the American founding fathers substituted *representative democracy* to direct democracy expressing popular power. Yet, as Ake observes, "representative democracy was a contradiction in terms. Citizens had to participate directly in the exercise of sovereignty or there is no democracy at all. The idea of representative democracy repudiated the very core of the traditional meaning of democracy, popular power."[30] Ake traces the origins of liberal democracy to two British social contract theorists, Thomas Hobbes and John Locke, who are widely acknowledged as the fathers of this political philosophy. For Hobbes, government exists mainly to maintain law and ensure the security of the subjects. This naturally leads him to offer an essentially minimalist theory of government according to which "the government which governs least, governs best." John Locke emphasizes government by consent and the obligations of rulers to the ruled, and he posits human rights, particularly the right of private property, which cannot be limited.[31] In its contemporary form, liberal democracy is synonymous with multiparty electoral competition. Ake concludes this analysis by observing that "the classical theory of liberal democracy is less an expression of democracy than its restriction. It does away entirely with the idea of popular power and it replaces the idea of self-government with that of the consent of the governed. Even so the consent of the governed is largely an abstraction which is not operationalized, especially by universal suffrage. It does not set much value on the idea of political participation . . . It is not about involvement in government but about minimizing government and its nuisance value."[32] In *Democracy and Development in Africa*, Ake offers an original and insightful analysis of the multidimensional African crisis and outlines the key elements of a new development paradigm that he proposes for Africa. Starting with the observation that "three decades of preoccupation with development in Africa have yielded meager returns," Ake points to the fallacy of analyzing development in terms of failure: "The problem is not so much that development has failed as that it was never really on the agenda in the first place." All the available evidence points to one inescapable conclusion: "Political conditions in Africa are the greatest impediment to development."[33] Thereupon Ake sets out to demonstrate how African politics has prevented the pursuit of development and the emergence of appropriate development programs.

Ake traces the history of the state in Africa to colonialism and the capitalist penetration of the continent. According to him, in spite of formal independence, the *postcolonial state* in Africa still retains the essential features that characterized the *colonial state* in Africa—namely, absolutism, arbitrariness, exclusion, but also political domination, social marginalization, cultural dependency, and economic exploitation. Like its predecessor, the postcolonial state is an apparatus of violence that relies for compliance on coercion rather than authority.[34] Put differently, "anti-colonial demands for self-rule in Africa achieved the vision of a quasi-independent state, but failed in transforming the structures of the post-colonial state or in imagining alternative conceptions of statehood independent of the European model."[35] In other words, it is because the African state is an essentially *alien* construct that it cannot possibly serve as an agent of development: "The major institution engrafted from the *core* to the *peripheries* following the European model of the nation-state, is *the state in Africa*. However, unlike its European model . . . *the state in Africa* is a force imposed on society from without. This inversion in the logic of state formation in Africa underlines its alienness. This alienness of the state in Africa—its lack of conformity with the expectations and practices of the people—is what makes it inadequate for its purpose in the continent."[36] It will be recalled that a similar argument is made by Kofi A. Busia, who, in *The Challenge of Democracy*, argues that "all the new nations of Africa have inherited a legacy of authoritarian political structures from their former rulers"[37] (see Chapter 3).

The African political elite handpicked by the former colonizers was essentially preoccupied with seizing and maintaining political power. Indeed, "the *struggle for power* was so absorbing that everything else, including development, was marginalized."[38] According to Ake, the contemporary African state is not a public entity but tends to be *privatized* in the sense that it is "appropriated to the service of *private interests* by the dominant faction of the elite."[39] More interested in *political survival* than in development, the new leaders of independent Africa gave precedence to *political domination* over social transformation and thus tended to be in conflict with the majority of their population. Unable and unwilling to satisfy their people's demands for economic redistribution and social justice, these leaders had to find something to replace the nationalist ideology of self-government and maintain a sense of common purpose: they adopted the *ideology of development*.

Too absorbed by the struggle for power and survival, the African leaders allowed the West to supply a *development paradigm* as a more specific form of a broader Western model of social transformation—namely, *modernization theory*. Moreover, these leaders allowed the international development community to provide the development paradigm and agenda for Africa, translated into development plans devised by expatriates. Because modernization theory assumes that the development of the underdeveloped areas of the world is implicitly a matter of becoming Western, this development paradigm is essentially useless as a tool of societal transformation and economic development precisely because it largely ignores the historical and cultural specificity of the African countries.[40] Evidently, this calls for a new development paradigm for Africa.

For Ake, the basic assumptions of a new development paradigm for Africa are as follows:

- Development is not economic growth.
- Development is not a project but *a process.*
- Development is the process by which people create and recreate themselves and their life circumstances to realize higher levels of civilization in accordance with their own choices and values.
- Development is something that people must do for themselves. If *people* are the end of development, they are also necessarily its agent and its means.
- Africa and the global environment are to be taken as they are and not as they ought to be.[41]

While these assumptions constitute the prevailing conventional wisdom of the development community, they have never been taken seriously and applied systematically. Doing so, says Ake, shall result in a markedly different way of approaching development from that prevailing today. He then goes on to discuss the kind of *democracy* that Africa needs. According to him, the suitable democracy for Africa should have the following four characteristics:

- a democracy in which people have some real *decision-making power*, which entails *decentralization* of power to local democratic formations
- a social democracy that places emphasis on concrete *political, social,* and *economic rights,* as opposed to a liberal democracy that emphasizes abstract political rights

- a democracy that puts as much emphasis on *collective rights* as it does on individual rights
- a democracy of *incorporation* as inclusive as possible, with a legislature in which nationality groups and mass organizations—such as youth and women groups, as well as trade unions—should be represented[42]

Given the weakening of the African political elites and the failure of the development project in Africa, Ake reckons that the prospects for democratization from within are favorable. Indeed, "*a democratic revolution* is needed to beat the crisis of underdevelopment. Africans are seeking democracy as a matter of survival." Such a people-based and people-centered democracy movement shall markedly differ from liberal democracy in the sense that "it will emphasize concrete *economic and social rights* rather than abstract political rights; it will insist on the democratization of economic opportunities, the social betterment of the people, and a strong social welfare system. To achieve these goals, it will have to be effectively participative and will have to draw on *African traditions* to adapt democracy to the cultural and historical experiences of ordinary people."[43] The development strategy derived from such a people-driven democratization process should, according to Ake, be based on the following values and principles:

- *A popular development strategy.* The primary principle of development strategy in Africa is that the people have to be the agents, the means, and the end of development.
- *Self-reliance.* This is about responsibility and must be practiced at all levels: community and household, national, regional, and federal.
- *Empowerment and confidence.* Self-reliance requires such confidence. Lack of confidence is a serious problem; it may well be the greatest obstacle to the development of Africa.
- *Self-realization rather than alienation.* What is happening now is an attempt to develop against the people. Development must take the people not as they ought to be but as they are and try to find how the people can move forward by their own efforts, in accordance with their own values.[44]

Claude Ake has very clearly and succinctly identified the causes and manifestations of Africa's social, economic, and political crisis. He has also proposed the broad outline—which circumstances did not allow him to further develop—of a suitable democratic system and a new development paradigm that constitute a way out of the crisis. That, in essence, is Ake's intellectual legacy to the African people in general and to the African academic community in particular. By its originality, perceptiveness, and relevance, Ake's contribution to African political thought assuredly deserves a place in the pantheon of the great African political thinkers, alongside such luminaries as Amilcar Cabral, Kwame Nkrumah, and Frantz Fanon.[45]

GODFREY MWAKIKAGILE

A Biographical Note

Godfrey Mwakikagile was born in Kigoma (western Tanzania) on October 4, 1949, in a family originally from the Rungwe District. He attended Songea Secondary School in Ruvuma region (southern Tanzania) and Tambaza High School in Dar es Salaam, the nation's capital. He was in the National Service in Bukoba (northwestern Tanzania). In Tanzania, he worked as an information officer in the Ministry of Information and Broadcasting, as well as a reporter for *The Standard* (later renamed *Daily News*) in Dar es Salaam. He went to the United States in November 1972 and attended Wayne State University (Detroit, MI), from which he graduated in 1975. In 1976, he attended Aquinas College (Grand Rapids, MI).

A prominent African public intellectual and prolific author—he has published more than thirty books since 1999—Godfrey Mwakikagile is considered one of the late president Julius Nyerere's most prominent biographers. His books deal mostly with postcolonial African history, politics, and economics. They include *Economic Development in Africa* (1999), *Nyerere & Africa: End of an Era* (4th edition, 2008), *Africa and the West* (2000), and *The Modern African State: Quest for Transformation* (2001).

The African Federal Government[46]

Godfrey Mwakikagile's work falls squarely within the "Statist" approach that focuses on *the state* as the main unit of analysis in African politics. In essence, statist scholars argue that African leaders "have created structures of domination that have enabled them to misuse their offices to reap personal gains at the expense of the pressing needs of the bulk of the population."[47] Mwakikagile begins his analysis by observing that while "the modern African state is the most dominant institution on the African continent," it is "a fragile institution because of its structural flaws." Basically, "African states operate as oppressive instruments of power."[48]

Like Claude Ake, Mwakikagile traces the history of the state in Africa to colonialism and the capitalist penetration of the continent. For him (as for Busia and Ake), in spite of formal independence, the *postcolonial state* in Africa still retains the essential features that characterized the *colonial state* in Africa. Mwakikagile describes the negative impact of this colonial inheritance on African societies and polities as follows: "The modern African state is an alien institution inherited from Europeans which has not been fully adapted to the realities of Africa. When the colonial rulers left, the institutional mechanisms of governance they introduced remained intact. In most cases, Africans inherited those structures without restructuring them to reflect the realities of African societies and accommodate diverse interests and conflicting social and political beliefs of the different groups which constituted the new nations. Ignoring the interests of some led to disaster, and continues to do so, as the history of African countries since independence sadly demonstrates."[49] Mwakikagile further elaborates on this important point: "As a creation of imperial rule, it is not surprising that the modern African state is structurally flawed. *It was not designed to serve African interests but to facilitate and consolidate colonial administration.*"[50] As previously observed by Busia and Ake, the postcolonial state is, according to Mwakikagile, essentially an apparatus of violence that relies for compliance on coercion rather than legitimacy: "Probably the most effective means the modern African state has used to perpetuate its existence and hold its people together has been arbitrary employment of coercive power—legally wielded almost exclusively by the state—to squash dissent . . . the modern African state remains corrupt and despotic, and inefficient except as a repressive apparatus."[51] To the extent that "they inherited its colonial institutional structures without correcting its structural flaws to make it a functional apparatus within the African context,"[52] the African leaders bear some of the responsibility for this state of affairs.

Mwakikagile then proceeds to a comprehensive analysis—which constitutes the core of *The Modern African State*—of state collapse in Liberia, anarchy and state disintegration in Sierra Leone and Somalia, ethnic cleansing in Rwanda and Burundi, modern slavery in Mauritania and Sudan, and the implosion of the state in the Congo following the fall of the Mobutu regime.[53] Mwakikagile also notes that between 1996 and 1998, 35 out of 53 countries in Africa—fully two-thirds—were wracked by civil war or conflict[54] and that in 1997 there were at least 90 private armies helping African governments to maintain or restore law and order in 53 African countries.[55] According to the author, this state of affairs helps explain the emergence of the African military as the most dominant and powerful institution in African politics.[56]

This exhaustive analysis leads Mwakikagile to conclude that "in Africa, the struggle for power is mostly conducted along ethnic and regional rather than class and ideological lines."[57] Consequently, this situation, he believes, "calls for a solution which, so far, has never been tried in Africa to resolve perpetual ethnic conflicts and other intra-state civil strife motivated by regional rivalries and hostilities." The solution, argues Mwakikagile, "is *ethnic self-determination* leading to the establishment of *ethno-states*—including those based on regional, cultural and linguistic affinity—in place of the modern African state in countries . . . where ethnic and regional conflicts threaten to destroy African nations as we know them today."[58] In other words, the ongoing fragmentation of African countries along ethnic and regional lines "seems to point to one solution: reorganization of the modern African state along federal lines with extensive *devolution of power* to the *regions* and *ethno-states*."[59]

As the cases of Rwanda and Burundi clearly show, the root cause of the problem lies in the colonial boundaries, "because they have confined people within their own countries although there is not enough room or fertile land for everybody in all those countries." As a result, "African leaders need to seriously consider loosening their borders—and even redrawing the map of Africa—in order to allow people to move freely across national borders to ease population pressures and provide economic opportunities elsewhere across the continent for people from less-endowed areas." In other words, argues Mwakikagile, the severity of the African predicament calls for nothing less than a closer union in the form of an *African confederation* or *African federal government*, starting with economic integration, leading to an *African common market*, and, eventually, resulting in a political union.[60] Concretely, Mwakikagile proposes the following plan for a Union of African States: "If the future of Africa lies in federation, that kind of federation could even be a giant federation of numerous autonomous units which have replaced the modern African state in order to build, on a continental or sub-continental scale, a common market, establish a common currency, a common defense, and may be even pursue a common foreign policy under some kind of central authority—including collective leadership on rotational basis—which Africans think is best for them."[61] Observing that a substantial degree of informal cross-border movement of people already exists in Africa—such as the back and forth movement of the Masai across the Kenya-Tanzania border—Mwakikagile believes that "the larger supra-national units . . . would function as a single entity allowing free movement and settlement of its peoples wherever land is available in the region." Mwakikagile offers an East African Federation composed of Kenya, Uganda, Tanzania, Rwanda, Burundi, and the Democratic Republic of the Congo (DRC) as an example of regional integration leading to larger supranational units.[62]

Mwakikagile also identifies the type of government best suited for the African situation as a *democracy by consensus*, which, in his view, would allow all social, ethnic, and regional factions to freely express themselves. Such a democracy should take the form of a *government of national unity*, inclusive of both the winners and losers in the electoral process, and would entail a multiparty system approved by national referendum; it should also be based on extreme decentralization down to the lowest grassroots level. Furthermore, in this democratic system the tenure of the president must be limited to one term (preferably five to six years), and the tenure of the members of the national legislatures to two three-year terms.[63] Mwakikagile then goes on to identify the institutions that such a federal government should include to ensure accountability and transparency:

- a *constituent national assembly* in each country tasked with writing the constitution, representative of the diverse and pluralistic nature of African countries, and thus composed of the representatives of all political parties and interests groups (i.e., members of the civil society), such as ethnic groups, trade unions, professional associations, student organizations, religious organizations, and women's groups
- an *independent judiciary* to hold everybody—elite and people alike—accountable
- an *independent press*, including several independent newspapers and radio stations, to air dissenting opinions and present alternative policies

- an *independent electoral commission* composed of members of all the different political parties in the country to monitor elections and check vote rigging
- an *independent police and security force* under neutral control[64]

In the final analysis, says Mwakikagile, the descent into ethnic conflict and civil war and the danger of secession in Africa can only be averted if power is given back to the people in a truly decentralized fashion: "Give them [the people] more power and freedom to manage their own affairs in their own localities and regions to make sure that no one is oppressing them, and also to assure them that they are an integral part of the nation like everybody else. *Let the people decide.* They know what is best for them far better than national leaders in distant capitals do. People want to lead themselves at the grassroots level, not to be told all the time what to do by those above."[65] Finally, Mwakikagile warns of dire consequences for Africa if his policy prescriptions are ignored: "All what we have suggested here can and must be done. Otherwise everything is going to spin out of control as the modern African state collapses from its own weaknesses because of its failure to forge unity in diversity on a democratic basis."[66]

MUENI WA MUIU

A Biographical Note

Mueni wa Muiu is a graduate of Howard University (Washington, DC), earning an MA in African studies in May 1991 and a PhD in political science in May 2003. Her dissertation was published in 2008 by Palgrave Macmillan (New York) under the title *The Pitfalls of Liberal Democracy and Late Nationalism in South Africa.* Her second book (coauthored with me) was published in 2009 by the same publisher under the title *A New Paradigm of the African State: Fundi wa Afrika.*

Mueni wa Muiu has been active in many academic associations and fora, most notably the African Studies Association, the Association of Third World Studies (ATWS), and the Council for the Development of Social Science in Africa (CODESRIA). She has presented more than fifty academic papers and published more than ten book chapters and articles (as well as ten book reviews) in refereed academic journals. In October 2001, the ATWS granted Mueni wa Muiu the Harold Isaacs Best Graduate Paper Award. The same organization granted her the Reddick Award for best article published in the *Journal of Third World Studies* in 2002. It should be noted that both awards were granted for her seminal research on *Fundi wa Afrika,* which is the subject of this section.

Mueni wa Muiu taught political science at Georgia Perimeter College in Clarkston, Georgia (2002–3), as well as at the University of North Carolina at Asheville (2003–4). In August 2004, she joined Winston-Salem State University (WSSU; Winston-Salem, North Carolina) as assistant professor of political science. In 2010, she was promoted to the rank of associate professor of political science in the Department of Social Sciences at WSSU.

FUNDI WA AFRIKA: A New Paradigm of the African State[67]

The starting point of Mueni wa Muiu's analysis is what many authors have called "the paradox of African development": "Why is it that a continent so richly endowed with natural resources and minerals is consistently rated as the poorest in the world? Why is it that contrary to what pertains in the rest of the world, Africans are still struggling for their basic human, political, economic and social rights?"[68] In other words, "why are African countries now by any social, economic and political indicators, at a lower level of development than they were at independence in spite of the billions of dollars of foreign aid poured into them? . . . why, of all continents, is Africa the only one that is actually regressing rather than progressing?"[69] Mueni wa Muiu further argues that none of the existing African studies theories, approaches, and paradigms—from modernization to statist—satisfactorily explains the "African predicament" or provides a realistic and workable exit option.[70] What is required, therefore, is nothing less than an entirely new paradigm in the study of African politics that she calls *Fundi wa Afrika* (meaning "builder" or "tailor" of Africa in the Ki-Swahili language of eastern Kenya).[71] According to the author, the constituent elements of this paradigm must include the following:

- an exhaustive and radical critique of existing paradigms of the African state
- relinking with and reviving indigenous African traditions, culture, languages, social structures, and political systems and institutions, appropriately modernized and adapted to current political, economic, and social conditions in Africa
- drawing ideas, knowledge, and inspiration from and building on the work of various African political thinkers such as Ibn Khaldun, Amilcar Cabral, Frantz Fanon, Kwame Nkrumah, Cheikh Anta Diop, Daniel Osabu-Kle, and Claude Ake
- taking a resolutely Africanist and Pan-Africanist perspective—namely, putting Africa and Africans first, emphasizing the fundamental cultural unity of Africa, and promoting the political and economic unity of Africans in Africa and in the diaspora[72]

In what sense does *Fundi wa Afrika* constitute a *new* paradigm in African studies? The authors claim that their theory departs from the statist approach—used by such scholars as Jean-François Bayart, Patrick Chabal, Jean-Pascal Daloz, Jeffrey Herbst, Richard Joseph, Mathurin Houngnikpo, Achille Mbembe, Abdi Ismail, and Ahmed I. Samatar—because it is both analytic and prescriptive:

1. It analyzes the creation and evolution of the African state (from indigenous to colonial to postcolonial) using a long-term historical perspective.
2. It shows how internal and external events and actors in Africa shaped the
   state and its leadership.
3. It prescribes what the ideal state and its leadership (as determined by
   Africans themselves) should be.[73]

From the point of view of social scientific research, *Fundi wa Afrika* introduces two major methodological innovations: (1) a long-term historical perspective and (2) a multidisciplinary approach. "We can only understand the
multifaceted crisis that affects most African countries today . . . by adopting
an interdisciplinary and long-term historical perspective."[74] The long-term
historical perspective was first conceived and applied by French historian Fernand Braudel—as the *longue durée*—to the study of the rise and fall of the
Mediterranean civilization and was used subsequently by Charles Tilly in the
study of capitalism and state formation in Europe.[75] It is interesting to note
in this regard that to the best of our knowledge, the *longue durée* has never
been systematically applied to the study of the evolution of African societies.[76] Typically, historians of Africa begin their studies from 1800 or 1850.[77]
From a long-term historical perspective, Mueni wa Muiu means from the
sixth century BCE (Kush/Nubia and Egypt) to the present. By using such
a perspective, the author is able to explain the current African predicament
by the systematic destruction of African states and the dispossession, exploitation, and marginalization of African people through successive historical
processes: the trans-Atlantic slave trade, imperialism, colonialism, and neocolonialism (now renamed globalization).[78] Muiu and I argue that "a multidisciplinary perspective is necessary because only then can we get a panoramic
view capable of fully explaining the conditions prevailing in contemporary
Africa." While such a perspective should ideally include history, archeology,
linguistics, literature, anthropology, sociology, geography, geopolitics, political science, and economics, practical and disciplinary constraints forced us to
limit ourselves to history, political science, geopolitics, and economics, and
also (to a lesser extent) to anthropology, sociology, and literature. Anticipat-
ing the criticism of those who might consider such a perspective too broad
and incredibly bold, we explain, "It is broad because what we present here
is a template for understanding Africa . . . *Fundi* is bold because in order
to find solutions that address the root of Africa's problems, rather than the
symptoms, one has to be bold . . . Such an approach enables us to highlight
the contribution of Africa to world civilization, as well as its potential for
economic development."[79]

  In *A New Paradigm of the African State: Fundi wa Afrika*, the *longue
durée* as well as the multidisciplinary perspective are embodied in three chapters. Chapter 2, "Indigenous African Political Systems and Institutions," is a
survey of state-building in ancient Africa (Egypt, Kush/Nubia, Axum, and
Carthage), in medieval Africa (Ghana, Mali, Songhay, and Kanem-Bornu),
as well as in eighteenth- and nineteenth-century West Africa (Segu, Oyo,

and Dahomey).[80] Chapter 3 analyses the evolution of the African colonial and postcolonial states,[81] while Chapter 4 takes on the theme of "Genocide, African Natural Resources and the West" in historical perspective.[82] Furthermore, *Fundi* uses two country case studies to test the validity of its hypothesis—the Democratic Republic of the Congo (DRC, ex-Zaïre)[83] and South Africa[84]—in each case analyzing the evolution of the country from indigenous to contemporary political systems.

Mueni wa Muiu is in full agreement with Claude Ake and Godfrey Mwakikagile when they observe that in spite of formal independence, the *postcolonial state* in Africa still retains the essential features that characterized the *colonial state* in Africa—namely, absolutism, arbitrariness, and exclusion, but also political domination, social marginalization, cultural dependency, and economic exploitation. Like its predecessor, argues Ake, the postcolonial state is an apparatus of violence that relies for compliance on coercion rather than legitimacy.[85] Likewise, Muiu's analysis parallels that of Mwakikagile when he observes that the modern African state is structurally flawed in the sense that "it was not designed to serve African interests but to facilitate and consolidate colonial administration."[86] Thus Muiu and I observe that the present African state is the product of successive historical processes—from slavery to colonialism to globalization—and thus "reflects the Western state but fails to perform the same functions." Moreover, we argue "that this Leviathan is a monster that functions as an agent of exploitation of the people by both African rulers and the West." We conclude, "The present state is not conducive to development because its nature—an exogenous structure without the interests, priorities and needs of Africans at heart—and its relationship with the West do not allow for any type of autonomous, popular development. In reality, the African state has been constructed in such a way that dependency on the West is inevitable."[87] According to us, in order to meet the specific priorities and needs of Africans, "the state must be reconfigured by retaining its positive (and adequately functioning) elements and by incorporating the still functional remnants of indigenous African institutions."[88]

The main practical aspects of *Fundi wa Afrika* are summarized by Muiu and me in 16 points as follows:

1. According to *Fundi wa Afrika*, the African state must be reconstructed based on African culture, history, traditions, priorities, and needs (however these are defined by Africans). It uses history to demonstrate that African political systems were radically and permanently altered after slavery to serve minority and Western needs. To reverse this trend, Africans must first recapture their economies. Such a development implies the control by Africans over the resources within their borders for the *sole benefit* of the African people.

2. The first priority of any legitimate leader in Africa must be to halt the progression of debilitating diseases still endemic in Africa, particularly AIDS, malaria, sleeping sickness, river blindness, bilharzia, and tuberculosis.

3. Africans should connect the rural (where the majority lives) with the urban areas on the basis of African culture. If Africans are to control their destiny, they must do so within their own culture.

4. Africans must transform their educational systems, using a new type of pedagogy and emphasizing such subjects as civic education, African history, and science and mathematics.

5. A new African leadership truly in the service of African people must be chosen from each level and based on ideals and principles that the people themselves will decide on.

6. African women must be the driving force of the political, economic, and social development of Africa.

7. In the context of globalization and the world economy, African countries must be selective in their trade policies in order to develop their human resources behind protective barriers.

8. In the reconstituted African state, the activities of nongovernmental organizations (NGOs) will be circumscribed and strictly regulated to ensure that their activities conform to the interests, priorities, and needs of Africans rather than those of the West.

9. In order to connect African states to each other and facilitate the inter-African movement of people, goods, and services, roads, railways, air routes, and telecommunication networks should be planned.

10. A comprehensive cultural policy in the area of radio and visual arts (including television and film) based on African culture and values should be introduced in Africa.

11. A reconstituted African state must protect children and the youth. Such a state must impose prohibitive fines on any group or individuals that promote the violation of the lives of children under the pretense of "African culture," "tourism," or "religion."

12. A reconstituted African state must also protect girls from genital mutilations, a practice carried over from ancient Egypt and Kush.

13. Every region of Africa should have a beautification and sanitation department providing electricity, water, and sanitation infrastructure to all the African cities.

14. Africa should have a continental army based on redrawn borders. Each state will contribute a contingent to a standing federal army to protect the continent.

15. The African "debt" must be totally written off, and a moratorium on debt repayment declared.

16. The development of an African identity will be encouraged and privileged over an ethnic identity; Africans in the diaspora who support the new state could invest in this state or settle there if they wish to.[89]

In *Fundi wa Afrika*—inspired in particular by the previous Pan-African projects of Kwame Nkrumah, Cheikh Anta Diop, and Godfrey Mwakikagile—we argue that a new, viable, and modern African state based on five political entities—the Federation of African States—should be built on the functional remnants of indigenous African political systems and institutions and based on African values, traditions, and culture.

In the *Federation of African States* (FAS), Africa will have one constitution and a common foreign and defense policy. Instead of the current 55 states, Africa will be divided into five super-states (see map of FAS, Chapter 4, p. 68). The new state of *Kimit* will include Algeria, Libya, Morocco, Egypt, Tunisia, and Western Sahara, plus the Arab population of Mauritania, Northern Sudan, and Northern Chad. *Mali* will include Benin, Burkina Faso, Cape Verde, Côte d'Ivoire, Gambia, Ghana, Guinea, Guinea-Bissau, Liberia, Mali, Niger, Nigeria, Senegal, Sierra Leone, and Togo, plus the African population of Mauritania. *Kongo* will include Congo (DRC), Congo Republic, Cameroon, Southern Chad, Central African Republic, Equatorial Guinea, Gabon, São Tome and Principe, Uganda, Rwanda, and Burundi. *Kush* will include southern Sudan, Ethiopia, Eritrea, Djibouti, Somalia-Somaliland, Kenya, Tanzania, Zanzibar, Seychelles, and Comoros. *Zimbabwe* will include Angola, Botswana, Namibia, Malawi, Mozambique, Madagascar, Mauritius, Lesotho, Swaziland, South Africa, Zambia, and Zimbabwe. The new federal capital city will be called Napata; it will not belong to any of the five states. Each region will have a key player, based on population and resources—for example, Kongo, Egypt, Ethiopia, Nigeria, and South Africa. FAS will be protected by a federal army made up of diverse members from the five states. All external economic relations will be conducted by the federal government. Economic and political power will be decentralized, giving people more input in the day-to-day activities of the federation.[90]

In FAS, power will be decentralized and start from the village councils, made up of the local people. This will be followed by a regional council of elders, then a national council that will be followed by the federal council of presidents. Each of the five regions of FAS will be governed by five rotating presidents on the basis of a federal system. Africa will have a popular democracy—based on accountability and responsibility—that will be organized from below. Since each section of the population will have representatives at all levels of government, power will be decentralized and the people will determine their destiny based on their interests, priorities, and needs.[91]

It now "behooves the African studies scholarly community to apply *Fundi* to specific country case studies to prove its validity."[92] Mueni wa Muiu and I have taken up our own challenge and are currently at work on a new book that applies the *Fundi* paradigm to a political history of Algeria, Côte d'Ivoire, Kenya, and Zimbabwe.[93] Furthermore, we argue that "*Fundi* can be used outside the continent to study any former colony in which the indigenous population still exists, such as Brazil, Bolivia, Haïti, Indonesia, or Iraq. All these countries experience basically the same conditions . . . they only differ in terms of degree."[94]

CONCLUSION

The Africanist-populist scholars surveyed in this chapter have heeded Fanon's admonition to Africans that they must be bold and innovative and develop their own ideas, concepts, and institutions based on African values, culture, and traditions. This alternative path to Western liberal democracy and capitalist development is precisely the line of thinking of an emerging African scholarship, exemplified by the four African scholars whose political ideas were examined in this chapter: Daniel T. Osabu-Kle, Claude Ake, Godfrey Mwakikagile, and Mueni wa Muiu. These ideas for a new, free, and self-reliant Africa are put forth by African scholars who have the best interest of the continent ant its people at heart. The Africanist-populist scholars are convinced that the solution of African problems lie within Africans themselves; they all advocate popular democracy and development, and they are all dedicated Pan-Africanists.

The central thesis put forward by Daniel Osabu-Kle is that "only a democracy compatible with the African cultural environment is capable of achieving the political conditions for successful development in Africa."[95] He calls this type *jaku* democracy. Osabu-Kle begins his analysis by observing that Africans don't have to choose between liberal democracy and socialism. Indeed, "Africans will only be able to solve their problems the African way."[96] For the "African personality" to be restored, argues Osabu-Kle, a process of mental decolonization must take place. This involves, in particular, a process of ideological re-education of the African society aimed at creating "a new African." In the political realm, Africans must modify and adapt indigenous African political systems and institutions to create a consociational (or consensual) democracy. Finally, Osabu-Kle (like Nkrumah before him) calls for the creation of a United States of Africa.

In *Democracy and Development in Africa*, Nigerian political scientist Claude Ake provides an insightful analysis of the African crisis and outlines the key elements of a new development paradigm. Like Kofi Busia (see Chapter 3), Ake observes that the African postcolonial state is essentially an unreformed colonial state characterized by authoritarianism; it is used by the African leaders as an instrument of coercion. Being an alien construct, argues Ake, the African state cannot possibly serve as an agent of development. Ake also shows that the contemporary African state has been privatized in the sense that it primarily serves the interests of the elites rather than those of the masses. Thus African leaders merely adopted the "ideology of development" as a smokescreen, pretending to do "something" for the country and its citizens (but in actual fact doing nothing). Ake then outlines the two core elements of a new, *people-centered* development paradigm for Africa:

1. *Popular development*—that is, a type of development in which *the people* are the agent, the means, and the end of development
2. *Popular democracy* in which *people* have real decision-making power

Claude Ake's major contribution to the advancement of social sciences in Africa is that he correctly identified the root causes of the African crisis and proposed an appropriate solution to this crisis in the form of a suitable democratic system and a new development paradigm.

Like Kofi Busia and Claude Ake, Godfrey Mwakikagile observes that "the modern African state is structurally flawed. It was not designed to serve African interests but to facilitate and consolidate colonial administration."[97] In addition, the African postcolonial state is also an apparatus of violence that relies for compliance on coercion rather than on legitimacy. Mwakikagile's central thesis is that ethnic conflict, civil war, and secession in Africa can only be avoided if power is given back to the people. The solution he proposes— based on the principle of "unity in diversity"—is ethnic self-determination based on ethno-states. Starting from the observation that that a substantial degree of informal, cross-border movement of people already exists in Africa, Mwakikagile's plan calls for redrawing the map of Africa to create an African confederation or African federal government that could take the form of a "Union of African States."

In *A New Paradigm of the African State: Fundi wa Afrika*, Mueni wa Muiu begins her analysis with an exposé of the "paradox of African development"— namely, why does a continent so richly endowed in natural resources and with such an enormous agricultural potential currently rank as the poorest in the world? Using a long-term historical perspective and a multidisciplinary approach, Muiu argues that the current African predicament may be explained by the systematic destruction of African states and the dispossession, exploitation, and marginalization of African people through successive historical processes: the trans-Atlantic slave trade, imperialism, colonialism, and neocolonialism (or globalization). Furthermore, Muiu agrees with Busia, Ake, and Mwakikagile that the postcolonial state is still a colonial structure and an instrument of violence and coercion.

Muiu's central thesis is that the African state must be reconfigured to meet the interests, priorities, and needs of African peoples; this involves (1) retaining the positive and adequately functioning elements of the contemporary political systems and (2) incorporating the still-functioning elements of indigenous African institutions. Muiu further argues that a new, viable, and modern African state must be created in the form of a Federation of African States (FAS) based on five sub-regional political entities : Kimit, Mali, Kongo, Kush, and Zimbabwe (see the map of FAS in Figure 4.1, p. 68). In FAS, power will be decentralized and based on a rotating presidency, with a common foreign and defense policy.

In the final analysis, the common elements in the political thought of Osabu-Kle, Ake, Mwakikagile, and Muiu are as follows:

- an *Africanist* perspective, based on the conviction that only Africans themselves will be able to solve their problems the African way, on the basis of African values, culture, and traditions, ultimately leading to the emergence of an *African consciousness* and a *new African*

- an analysis of the African postcolonial state as an unreformed, authoritarian colonial state based on violence and coercion rather than on consensus
- centrality of *the people*, viewed as agent, means, and main beneficiary of democracy and development
- promotion of *popular development* and *popular democracy*, with the people as main agent and beneficiary
- the necessity for *African unity* and thus to reconfigure the African state, whether in the form of a *Union of African States, United States of Africa*, or *Federation of African States*

FURTHER READING

Ake, Claude, *Democracy and Development in Africa* (Washington, DC: The Brookings Institution, 1996).

Martin, Guy, "Reflections on Democracy and Development in Africa: The Intellectual Legacy of Claude Ake," *Ufahamu* 26, no. 1 (Winter 1998): 102–9.

Muiu, Mueni wa, "*Fundi wa Afrika*: Toward A New Paradigm of the African State," *Journal of Third World Studies* 19, no. 2 (Fall 2002): 23–42.

Muiu, Mueni wa, and Guy Martin, *A New Paradigm of the African State: Fundi wa Afrika* (New York: Palgrave Macmillan, 2009).

Mwakikagile, Godfrey, *The Modern African State: Quest for Transformation* (Huntington, NY: Nova Science Publishers, 2001).

Osabu-Kle, Daniel T., *Compatible Cultural Democracy: The Key to Development in Africa* (Peterborough, Ontario: Broadview Press, 2000).

———✦❈✦———

THE TRANSFORMATIVE POWER
OF IDEAS AND VALUES

TOWARD PEACE, DEVELOPMENT,
AND DEMOCRACY IN AFRICA

African political thought refers to the original ideas, values, and blueprints for a better Africa that inform African political systems and institutions from the ancient period to the present. African political thought also refers to political theories and ideologies developed by various African scholars and statesmen, as enunciated in their speeches, autobiographies, writings, and policy statements. Political thought usually precedes and informs political action; the latter, in turn, influences political thought. Political theory and political practice are thus inextricably linked. In other words, African political thought provides practical solutions to political, economic, social, and cultural problems, and it varies according to historical circumstances and a constantly changing African and world political environment.

A major distinction was made between indigenous and modern African political thought. The former was developed during the so-called golden age of African history and refers to the governance of ancient kingdoms and empires (such as Egypt, Kush/Nubia, Axum, Ghana, Mali, Songhay, and Kanem-Bornu), but it was also developed by such scholars as Ibn Khaldun, Al Bekri, and Ibn Battuta and is associated with indigenous African political systems and institutions. Modern African political thought emerged in the late nineteenth and early twentieth centuries and was developed by African scholars such as James Africanus Horton, Edward Wilmot Blyden, and Kofi A. Busia.

All the modern African authors/statesmen surveyed in this book exhibit a number of common characteristics. First, they are both political thinkers and political statesmen/activists, linking theory and practice as all great philosopher-kings have done throughout history. Second, all have, to various degrees, been influenced by the Marxist-Leninist ideology. Third, they are all truly dedicated to the welfare and well-being of their countries and people. As such, they were all dedicated African nationalists. Fourth, they ruled for a relatively short period of time (sometimes not at all), and many died in the prime of their lives (often at the hands of agents of Western powers), as the cases of Amilcar Cabral, Frantz Fanon, Patrice Lumumba, Thomas Sankara, Agostinho Neto, Eduardo Mondlane, Samora Machel, and Steve Biko clearly illustrate. As a result, these statesmen/activists were unable to see their policies mature and bear fruit.

This textbook is, to the best of our knowledge, the very first attempt to synthesize African political thought into one single thematic volume. There are other features that make this volume unique and original. For one thing, it is the first book in which indigenous African political ideas and values (from antiquity to the nineteenth century) are examined alongside modern African political ideas (from the nineteenth century to the present). Furthermore, it is also the very first time that the emergence of Islamic values and ideas on governance between the second and eighth centuries in North, Western, Central, and Eastern Africa are studied in relation to indigenous African values and ideas on governance. Finally, contrary to existing works on the subject, this textbook focuses primarily on the *ideas* and the common themes that bind them rather than on the *individuals*—whether scholars, statesmen, or leaders—themselves.

Chapter 1 consisted of an overview of the political ideology of indigenous African political systems and institutions, from antiquity to the nineteenth century. We showed that those systems and institutions were traditionally based on kinship, ancestry, and the rule of law; furthermore, they were essentially democratic in that they were based on an elaborate system of checks and balances, and they involved ordinary people in the political decision-making process. Moreover, the African leader was accountable for his actions at all times. The purpose of this analysis is not to reclaim a nostalgic "golden age" but rather to identify the still functioning elements of the indigenous African political systems and institutions that could be incorporated into a reconfigured African state and fused with the positive elements of modern African political systems, as advocated by such scholars as Daniel Osabu-Kle and Mueni wa Muiu and as experimented in practice by Amilcar Cabral, Samora Machel, Thomas Sankara, and Julius Nyerere.

In Chapter 2, we examined the influence of Islamic values and ideas on indigenous African political systems and institutions, from the tenth to the nineteenth centuries. Islam as a religion and way of life is one of the fundamental aspects of African civilization. The period from the seventh to the sixteenth centuries witnessed the progressive Islamization of the states and societies of North Africa, the Western and Central Sudan, Ethiopia, Somalia, the East African coastal areas, and the Indian Ocean islands. In West Africa, Islam spread mostly to the urban commercial and political centers among the ruling elite and the aristocracy, leading to the emergence of a clerical class (*ulama*) in these urban centers. The majority of the people—mostly peasants living in the rural areas—were barely influenced by Islam and remained faithful to their indigenous African beliefs. As a result, Islam in the Western Sudan was very much a *mixed religion* that included elements of the Berber and other indigenous African religions.

The available historical evidence shows that from the eleventh to the eighteenth century, a process of *Africanization of Islam* took place. This process of mutual cross-fertilization resulted from a fusion of elements of Islamic religion, culture, and values with elements of indigenous African religion, culture, and values that produced a *mixed religion* retaining aspects of both. Nineteenth-century Islamic revival in the Western Sudan took the form of a militant Messianic movement and a social revolution, leading to the creation of a new political entity, the Islamic theocratic state, which collided with preexisting indigenous African political systems and institutions. Unfortunately, the two systems could not be reconciled, and the theocratic states failed primarily because they were not based on indigenous values, traditions, and institutions.

Chapter 3 begins with an overview of the image of Africa as the "Dark Continent" and Africans as "primitive" and "uncivilized" constructed by Europeans—under the influence of social Darwinism—from the sixteenth century onward. The chapter then focused on the French colonial policies of assimilation and association as well as on the British policy of "Indirect Rule"; it also examined the rise of economic and political liberalism in nineteenth century Europe as a background to the rise of "humanitarianism." The next section focused on a small Western-educated West African intellectual elite—Edward W. Blyden, James Africanus Horton, and Joseph E. Casely Hayford—which attempted to reconcile Western systems of thought with African values, culture, and traditions—or Western liberalism with African democracy. The last section examined the ideas of two prominent African advocates of liberal democracy: Kofi Busia of Ghana, who believed in the universal character of liberal democracy, and Kenneth Kaunda of Zambia, who advocated the political ideology of African humanism.

Chapter 4 examined Pan-Africanism and African unity, from ideal to practice. According to the standard-bearers of Pan-Africanism during the early post-independence period—Kwame Nkrumah, Ahmed Ben Bella, Patrice Lumumba, Ahmed Sékou Touré, and Modibo Kéïta—the African states should aim for immediate political and economic integration in the form of a "United States of Africa" consisting of an African Common Market, African Monetary Union, African Military High Command, and a continent-wide Union Government. Alas, the continental organization that was eventually set up on May 25, 1963—the Organization of African Unity (OAU)— reflected the views of the functionalist/gradualist African leaders (such as Félix Houphouët-Boigny, Nnamdi Azikiwe, and Jomo Kenyatta), who advocated a gradual, step-by-step approach to African integration based on cooperation in non-controversial, technical, and economic areas. After Kwame Nkrumah's demise in February 1966, Muammar Qaddafi of Libya assumed the mantle of leader of the Pan-Africanist movement and actively promoted the project of a Union of African States as advocated by Nkrumah in *Africa Must Unite* (1963). Unfortunately, the African Union (AU) that was created in May 2002 does not significantly differ from its predecessor, the OAU, as it is modeled on the European Union.

The chapter then surveyed past and current proposals for a revision of the map of Africa and a reconfiguration of the African states put forward by various authors, notably Cheikh Anta Diop, Marc-Louis Ropivia, Makau wa Mutua, Arthur Gakwandi, Joseph Ki-Zerbo, Daniel Osabu-Kle, Godfrey Mwakikagile, Pelle Danabo, and Mueni wa Muiu. These projects are premised on the belief that unity is an essential prerequisite to the achievement of development, peace, and security in Africa. While each of these proposals has merit, most are not grounded in an overarching political framework, and they lack specificity in terms of the actual structure and functioning of the reconfigured states. We concluded that only with the realization of Mueni wa Muiu's project for state reconfiguration in Africa—A Federation of African States (FAS) based on five subregional units and total political and economic integration with a rotating presidency—will African's "Dream of Unity" finally become reality.[1]

Chapter 5 surveyed the political, economic, social, and cultural dimensions of the socialist-populist ideology from a distinctly *socialist* perspective. Note that in the socialist-populist ideology, the emphasis is on *socialist*. The common characteristics of the leaders associated with this ideology—Patrice Lumumba, Ahmed Ben Bella, Amilcar Cabral, and Samora Machel—are their short tenure of office, their preference for democratic governance, their populism, and (for the last three) the fact that they achieved independence as a result of an armed struggle. We noted striking similarities in the political ideologies of Amilcar Cabral and Samora Machel: the need for an ideology and to link theory and practice, the primacy of the political, the need to return to the source and create a new man, and acknowledging that the people must be the agents and main beneficiaries of democracy and development. Not surprisingly, the same common characteristics apply to the socialist-populist leaders surveyed in Chapter 6.

Chapter 6 continued the survey—started in Chapter 5—of the political, economic, social, and cultural dimensions of the socialist-populist ideology from a distinctly *socialist* perspective. The chapter focused specifically on the statesmen who, in spite of their socialist rhetoric, used the socialist-populist ideology primarily as an instrument of control and coercion: Kwame Nkrumah of Ghana, Ahmed Sékou Touré of Guinea, Modibo Kéïta of Mali, and Julius K. Nyerere of Tanzania. We observed a significant degree of convergence in the way in which Nkrumah, Touré, and Kéïta conceived of African socialism. These three leaders all viewed African socialism as grounded in African indigenous values, culture, and traditions; as people-centered, aiming at the creation of "a new man"; and as aiming at creating a Union of African States as a first stage toward the eventual establishment of a United States of Africa. We also remarked that Julius Nyerere's concept of African socialism

(*Ujamaa*) differed somewhat from that of the previous three leaders. For Nyerere, African socialism was a universal concept and an "attitude of mind"; it was firmly grounded in African culture and traditions, and it was realized through a self-reliant strategy of development. What all these statesmen have in common is a deep and abiding faith in the power of African socialism to radically and durably transform their societies in a way that would satisfy the basic economic and social needs of their peoples, thereby significantly improving their standard of living.

Chapter 7 consisted of an overview of the political, economic, social, and cultural dimensions of the populist-socialist ideology from a distinctly *populist* perspective, from the early 1960s to the present. By "populist-socialist" we refer to states that adhere to socialism but do not stress (or even reject) Marxism. The intellectuals/statesmen reviewed in that chapter were both theoreticians and practitioners who genuinely sought to improve the living conditions of their people by attempting to implement policies of political, economic, social, and cultural transformation. In that chapter, we noted the striking similarities between the political ideas of Frantz Fanon and Thomas Sankara: the essential nature of ideology; the need for a specifically African political thought based on African values, culture, traditions, and history; cultural liberation and mental decolonization, leading to an African consciousness and the creation of a "new man"; the need for the people to be the main actor and beneficiary of democracy and development in Africa; and the need for African unity to be based on the people rather than on the governments and the elites.

The third section of the chapter focused on Muammar Qaddafi's Third Universal Theory, as exposed in the three volumes of *The Green Book*; it advocates "people power" in the form of a direct democracy with popular assemblies and people's committees, a socialist economy based on equitable distribution of resources among citizens, and the achievement of a substantial degree of political and economic unity in the form of a Union of African States. Finally, the fourth section of that chapter surveyed Steve Biko's ideology of Black Consciousness, an ideology of psychological liberation and cultural emancipation of the African man in South Africa. A major dimension of this ideology is its redefinition of "non-whites" as "blacks" to designate the African, Colored, and Indian/Asian communities in the country.

What this survey of the political thought of Fanon, Sankara, Qaddafi, and Biko teaches us is that if popular democracy and development are to succeed in Africa, African people must stop blindly following the West and must be bold and innovative. In other words, it is essential that Africans develop their own ideas, concepts, and institutions on the basis of African values, culture, and traditions. This alternative path to Western liberal democracy and capitalist development is precisely the line of thinking of an emerging African scholarship exemplified by Daniel Osabu-Kle, Claude Ake, Godfrey Mwakikagile, and Mueni wa Muiu, whose political ideas were examined in Chapter 8.

The Africanist-populist scholars surveyed in Chapter 8 have heeded Fanon's admonition to Africans that they must be bold and innovative and develop their own ideas, concepts, and institutions based on African values, culture, and traditions. Thus Daniel Osabu-Kle, Claude Ake, Godfrey Mwakikagile, and Mueni wa Muiu—who all have the best interest of Africa and its people at heart—have, each in their own way, developed ideas for a new, free, and self-reliant Africa.

As previously stated, African political thought provides practical solutions to political, economic, social, and cultural problems, and it varies according to historical circumstances and a constantly changing African and world political environment. The fact that Africa is currently facing a multidimensional crisis—political, economic, social, and cultural—of epic proportions is not in dispute. Ethno-regional and religious conflict, intra and interstate wars, droughts, famine, diseases, epidemics, malnutrition, and state collapse, fragmentation, and disintegration are the norm rather than the exception in Africa today. There is no doubt that the extreme severity of the African crisis—or, rather, of the African predicament—calls for drastic solutions and radical remedies. As the French saying goes, *"aux grand maux les grand remèdes"* (extreme crises call for drastic remedies). Mueni wa Muiu and I concluded *Fundi wa Afrika* by addressing the following call to action to every African:

> Africans, is this the Africa we want? How many more of us will have to die as a result of senseless wars before we realize that our own salvation and that the solution to all our problems lie not without, but within ourselves? Let us move beyond mere survival; let us refuse to remain passive victims of a perceived pre-ordained fate and let us become the initiators and agents of our own development. Indeed, as Fanon urges us to do, let us create a new African. Therein resides the secret of Africa's resolution of its predicament, and the key to its future development.[2]

Ideas matter. The majority of the statesmen/scholars reviewed in this book demonstrate the power of political ideas as they helped transform the various African societies involved. An ideology is essential as a guide to action in a new society. Political theory and political practice are inextricably linked. As Fanon cogently remarked, "the greatest danger that threatens Africa is the absence of ideology."[3] Heeding Fanon's admonition to "turn over a new leaf," "work out new concepts," and "set afoot a new man,"[4] the Africanist-populist scholars—exemplified by Claude Ake and Mueni wa Muiu—have, indeed, been bold and innovative in their quest for new ideas and new concepts—based on African values, culture, and traditions—to create a free and self-reliant Africa and a new African. More specifically, these Africanist-populist scholars offer an *Africanist* perspective based on the conviction that the solution of African problems lie within African themselves; they consider *the people* as the agent, means, and main beneficiary of democracy and development; and they are all convinced *Pan-Africanists*, variously calling for the advent of a Union of African States, United States of Africa, or Federation of African States. May they inspire a new generation of African scholars to follow in their footsteps, take up the challenge, and come up with new ideas and concepts for peace, development, and democracy in Africa.

NOTES

INTRODUCTION

1. Pioneering works on African political thought include J. Ayo Langley, *Pan-Africanism and Nationalism in West Africa: A Case Study in Ideology and Social Classes* (Oxford: Clarendon Press, 1973); William H. Friedland and Carl G. Rosberg Jr., eds., *African Socialism* (Stanford, CA: Stanford University Press, 1964); Claude Wauthier, *The Literature and Thought of Modern Africa* (Washingron, DC: Three Continents Press, 1979 [1964]); Robert W. July, *The Origins of Modern African Thought* (London: Faber and Faber, 1968); Henry S. Wilson, ed., *Origins of West African Nationalism* (London: Macmillan/St. Martin's Press, 1969); Yves Bénot, *Idéologies des Indépendances Africaines*, 2nd ed. (Paris: François Maspéro, 1972); Gideon C. M. Mutiso and S. W. Rohio, eds., *Readings in African Political Thought* (London: Heinemann, 1975); and Carl G. Rosberg Jr. and Thomas M. Callaghy, *Socialism in Sub-Saharan Africa* (Berkeley: Institute of International Studies, University of California, 1979).

   A more recent—though fairly superficial—compendium is that of Peter Boele van Hensbroek, *Political Discourses in African Thought, 1860 to the Present* (Westport, CT: Praeger Publishers, 1999); see also Crawford Young, *Ideology and Development in Africa* (New Haven, CT: Yale University Press, 1982) and P. L. E. Idahosa, *The Populist Dimension to African Political Thought: Critical Essays in Reconstruction and Retrieval* (Trenton, NJ: Africa World Press, 2004).

2. Boele van Hensbroek, *Political Discourses in African Thought, 1860 to the Present*, 1.

3. Henry L. Bretton, *The Rise and Fall of Kwame Nkrumah* (London: Pall Mall, 1966), 158.

4. See for instance Daniel Chu and Elliot Skinner, *A Glorious Age in Africa: The Story of Three Great African Empires* (Garden City, NY: Zenith Books/Doubleday, 1965); Margaret Shinnie, *Ancient African Kingdoms* (London: Edward Arnold, 1965); Roland Oliver, ed., *The Middle Age of African History* (London: Oxford University Press, 1967); and Basil Davidson, *African Civilization Revisited: From Antiquity to Modern Times* (Trenton, NJ: Africa World Press, 1991).

5. Thomas Hodgkin, *Nationalism in Colonial Africa* (New York: New York University Press, 1957), 23; Basil Davidson, *Which Way Africa? The Search for a New Society* (Harmondsworth, UK: Penguin Books, 1967), 53–57.

6. On this topic, see Marina and David Ottaway, *Afrocommunism*, 2nd ed. (New York: Africana Publishing Company, 1986); Edmond J. Keller and Donald Rothchild, eds., *Afro-Marxist Regimes: Ideology and Public Policy* (Boulder, CO: Lynne Rienner Publishers, 1987); Crawford Young, *Ideology and Development in Africa* (New Haven: Yale University Press, 1982), chapter 3, 22–96. See also the "Marxist

Regimes Series" edited by Bogdan Szajkowsi at Pinter Publishers (London and New York), which includes case studies ("Politics, Economics & Society") of Angola, Benin, Burkina Faso, Cape Verde, Congo, Ethiopia, Ghana, Guinea-Bissau, Madagascar, Mozambique, São Tomé and Principe, and Zimbabwe.

7. See in particular F. Abiola Irele, *The Négritude Moment: Explorations in Francophone African & Caribbean Literature & Thought* (Trenton, NJ: Africa World Press, 2010); F. Abiola Irele, *Négritude et condition africaine* (Paris: Editions Karthala, 2008); Stanislas S. Adotevi, *Négritude et Négrologues* (Paris: Le Castor Astral, 1998); Irving Leonard Markovitz, *Léopold Sédar Senghor & the Politics of Négritude* (New York: Atheneum, 1969); Léopold Sédar Senghor, *Literté 1: Négritude et Humanisme* (Paris: Éditions du Seuil, 1964); Marcien Towa, *Léopold Sédar Senghor: Négritude ou Servitude?* (Yaoundé: Éditions CLE, 1976); Janet G. Vaillant, *Black, French, and African: A Life of Léopold Sédar Senghor* (Cambridge, MA: Harvard University Press, 1990); and Claude Wauthier, *L'Afrique des Africains: Inventaire de la Négritude* (Paris: Éditions du Seuil, 1964); translated into English as *The Literature and Thought of Modern Africa*, 2nd ed. (Washington, DC: Three Continents Press, 1979).

8. See in particular Léopold S. Senghor, *Liberté II: Nation et Voie Africaine du Socialisme* (Paris: Éditions du Seuil, 1971); Charles F. Andrain, "Guinea & Senegal: Contrasting Types of African Socialism," In *African Socialism*, ed. William H. Friedland and Carl G. Rosberg Jr. (Stanford, CA: Stanford University Press, 1964), 160–74; Yves Bénot, *Idéologies des Indépendances africaines*, 2nd ed. (Paris: François Maspéro, 1972), 191–306; and Louis V. Thomas, *Le Socialisme et l'Afrique*, 2 vols. (Paris: Le Livre Africain, 1966).

9. Note that the populist-socialist regime of John Jerry Rawlings in Ghana lasted only from 1979 to 1983; from 1983 to 1992, Rawlings abandoned populism and introduced liberal political and economic policies under intense pressure from Western powers and international financial institutions (International Monetary Fund and World Bank); on this subject, see in particular Kweku G. Folson, "Ideology, Revolution and Development: The Years of J.J. Rawlings in Ghana," in Okwudiba Nnoli, ed., *Government and Politics in Africa: A Reader* (Harare: AAPS Books, 2000), 124–50; and Emmanuel Hansen, *Ghana Under Rawlings: Early Years* (Lagos: Malthouse Press Limited/AAPS, 1991).

10. When president Léopold Senghor initiated multiparty democracy in Senegal in 1977, Cheikh Anta Diop created a leftist opposition party, the *Rassemblement National Démocratique* (RND: National Democratic Rally). As a result of the legislative elections of 1983 under president Abdou Diouf, Cheikh Anta Diop became the one and only RND deputy in the national assembly; he died shortly thereafter, in February 1986. See Pathé Diagne, *Cheikh Anta Diop et l'Afrique dans l'histoire du monde* (Paris: L'Harmattan/Sankoré, 2002), 45–46. Taking advantage of the liberalization of the regime in Burkina Faso, Joseph Ki-Zerbo founded a progressive, Pan-African party, the *Parti pour la démocratie et le progrès* (PDP: Party for Democracy and Progress), in 1992, of which he became chairman. In the May 1997 legislative elections, the PDP won 10 percent of the votes and 6 (out of 111) seats in the national assembly, thereby becoming the country's main opposition party. However, Joseph Ki-Zerbo resigned from his chairmanship of the PDP in 1998 and joined a short-lived antigovernment civil society coalition. He died in December 2006. See Joseph Ki-Zerbo with René Holenstein, *A quand l'Afrique?* (Geneva: Éditions de l'Aube/Éditions d'en bas, 2003), 189–96.

CHAPTER 1

1. K. A. Busia, *Africa in Search of Democracy* (New York: Frederick A. Praeger, 1967), 9.

2. J. Yoyotte, "Pharaonic Egypt: Society, Economy and Culture," in *General History of Africa; II: Ancient Civilizations of Africa*, ed. G. Mokhtar (Paris: Unesco/Heinemann, 1981), 130.

3. In the context of indigenous African political systems and institutions, the term *leader* refers to all the persons in charge of a political unit, be it lineage or village (chief), kingdom (king), or empire (emperor).

4. K. A. Busia, *Africa in Search of Democracy*, 7, 9, 26.

5. For an overview of indigenous African political systems and institutions, see Cheikh Anta Diop, *L'Afrique Noire Pré-Coloniale* (Paris: Présence Africaine, 1960), translated into English as *Precolonial Black Africa* (Chicago: Lawrence Hill Books, 1987); George B. N. Ayittey, *Indigenous African Institutions* (Ardsley-on-Hudson, NY: Transnational Publishers, 1991); Ayittey, *Africa Betrayed* (New York: St. Martin's Press, 1992), chapter 3, 37–77; Pathé Diagne, *Pouvoir politique traditionnel en Afrique occidentale* (Paris: Présence Africaine, 1968); and Mueni wa Muiu and Guy Martin, *A New Paradigm of the African State: Fundi wa Afrika* (New York: Pagrave Macmillan, 2009), chapter 2, 22–47. The classical *exposé* of the (dubious) distinction between "state" and "stateless" societies is found in M. Fortes and E. E. Evans-Pritchard, eds., *African Political Systems* (London: Oxford University Press, 1940).

6. Djibril Tamsir Niane, *Soundjata ou l'Épopée Mandingue*, 3rd ed. (Paris: Présence Africaine, 1960), translated into English as *Sundiata: An Epic of Old Mali* (Harlow, UK: Longman, 1965); Fa-Digi Sisoko, *The Epic of Son-Jara: A West African Tradition*, trans. John William Johnson (Bloomington: Indiana University Press, 1992); CELHTO, *La Charte de Kurukan Fuga: Aux sources d'une pensée politique en Afrique* (Paris: L'Harmattan/SAEC, 2008), article 8, 45 ("The Kéita clan is designated as the ruling clan of the Empire").

7. Elliott P. Skinner, *The Mossi of The Upper Volta: The Political Development of a Sudanese People* (Stanford, CA: Stanford University Press, 1964), 127, 138.

8. As stipulated in article 1 of the Mande Charter (*La Charte de Kurukan Fuga*, 41).

9. Basil Davidson, *The Lost Cities of Africa*, rev. ed. (Boston: Little, Brown and Co., 1970), 87.

10. J. K. Fynn, *Asante and its Neighbours, 1700–1807* (Evanston, IL: Northwestern University Press, 1971), 33, 55.

11. Colin M. Turnbull, *The Lonely African* (New York: Clarion Book/Simon & Schuster, 1962), 94.

12. K. A. Busia, *Africa in Search of Democracy* (New York: Frederick A. Praeger, 1967), 24.

13. Busia, *Africa in Search of Democracy*, 24–25.

14. K. A. Busia, *The Position of the Chief in the Modern Political System of Ashanti* (London: Oxford University Press/International African Institute, 1951), 21–22.

15. Busia, *Africa in Search of Democracy*, 23.

16. Ayittey, *Indigenous African Institutions*, 71–149; Ayittey, *Africa Betrayed*, 37–48.

17. Busia, *Africa in Search of Democracy*, 25–26.

18. Gaston Maspéro, *Au Temps de Ramsès et d'Assourbanipal: Égypte et Assyrie Anciennes*, 6th ed. (Paris: Librairie Hachette, 1912), 11–17.

19. J. Yoyotte, "Pharaonic Egypt: Society, Economy and Culture," 121.

20. A. Abu Bakr, "Pharaonic Egypt," in *General History of Africa; II: Ancient Civilizations of Africa*, ed. G. Mokhtar, 100; Christopher Ehret, *The Civilizations of Africa: A History to 1800* (Charlottesville: University Press of Virginia, 2002), 148–49.

21. Cheikh Anta Diop, *L'Unité culturelle de l'Afrique Noire*, 2nd ed. (Paris: Présence Africaine, 1982), 109–11.

22. J. Leclant, "The Empire of Kush: Napata and Meroe," in *General History of Africa: II Ancient Civilizations of Africa*, ed. G. Mokhtar, 278–97; A. A. Hakem, "The Civilization of Napata and Meroe," ibid., 298–325; Stanley Burstein, ed., *Ancient African Civilizations: Kush and Axum* (Princeton, NJ: Markus Wiener Publishers, 1998), 60–61, 65; and Muiu and Martin, *A New Paradigm of the African State*, 28.

23. *La Charte de Kurukan Fuga*, articles 14 and 16, 47.

24. Madina Ly-Tall, *Contribution à l'Histoire de l'Empire du Mali (XIIIe-XVIe siècles)* (Dakar: Les Nouvelles Éditions Africaines, 1977), 159–61.

25. Kenneth S. Carlston, *Social Theory and African Tribal Organization* (Urbana: University of Illinois Press, 1968), 310, 109.

26. *La Charte de Kurukan Fuga*, articles 24 & 25, 51.

27. Said Hamdun and Noel King, *Ibn Battuta in Black Africa* (Princeton, NJ: Markus Wiener Publishers, 1975), 58.

28. On indigenous legal institutions and customary laws, see in particular George B. N. Ayittey, *Indigenous African Institutions*, chapter 2, 39–69.

29. *La Charte de Kurukan Fuga*, article 7, 45.

CHAPTER 2

1. I. Hrbek, "Africa in the Context of World History" in *General History of Africa III: Africa from the Seventh to the Eleventh Century*, ed. M. El Fasi and I. Hrbek (Paris: Unesco, 1988), 1.

2. Hrbek, "Africa in the Context of World History," 6–7. According to the historians of Africa, the "Western Sudan" refers to sub-Saharan West Africa, from the Senegal river to the Niger Bend, and included such prominent medieval African states as Ghana, Mali, and Songhay; the "Central Sudan" refers to sub-Saharan West-Central Africa, from southern Niger and northern Nigeria to the Lake Chad Basin, and included such states as Bagirmi, Kanem, and Bornu. Both Western and Central Sudan are not to be confused with the present-day countries of Sudan and Southern Sudan.

3. Hrebek, "Africa in the Context of World History," 7–8. On the significance of the gold trade in state formation in North Africa, see also Yves Lacoste, *Ibn Khaldoun: Naissance de l'histoire, passé du tiers monde* (Paris: François Maspéro, 1980), 25–30. The strategic significance of gold in the economies of the medieval West African states is well captured in Edward W. Bovill, *The Golden Trade of the Moors: West African Kingdoms in the Fourteenth Century* (Princeton, NJ: Markus Wiener Publishers, 1995), 98–131; and Nehemia Levtzion, *Ancient Ghana and Mali* (New York: Africana Publishing Co., 1980), 124–35; see also Madina Ly-Tall, *Contribution à l'Histoire de l'Empire du Mal (XIIIe-XVIe sièclesi)* (Dakar:

Les Nouvelles Éditions Africaines, 1977), 102–7. Recent historical research has revealed that the so-called Almoravid conquest of Awdaghost (1054–55) and the Kingdom of Ghana (1076–77) were somewhat exaggerated, as this chapter later explains.

4. Hrbek, "Africa in the Context of World History," 8–10. On the Arab scholars and merchants, see Nehemia Levtzion and Jay Spaulding, eds., *Medieval West Africa: Views from Arab Scholars and Merchants* (Princeton, NJ: Markus Wiener Publishers, 2003).

5. Zakari Dramani-Issifou, "Islam as a Social System in Africa since the Seventh Century," in *General History of Africa III*, 92–93, see also 112–13.

6. Elikia M'Bokolo, *Afrique Noire: Histoire et Civilisations. Tome I: Jusqu'au XVIIIe siècle* (Paris: Hatier, 1995), 104.

7. M. El Fasi and I. Hrbek, "The Coming of Islam and the Expansion of the Muslim Empire," in *General History of Africa III*, 39–40; M'Bokolo, *Afrique Noire*, 117.

8. Nehemia Levtzion, *Ancient Ghana and Mali* (New York. Africana Publishing, 1980), 204; M'Bokolo, *Afrique Noire*, 117.

9. El Fasi and Hrbek, "The Coming of Islam," 47–55.

10. M. El Fasi and I. Hrbek, "Stages in the Development of Islam and Its Dissemination in Africa," in *General History of Africa III*, 59, see also 56–59.

11. Ibid., 68–71.

12. A. G. Hopkins, *An Economic History of West Africa* (New York: Columbia University Press, 1973), 64.

13. El Fasi and Hrbek, "Stages in the Development of Islam," 72, see also 71–72.

14. Al-Bakri, *Description de l'Afrique septentrionale* (1913), as quoted by El Fasi and Hrbek, "Stages in the Development of Islam," 73; and Levtzion, *Ancient Ghana and Mali*, 43–52. On the early Islamic influence in Gao, see M'Bokolo, *Afrique Noire*, 105.

15. El Fasi and Hrbek, "Stages in the Development of Islam," 73–74.

16. Levtzion, *Ancient Ghana and Mali*, 184.

17. M. Hiskett, *The Development of Islam in West Africa* (London: Longman, 1984), 23; Levtzion, *Ancient Ghana and Mali*, 185–88; J. Spencer Trimingham, *A History of Islam in West Africa* (London: Oxford University Press, 1970), 47–60.

18. Levtzion, *Ancient Ghana and Mali*, 73–83, 190–99; Trimingham, *A History of Islam in West Africa*, 60–83.

19. El Fasi and Hrbek, "Stages in the Development of Islam," 78, see also 75–78. On the Timbuktu scholars, see also Sékéné Mody Cissoko, *Tombouctou et l'Empire Songhay* (Dakar: Les Nouvelles Éditions Africaines, 1975), 187–93; Levtzion, *Ancient Ghana and Mali*, 200–207; M'Bokolo, *Afrique Noire*, 115–17.

20. El Fasi and Hrbek, "Stages in the Development of Islam," 76, see also 75–76.

21. Ibid., 80, see also 78–80.

22. Ibid., 80–81. On Mossi resistance to Islamization, see also Cissoko, *Tombouctou et l'Empire Songhay*, 186.

23. El Fasi and Hrbek, "Stages in the Development of Islam," 81.

24. Dramani-Issifou, "Islam as a Social System in Africa," 94, see also 92–94 (emphasis in the original).

25. Ibid., 96, see also 93–97.

26. Ibid., 97–104; and M'Bokolo, *Afrique Noire*, 107–8. On the *marabout*, see also Cheikh Anta Diop, *L'Afrique Noire Pré-Coloniale* (Paris: Présence Africaine, 1960), 124–26, translated into English by Harold J. Salemson as *Precolonial*

Black Africa: A Comparative Study of the Political & Social Systems of Europe and Black Africa, from Antiquity to the Formation of Modern States (Chicago: Lawrence Hill Books, 1987), 167–69.

27. Diop, *L'Afrique Noire Pré-Coloniale*, 123–24; Diop, *Precolonial Black Africa*, 165–66.

28. Dramani-Issifou, "Islam as a Social System in Africa," 107, see also 104–7.

29. Cissoko, *Tombouctou et l'Empire Songhay*, 194–95.

30. Ibid., 108, see also 107–8. On the conversion of the king of Malal, see also Levtzion, *Ancient Ghana and Mali*, 188–89; and M'Bokolo, *Afrique Noire*, 106–7.

31. Dramani-Issifou, "Islam as a Social System in Africa," 108; M'Bokolo, *Afrique Noire*, 110.

32. Levtzion, *Ancient Ghana and Mali*, 190.

33. Joseph Ki-Zerbo, *Histoire de l'Afrique Noire, d'Hier à Demain* (Paris: Hatier, 1978), 136 (translated from the French by the author, as elsewhere in this book).

34. The handbook was entitled *Answers to the Questions of the Emir al-Hadjdj Abdullah ibn Abu Bakr*, in Dramani-Issifou, "Islam as a Social System in Africa," 109–10; see also Cissoko, *Tombouctou et l'Empire Songhay*, 187.

35. Dramani-Issifou, "Islam as a Social System in Africa," 110.

36. Cissoko, *Tombouctou et l'Empire Songhay*, 177–79.

37. Dramani-Issifou, "Islam as a Social System in Africa," 115–18; and Cissoko, *Tombouctou et l'Empire Songhay*, 175–80. On the Bamana kingdom of Segu, see Sundiata A. Djata, *The Bamana Empire by the Niger: Kingdom, Jihad and Colonization, 1712–1920* (Princeton, NJ: Markus Wiener Publishers, 1997).

38. Levtzion, *Ancient Ghana and Mali*, 200. Cissoko observes the same process at work in the Songhay Empire: "Islam became a truly African faith in the eastern part of the Western Sudan as a result of missionary activity, at which point Islam ceased to be a foreign religion. During the fifteenth century, it was assimilated by the local populations, which adapted it to their indigenous values. Having penetrated the rural areas and traditionally non-Muslim regions, Islam became 'indigenized' as it blended with indigenous beliefs. The *marabout* and the magician lived side-by-side and often practiced the same rituals . . . Islam has become a truly Sudanese belief, and it has transformed the moral and spiritual values of the population of this region" (Cissoko, *Tombouctou et l'Empire Songhay*, 188).

39. Arnold J. Toynbee, *A Study of History*, vol. 3, *The Growth of Civilizations*, 2nd ed. (London: Oxford University Press, 1935), 322.

40. N. J. Dawood, ed., *The Muqaddimah: An Introduction to History*, by Ibn Khaldûn, trans. Franz Rosenthal (Princeton, NJ: Bollingen Series/Princeton University Press, 1967), ix.

41. Yves Lacoste, *Ibn Khaldoun*, 229–39, 259–267; Jamil Sayah, *Philosophie politique de l'Islam. L'Idée de l'État, de Ibn Khaldoun à Aujourd'hui* (Paris: L'Atelier de l'Archer, 2000), 11–21; Enid Hill, "Ibn Khaldûn," in *The Oxford Companion to Politics of the World*, 2nd ed., ed. Joel Krieger (New York: Oxford University Press, 2001), 379.

42. Mohammed Talbi, *Ibn Khaldûn: Sa vie, son oeuvre* (Tunis: Maison Tunisienne de l'Édition, 1973), 44; quoted in Ibn Khaldûn, *The Muqaddimah: An Introduction to History*, trans. Franz Rosenthal (Princeton, NJ: Bollingen Series/Princeton University Press, 2005 [1958]), xv.

43. Dawood, ed., *The Muqaddimah*, xi.

44. Hill, "Ibn Khaldûn," 379; Dawood, ed., *The Muqqadimah*, xii; Khaldûn, *The Muqaddimah*, 123–261.

45. Khaldûn, *The Muqaddimah*, 123–261; Lacoste, *Ibn Khaldoun*, 123–35; Sayah, *Philosophie politique de l'Islam*, 54–87, 119–44.

46. Trimingham, *A History of Islam in West Africa*, 161, see also 160–61; M'Bokolo, *Afrique Noire*, 45–49.

47. Trimingham, *A History of Islam in West Africa*, 161–62; M'Bokolo, *Afrique Noire*, 49–51.

48. Murray Last, "The Sokoto Caliphate and Borno," in *General History of Africa VI: Africa in the Nineteenth Century until the 1880s*, ed. J. F. Ade Ajayi (Paris: Unesco, 1989), 562–87; Trimingham, *A History of Islam in West Africa*, 162; M'Bokolo, *Afrique Noire*, 51–52.

49. Madina Ly-Tall, "Massina and the Torodbe (Tukulor) Empire until 1878," in *General History of Africa VI*, 600–611; M'Bokolo, *Afrique Noire*, 52–53; Amadou Hampaté Ba and Jacques Daget, *L'Empire Peul du Macina I: 1818–1853* (Paris: Mouton, 1962).

50. Ly-Tall, "Massina and the Torodbe (Tukulor) Empire," 611–35; M'Bokolo, *Afrique Noire*, 53–56; B. O. Oloruntimehin, *The Segu Tukulor Empire* (New York: Humanities Press, 1972); Yves-J. Saint-Martin, *L'Empire Toucouleur, 1848–1897* (Paris: Le livre africain, 1970).

51. M'Bokolo, *Afrique Noire*, 55–56.

52. Trimingham, *A History of Islam in West Africa*, 233 (emphasis added).

CHAPTER 3

1. V. Y. Mudimbe, *The Invention of Africa: Gnosis, Philosophy, and the Order of Knowledge* (Bloomington: Indiana University Press, 1988), 20.

2. Kevin C. Dunn, *Imagining the Congo: The International Relations of Identity* (New York: Palgrave Macmillan, 2003), 4–6; Joseph Conrad, *Heart of Darkness* with *The Congo Diary*, ed. Robert Hampson (London: Penguin Books, 1995).

3. Robert W. July, *The Origins of Modern African Thought: Its Development in West Africa during the Nineteenth and Twentieth Centuries* (London: Faber and Faber, 1968), 30.

4. By 1922, there were less than 100 citizens in the French African colonial empire, mostly concentrated in the four *communes de plein exercice* (full-fledged municipalities) of Dakar, Gorée, Rufisque, and Saint-Louis in Senegal. Similarly, by 1936, the French colony of Algeria numbered only 2,500 Algerian Muslim *évolués* with full citizenship rights.

5. John Chipman, *French Power in Africa* (Cambridge, MA: Basil Blackwell, 1989), 61–84; Robert Aldrich and John Connell, "Francophonie," in *France in World Politics*, ed. Aldrich and Connell (London: Routledge, 1989), 170–93; Anton Andereggen, *France's Relationship with Subsaharan Africa* (Westport, CT: Praeger Publishers, 1994), 93–103; Guy Martin, "Francophone Africa in the Context of Franco-African Relations" in *Africa in World Politics: Post-Cold War Challenges*, 2nd ed., ed. John W. Harbeson and Donald Rothchild (Boulder, CO: Westview Press, 1995), 164–65.

6. Michael Crowder, *West Africa under Colonial Rule* (London: Hutchinson, 1968), 168–69.

7. Crowder, *West Africa under Colonial Rule*, 169; Sir F. D. Lugard, *The Dual Mandate in British Tropical Africa* (Edinburgh: William Blackwood and Sons, 1922).

8. July, *The Origins of Modern African Thought*, 26–30.

9. Peter Boele van Hensbroek, *Political Discourses in African Thought* (Westport, CT: Praeger Publishers, 1999), 39.

10. Boele van Hensbroek, *Political Discourses in African Thought*, 42.

11. July, *The Origins of Modern African Thought*, 208–33; Henry S. Wilson, ed., *Origins of West African Nationalism* (London: Macmillan, 1969), 227–62; Norbert C. Brockman, *An African Biographical Dictionary* (Santa Barbara, CA: ABC-CLIO, 1994), 56; Hakim Adi and Marika Sherwood, *Pan-African History: Political Figures from Africa and the Diaspora since 1787* (London: Routledge, 2003), 11–15.

12. July, *The Origins of Modern African Thought*, 110–29; Wilson, *Origins of West African Nationalism*, 157–225; Brockman, *An African Biographical Dictionary*, 145; Adi and Sherwood, *Pan-African History*, 86–89.

13. July, *The Origins of Modern African Thought*, 433–57; Wilson, *Origins of West African Nationalism*, 309–80; Brockman, *An African Biographical Dictionary*, 75–76; Adi and Sherwood, *Pan-African History*, 82–85.

14. Brockman, *An African Biographical Dictionary*, 69.

15. Kofi A. Busia, *The Challenge of Africa* (New York: Frederick A. Praeger, 1962), 68–69.

16. Ibid., 66.

17. Ibid., 142.

18. Kofi A. Busia, *Africa in Search of Democracy* (New York: Frederick A. Praeger, 1967), 9, 16.

19. Busia, *Africa in Search of Democracy*, 20.

20. Ibid., 111, see also 52, 91.

21. Ibid., 167.

22. Ibid., 170–72.

23. Brockman, *An African Biographical Dictionary*, 167–68; Kenneth D. Kaunda, *Zambia Shall Be Free: An Autobiography* (London: Heinemann Educational Books, 1962).

24. Kaunda's admiration for Jesus and Gandhi is mentioned in Fergus MacPherson, *Kenneth Kaunda of Zambia: The Times and the Man* (New York: Oxford University Press, 1974), 308, see also 104–5, 308–10. The characterization of Nkrumah is by David Birmingham, *Kwame Nkrumah: The Father of African Nationalism*, revised edition (Athens: Ohio University Press, 1998).

25. Quoted in MacPherson, *Kenneth Kaunda of Zambia*, 309–10; Kaunda, *Zambia Shall Be Free*, 140, 152.

26. Kaunda, *Zambia Shall Be Free*, 143, 149, 158.

27. Ibid., 142 (emphasis in the original).

28. Ibid., 152.

29. Quoted in MacPherson, *Kenneth Kaunda of Zambia*, 310.

30. Marina and David Ottaway, *Afrocommunism*, 2nd ed. (New York: Africana Publishing, 1986), 44.

CHAPTER 4

1. Kwame Nkrumah, *Africa Must Unite* (New York: International Publishers, 1970).

2. Joseph-Roger de Benoist, *La Balkanisation de l'Afrique Occidentale Française* (Dakar: Les Nouvelles Éditions Africaines, 1979); Sékéné-Mody Cissoko, *Un Combat pour l'Unité de l'Afrique de l'Ouest: La Fédération du Mali (1959–1960)* (Dakar: Les Nouvelles Éditions Africaines du Sénégal, 2005); William J. Foltz, *From French West Africa to the Mali Federation* (New Haven: Yale University Press, 1965); Guédel Ndiaye, *L'Èchec de la Fédération du Mali* (Dakar: Les Nouvelles Éditions Africaines, 1980).

3. Cheikh Anta Diop, *Black Africa: The Economic and Cultural Basis for a Federated State*, rev. ed. (Chicago, IL: Lawrence Hill Books, 1987); Marc-Louis Ropivia, *Géopolitique de l'Intégration en Afrique Noire* (Paris: L'Harmattan, 1994); Makau wa Mutua, "Why Redraw the Map of Africa: A Moral and Legal Inquiry," *Michigan Journal of International Law* 16 (Summer 1995), 1113–76; Arthus S. Gakwandi, "Towards a New Political Map of Africa," in *Pan-Africanism: Politics, Economy and Social Change in the Twenty-first Century*, ed. Tajudeen Abdul-Raheem (New York: New York University Press, 1996), 181–90; Joseph Ki-Zerbo, *A Quand l'Afrique? Entretiens avec Rene Holenstein* (Geneva: Éditions d'en bas, 2003); Daniel Osabu-Kle, *Compatible Cultural Democracy: The Key to Development in Africa* (Peterborough, Ontario: Broadview Press, 2000); Godfrey Mwakikagile, *The Modern African State: Quest for Transformation* (Huntington, NY: Nova Science Publishers, 2001); Pelle D. Danabo, *From Africa of States to United Africa: Towards Africana Democracy*, Ph.D. dissertation (Lawrence: University of Kansas, 2008); Mueni wa Muiu and Guy Martin, *A New Paradigm of the African State: Fundi wa Afrika* (New York: Palgrave Macmillan, 2009).

4. Muiu and Martin, *A New Paradigm of the African State*, 195–216.

5. P. Olisanwuche Esedebe, *Pan-Africanism: The Idea and Movement, 1776–1991*, 2nd ed. (Washington, DC: Howard University Press, 1994), 3–38; Colin Legum, *Pan-Africanism: A Short Political Guide* (London: Pall Mall Press, 1962), 13–37; Vincent Bakpetu Thompson, *Africa and Unity: The Evolution of Pan-Africanism* (London: Longman, 1969), 3–41; Klaas Van Walraven, *Dreams of Power: The Role of the Organization of African Unity in the Politics of Africa* (Aldershot, UK: Ashgate, 1999), 75–100.

6. Colin Grant, *Negro with a Hat: The Rise and Fall of Marcus Garvey* (New York: Oxford University Press, 2008).

7. Colin Legum, *Pan-Africanism*, 94–96; Van Walraven, *Dreams of Power*, 89–90; Claude Wauthier, *The Literature and Thought of Modern Africa*, 2nd English language ed. (Washington, DC: Three Continents Press, 1979).

8. Esedebe, *Pan-Africanism*, 137–64.

9. Thompson, *Africa and Unity*, 126–27.

10. Other prominent Pan-Africanist leaders included Ahmed Ben Bella (Algeria); Barthélémy Boganda (Central African Republic); Modibo Kéïta (Mali); Patrice Lumumba (Congo); Gamal Abdel Nasser (Egypt); and Ahmed Sékou Touré (Guinea). It is interesting to note in this regard that in an interview with Cuban author Jorge Castañeda in Switzerland in 1966, Ahmed Ben Bella revealed the existence of an informal "Group of Six" (Nkrumah, Nyerere, Sékou Touré, Nasser, Modibo Kéïta, and Ben Bella); it is alleged that this group worked

secretly within the Organization of African Unity (OAU) on a number of issues, including the Congo and African liberation, excluding other African leaders.

11. Kwame Nkrumah, *Neo-Colonialism: The Last Stage of Imperialism* (London: Heinemann, 1968), 30.

12. Esedebe, *Pan-Africanism*, 171–73; Legum, *Pan-Africanism*, 55–59; Thompson, *Africa and Unity*, 147–48, 173; Van Walraven, *Dreams of Power*, 84–97; I. William Zartman, *International Relations of the New Africa* (Lanham, MD: University Press of America, 1987), 96–102, 126–33.

13. Nkrumah, *Africa Must Unite*, v, 217.

14. Nkrumah, *Africa Must Unite*, 187; Guy Martin, "Africa and the Ideology of Eurafrica: Neo-Colonialism or Pan-Africanism?" *The Journal of Modern African Studies* 20, no. 2 (June 1982), 221–38.

15. Kwame Nkrumah, quoted in Legum, *Pan-Africanism*, 119 (emphasis in the original).

16. Nkrumah, *Africa Must Unite*, 216–22.

17. Reginald H. Green and Ann Seidman, *Unity or Poverty? The Economics of Pan-Africanism* (Baltimore, MD: Penguin Books, 1968), 22–23 (emphasis in the original).

18. Mouammar Kadhafi, *Dans le Concert des Nations; Libres propos et entretiens avec Edmond Jouve* (Paris: Éditions de l'Archipel, 2004), 82–84.

19. Kadhafi, *Dans le Concert des Nations*, Annex V, 223–35.

20. Ignace Kissangou, *Une Afrique, un espoir* (Paris: L'Harmattan, 1996), 9–18, 115–23, 131–38.

21. Other African leaders associated with this school of thought included Nnamdi Azikiwe (Nigeria); Hastings Kamuzu Banda (Malawi); Jomo Kenyatta (Kenya); Leon M'Ba and his successor Albert-Bernard Bongo (Gabon); Julius K. Nyerere (Tanzania); Philibert Tsiranana (Madagascar); and Haile Selassie (Ethiopia).

22. Esedebe, *Pan-Africanism*, 165–225; David Francis, *Uniting Africa: Building Regional Peace and Security Systems* (Burlington, VT: Ashgate Publishing, 2006), 21–24; Thompson, *Africa and Unity*, 181–99; Van Walraven, *Dreams of Power*, 142–53; and Zartman, *International Relations in the New Africa*, 34–41.

23. Guy Martin, *Africa in World Politics: A Pan-African Perspective* (Trenton, NJ: Africa World Press, 2002), 280.

24. Cheikh Anta Diop, *Les Fondements Économiques et Culturels d'un État Fédéral d'Afrique Noire*, 2nd ed. (Paris: Présence Africaine, 1974), translated into English by Harold J. Salemson as *Black Africa: The Economic & Cultural Basis for a Federated State*, revised ed. (Chicago: Lawrence Hill Books, 1987).

25. Cheikh Anta Diop, *Nations Nègres et Culture*, 3rd edition, 2 vols. (Paris: Présence Africaine, 1979).

26. Diop, *Les Fondements*, 11–29; Diop, *Black Africa*, 3–14.

27. Diop, *Les Fondements*, 30–37; Diop, *Black Africa*, 15–20.

28. Diop, *Les Fondements*, 56–80; Diop, *Black Africa*, 37–56.

29. Diop, *Les Fondements*, 46–52, 56–80, 110–22; Diop, *Black Africa*, 29–31, 37–56, 79–89.

30. Martin, *Africa in World Politics*, 275–76.

31. Marc-Louis Ropivia, *Géopolitique de l'Intégration en Afrique Noire* (Paris: L'Harmattan, 1994), 23.

32. Ibid., 41–43.

33. Ibid., 180–86.

34. Ibid., 183.

35. Ibid., 207–11; Muiu and Martin, *A New Paradigm of the African State*, 20.
36. Makau wa Mutua, "Redrawing the Map along African Lines," *The Boston Globe*, September 22, 1994, 17; Mutua, "Why Redraw the Map of Africa"; Martin, *Africa in World Politics*, 278–79.
37. Arthur S. Gakwandi, "Towards a New Political Map of Africa," 181–82.
38. Ibid., 183.
39. Ibid., 187–89.
40. Ibid., 188.
41. Joseph Ki-Zerbo, *Histoire de l'Afrique Noire, d'Hier à Demain* (Paris: Hatier, 1978), 631, 643.
42. Ki-Zerbo, *A Quand l'Afrique?*, 45, 76–82.
43. Osabu-Kle, *Compatible Cultural Democracy*, 279–80.
44. Mwakikagile, *The Modern African State*, 215-16.
45. Ibid., 121.
46. Ibid., 216.
47. Danabo, *From Africa of States to United Africa*, 1–2.
48. Ibid., 129–34.
49. Ibid., 159.
50. Ibid., 161.
51. Muiu and Martin, *A New Paradigm of the African State*.
52. Ibid., 207–8.
53. Ibid., 208–9.
54. Nkrumah, *Africa Must Unite*, 219.
55. Mwakikagile, *The Modern African State*, 121.
56. Julius K. Nyerere, "Reflections," in *Reflections on Leadership in Africa: Forty Years After Independence: Essays in Honor of Mwalimu Julius K. Nyerere on the Occasion of his 75th Birthday*, ed. Haroub Othman (Dar es Salaam: Institute of Development Studies/University of Dar es Salaam, 2000), quoted in John S. Saul, *The New Liberations Struggle: Capitalism, Socialism, and Democracy in Southern Africa* (New York: Monthly Review Press, 2005), 159.
57. Ki-Zerbo, *Histoire de l'Afrique Noire*, 64; Ki-Zerbo, *A Quand l'Afrique?*, 160.
58. Ki-Zerbo, *Histoire de l'Afrique Noire*, 632, 640–41.

CHAPTER 5

1. Crawford Young, *Ideology and Development in Africa* (New Haven, CT: Yale University Press, 1982), 12.
2. Young, *Ideology and Development in Africa*, 100–103.
3. Crawford Young, *Politics in the Congo: Decolonization and Independence* (Princeton, NJ: Princeton University Press, 1965), 277.
4. Madeleine G. Kalb, *The Congo Cables: The Cold War in Africa, From Eisenhower to Kennedy* (New York: Macmillan, 1982), 128–56. Chapter 6 is titled "Getting Rid of Lumumba: Fair Means or Foul."
5. The Congo crisis, as well as the life, times, and death of Patrice Lumumba, are among some of the best-documented events/leaders in African political history. Among the most notable works in this regard, one should mention Yves Bénot, *La Mort de Lumumba* (Paris: Éditions Chaka, 1991); Colette Braeckman, *Lumumba, un crime d'État* (Bruxelles: Les Éditions Aden, 2002); Conor

Cruise O'Brien, *To Katanga and Back: A UN Case History* (New York: Universal Library/Grosset and Dunlap, 1966); Pierre De Vos, *Vie et mort de Lumumba* (Paris: Calmann-Lévy, 1961); Ludo de Witte, *The Assassination of Lumumba* (London: Verso, 2001); Ch. Didier Gondola, *The History of Congo* (Westport, CT: Greenwood Press, 2002): 97–129; Thomas Kanza, *Conflict in the Congo: The Rise and Fall of Lumumba* (Baltimore, MD: Penguin Books, 1972); Kwame Nkrumah, *Challenge of the Congo* (London: Panaf Books, 1967); Georges Nzongola-Ntalaja, *The Congo from Leopold to Kabila: A People's History* (London: Zed Books, 2002): 61–120; and Panaf Books, *Patrice Lumumba* (London: Panaf Books, 1973).

See also Hakim Adi and Marika Sherwood, *Pan-African History: Political Figures from Africa & the Diaspora since 1787* (London: Routledge, 2003), 113–16; Norbert C. Brockman, *An African Biographical Dictionary* (Santa Barbara, CA: ABC-CLIO, 1994), 195–96; Mueni wa Muiu and Guy Martin, *A New Paradigm of the African State: Fundi wa Afrika* (New York: Palgrave Macmillan, 2009), 120–25; and Benoit Verhaegen, "Patrice Lumumba," in *Les Africains*, vol. 2, ed. Charles-André Julien et. al. (Paris: Éditions Jeune Afrique, 1977), 187–219.

6. Patrice Lumumba, *Le Congo, terre d'avenir, est-il menaçé?* (Bruxelles: Office de Publicité, 1961), translated into English as *Congo, My Country* (London: Pall Mall Press, 1962); see also Yves Bénot, *Idéologies des Indépendances africaines*, 2nd ed. (Paris: François Maspéro, 1972), 118n74.

7. Lumumba, *Le Congo, terre d'avenir*, 191–209; quoted in Crawford Young, *Politics in the Congo: Decolonization and Independence* (Princeton, NJ: Princeton University Press, 1965), 277.

8. Jean Van Lierde, ed., *Lumumba Speaks: The Speeches and Writings of Patrice Lumumba, 1958–1961* (Boston: Little, Brown & Co., 1972), 57 (emphasis in the original), originally published in French as *La Pensée politique de Patrice Lumumba* (Paris: Présence Africaine, 1962).

9. Van Lierde, ed., *Lumumba Speaks*, 74.

10. Ibid., 70–71.

11. Ibid., 320.

12. Ibid., 224, 344, 350.

13. Lumumba's characterization as a "mad dog" is attributed to then CIA director Allen Dulles.

14. Adi and Sherwood, *Pan-African History*, 7–10; Paul E. Sigmund Jr., ed., *The Ideologies of the Developing Nations* (New York: Frederick A. Praeger, 1963), 145–46; Claire Arsenault, "Ahmed Ben Bella: le long et mouvementé parcours du premier président de l'Algérie indépendante," *Radio France Internationale* website, April 11, 2012, retrieved April 18, 2012, http://www.rfi.fr.

15. "The Future of Algeria," interview of Ben Bella with Maria Macciochi in *L'Unita* (August 13, 1962), reproduced in Paul E. Sigmund Jr., ed., *The Ideologies of the Developing Nations*, 146 (editor's translation from the French).

16. Ibid., 147.

17. Ibid., 146–7.

18. Benjamin Stora, *Algeria, 1830–2000: A Short History* (Ithaca, NY: Cornell University Press, 2001), 134.

19. Ibid., 149.

20. Ibid., 147–49.

21. Ahmad Ben Bella, "Néo-colonialisme et socialisme," in *La pensée politique arabe contemporaine*, ed. Anouar Abdel-Malek (Paris: Éditions du Seuil, 1970), 249–57.

22. Stora, *Algeria, 1830–2000*, 139; Benjamin Stora, *Histoire de l'Algérie depuis l'indépendance. 1. 1962–1988* (Paris: La Découverte, 2001), 29–30.

23. Alistair Horne, *A Savage War of Peace: Algeria, 1954–1962*, 4th ed. (New York: New York Review Books, 2006), 540; see also William B. Quandt, *Revolution and Political Leadership: Algeria, 1954–1962* (Cambridge, MA: The MIT Press, 1969), 204–35. Quandt observes that "instead [of a process of collegial decision-making] he [Ben Bella] chose to centralize influence in his own hands, and those who did not submit to his authority were soon excluded from government positions" (205).

24. Adi and Sherwood, *Pan-African History*, 16–19; Brockman, *An African Biographical Dictionary*, 73–74; Patrick Chabal, *Amilcar Cabral: Revolutionary Leadership & People's War* (Trenton, NJ: Africa World Press, 2003), 29–53; Ronald H. Chilcote, *Amilcar Cabral's Revolutionary Theory and Practice: A Critical Guide* (Boulder, CO: Lynne Rienner Publishers, 1991), 3–22.

25. Richard Handyside, ed., *Revolution in Guinea: Selected Texts by Amilcar Cabral* (New York: Monthly Review Press, 1969), 92–93.

26. Ibid., 92.

27. Basil Davidson, *The Liberation of Guiné: Aspects of an African Revolution* (Baltimore, MD: Penguin Books, 1969), 73 (emphasis in the original).

28. Handyside, ed., *Revolution in Guinea*, 107.

29. Ibid., 102.

30. Davidson, *Liberation of Guiné*, 76.

31. Africa Information Service, ed., *Return to the Source: Selected Speeches by Amilcar Cabral* (New York: Monthly Review Press, 1973), 43–44; see also Chilcote, *Amilcar Cabral's Revolutionary Theory and Practice*, 39–40.

32. Handyside, ed., *Revolution in Guinea*, 107.

33. Lars Rudebeck, "Socialist-Oriented Development in Guinea-Bissau," in *Socialism in Sub-Saharan Africa: A New Assessment*, ed. Carl G. Rosberg and Thomas M. Callaghy (Berkeley, CA: Institute of International Studies/University of California, 1979), 325–26.

34. Patrick Chabal, *Amilcar Cabral*, 168.

35. Ibid.

36. Ibid.; P. L. E. Idahosa, *The Populist Dimension to African Political Thought: Critical Essays in Reconstruction & Retrieval* (Trenton, NJ: Africa World Press, 2004), 191–205; and Rudebeck, "Socialist-Oriented Development in Guinea-Bissau," 322–44.

37. Handyside, ed., *Revolution in Guinea*, 86–87, 89.

38. Brockman, *An African Biographical Dictionary*, 201–2; Samora Machel, *Le Processus de la Révolution Démocratique Populaire au Mozambique: Textes du Président du FRELIMO, 1970–1974* (Paris: L'Harmattan, 1977), 9–16; Barry Munslow, ed., *Samora Machel: An African Revolutionary; Selected Speeches & Writings* (Harare: The College Press, 1987), xi–xxvii.

39. Machel, *Le Processus de la Révolution Démocratique Populaire au Mozambique*, 53.

40. Ibid. (translation from the French by the author, as elsewhere in this chapter).

41. "Special Mozambique," *Afrique-Asie* 109 (May 17–30, 1976), 4; Edward A. Alpers, "The Struggle for Socialism in Mozambique, 1960–1972," in *Socialism*

in Sub-Saharan Africa: A New Assessment, ed. Carl G. Rosberg and Thomas M. Callaghy (Berkeley, CA: Institute of International Studies/University of California, 1979), 274.

42. Samora Machel, *Mozambique: Revolution or Reaction?* (Richmond, BC: LSM Press, 1975), 8.

43. Quoted in Edward A. Alpers, "The Struggle for Socialism in Mozambique, 1960–1972," 275.

44. Machel, *Mozambique*, 7, 9 (emphasis added).

45. Marina and David Ottaway, *Afrocommunism*, 2nd ed. (New York: Africana Publishing, 1986), 77.

46. Machel, *Mozambique*, 9, 14.

47. Munslow, ed., *Samora Machel*, 16–17.

48. Machel, *Mozambique*, 8, 18.

49. Munslow, ed., *Samora Machel*, 15 (emphasis added).

50. Ibid.

51. Machel, *Mozambique*, 14, 19.

52. This section relies heavily of the insightful analysis of Marina and David Ottaway in *Afrocommunism*, 71, 81–83.

53. Ibid., 13–18; Machel, *Le Processus de la Révolution Démocratique Populaire au Mozambique*, 159–250; Munslow, ed., *Samora Machel*, 109–84.

CHAPTER 6

1. Kwame Nkrumah, *Towards Colonial Freedom: Africa in the Struggle against World Imperialism* (London: Heinemann, 1962), xv.

2. There is a prolific literature on Kwame Nkrumah's life, times, and politics. Among the most notable works are Tawia Adamafio, *By Nkrumah's Side: The Labour and the Wounds* (London: Rex Collings, 1982); David Birmingham, *Kwame Nkrumah: The Father of African Nationalism*, rev. ed. (Athens: Ohio University Press, 1998); Henry L. Bretton, *The Rise and Fall of Kwame Nkrumah* (London: Pall Mall, 1966); Basil Davidson, *Black Star: A View of the Life & Times of Kwame Nkrumah* (Oxford, UK: James Currey, 2007); Kofi Buenor Hadjor, *Nkrumah and Ghana: The Dilemma of Post-Colonial Power* (London: Kegan Paul International, 1988); Samuel G. Ikoku, *Le Ghana de Nkrumah* (Paris: François Maspéro, 1971); June Milne, *Kwame Nkrumah: A Biography* (London: Panaf Books, 1999); Kwame Nkrumah, *Ghana: The Autobiography of Kwame Nkrumah* (London: Thomas Nelson and Sons, 1959); David Rooney, *Kwame Nkrumah: The Political Kingdom in the Third World* (New York: St. Martin's Press, 1988); David Rooney, *Nkrumah: L'homme qui croyait à l'Afrique* (Paris: JA Livres, 1990); and Yuri Smertin, *Kwame Nkrumah* (New York: International Publishers, 1987). See also Hakim Adi and Marika Sherwood, *Pan-African History: Political Figures from Africa & the Diaspora since 1787* (London: Routledge, 2003), 143–46; and Norbert C. Brockman, *An African Biographical Dictionary* (Santa Barbara, CA: ABC-CLIO, 1994), 265–67.

3. Kwame Nkrumah, *Consciencism: Philosophy and Ideology for Decolonization*, rev. ed. (New York: Monthly Review Press, 1970), 59.

4. Nkrumah, *Consciencism*, 78.

5. Thomas Hodgkin, unpublished article on Ghana, cited by Dennis Austin, *Politics in Ghana, 1946–1960* (London: Oxford University Press, 1964), 40.

6. Kwame Nkrumah, *Ghana: The Autobiography of Kwame Nkrumah* (London: Thomas Nelson & Sons, 1959), v.

7. Kwame Nkrumah, *Handbook of Revolutionary Warfare* (London: Panaf Books, 1968), 25.

8. Nkrumah, *Ghana*, 37. Nkrumah also mentions Plato, Aristotle, Descartes, Kant, Schopenhauer, and Nietzsche as other authors who "awakened my philosophical conscience" while a student in the United States. Nkrumah, *Consciencism*, 2.

9. Nkrumah, *Ghana*, 37.

10. Kwame Nkrumah, "Guide to Party Action," First Address to the Seminar, Winneba Ideological School, February 3, 1962, 3. It is interesting to note that Nkrumah's concept of "Marxism" is broad and includes such other Marxist theoreticians and political leaders/activists as Lenin, Trotsky, Rosa Luxembourg, and Mao Ze-Dong.

11. Nkrumah, *Towards Colonial Freedom*, 11.

12. Kwame Nkrumah, *Neo-Colonialism: The Last Stage of Imperialism* (London: Heinemann, 1965).

13. Nkrumah, *Handbook of Revolutionary Warfare*, 29, 28 (emphasis added).

14. Nkrumah, *Ghana*, 37.

15. Nkrumah, *Handbook of Revolutionary Warfare*, 27.

16. Nkrumah, *Consciencism*, 84.

17. Nkrumah, *Ghana*, 10.

18. Nkrumah, *Consciencism*, 68, 70.

19. Ali A. Mazrui and Toby Kleban Levine, eds., *The Africans: A Reader* (New York: Praeger Publishers, 1986), xv.

20. Kwame Nkrumah, *I Speak of Freedom* (London: Heinemann, 1961), 2.

21. Nkrumah, *Ghana*, 85, see also chapter 10, 91–101.

22. Nkrumah, *I Speak of Freedom*, 164.

23. Kwame Nkrumah and *The Spark* editors, *Some Essential Features of Nkrumaism* (New York: International Publishers, 1965), 5.

24. Kofi Baako's lectures, as reproduced in *The Ghanaian Times* (Accra), January 24, 25, 26, 28, 29, 1961 (emphasis added). On the concept of "African Socialism," see William H. Friedland and Carl G. Rosberg Jr., eds., *African Socialism* (Stanford, CA: Stanford University Press, 1964), 3–11; and Carl G. Rosberg and Thomas M. Callaghy, *Socialism in Sub-Saharan Africa: A New Assessment* (Berkeley, CA: Institute of International Studies/University of California, 1979), 1–11.

25. Nkrumah, *Consciencism*, 103.

26. On this episode, see in particular Georges Chaffard, *Les Carnets Secrets de la Décolonisation*, vol. 2 (Paris: Clamann-Lévy, 1967), 193–200; Philippe Gaillard, ed., *Foccart Parle: Entretiens avec Philippe Gaillard*, vol. 1 (Paris: Fayard/Jeune Afrique, 1995), 161–66; Charles de Gaulle, *Mémoires d'Espoir: Le Renouveau, 1958–1962* (Geneva: Éditions Famot, 1981), 59–61; and Pierre Messmer, *Les Blancs s'en Vont: Récits de décolonization* (Paris: Albin Michel, 1998), 145–51.

27. Lapido Adamolekun, *Sékou Touré's Guinea: An Experiment in Nation Building* (London: Methuen, 1976); Adi and Sherwood, *Pan-African History*, 177–80; B. Ameillon, *La Guinée, bilan d'une indépendance* (Paris: François Maspéro, 1964); Brockman, *An African Biographical Dictionary*, 350–52; Victor D. Du Bois, "Guinea," in *Political Parties & National Integration in Tropical Africa*, ed. James S. Coleman and Carl G. Rosberg Jr. (Berkeley: University of California Press, 1964), 186–215; Fernand Gigon, *Guinée: État-pilote* (Paris: Plon, 1959);

Ibrahima Baba Kaké, *Sékou Touré: le héros et le tyran* (Paris: Jeune Afrique Livres, 1987); Sidney Taylor, ed., *The New Africans: A Guide to the Contemporary History of Emergent Africa and Its Leaders* (London: Paul Hamlyn, 1967), 193–95.

28. Quoted in Fernand Gigon, *Guinée, État-Pilote* (Paris: Plon, 1959), 29; and Claude Riviere, *Guinea: The Mobilization of a People* (Ithaca, NY: Cornell University Press, 1977).

29. Sékou Touré's collection of speeches and other writings were published by the Press Office of the Presidency of the Republic of Guinea between 1961 and 1982. His more theoretical writings include *La Guinee et l'emancipation africaine* (Paris: Présence Africaine, 1959); *Expérience Guinéenne et Unité Africaine*, 2nd ed. (Paris: Présence Africaine, 1961); and *L'Afrique et la Révolution* (Paris: Présence Africaine, 1965).

30. Ahmed Sékou Touré, *La Lutte du Parti Démocratique de Guinée pour l'émancipation africaine: La Planification économique* [V] (Conakry, 1969), 281. See also Ladipo Adamolekun, "The Socialist Experience in Guinea," in *Socialism in Sub-Saharan Africa*, 61–64; and Yves Bénot, *Idéologies des Indépendances africaines*, 2nd ed. (Paris: François Maspéro, 1972), 267–71.

31. Sékou Touré in an interview with Fernand Gigon, *Guinee, État-PIlote* (Paris: Plon, 1959), 29.

32. Sékou Touré, *La Lutte du PDG pour l'émancipation africaine* [V], 311.

33. Sékou Touré, *Huitième Congrès du Parti Démocratique de Guinée* (Conakry, 1967), 14; *Horoya* (PDG Daily, Conakry), August 31, 1978.

34. *Bulletin d'Information du BPN* [National Political Bureau of the PDG], Conakry, no. 94 (1970), 98.

35. Ahmed Sékou Touré, *The Political Action of the Democratic Party of Guinea for the Emancipation of Guinean Youth* (Cairo: Presses de la Société Orientale de Publicité, 1961), 108; see also Charles F. Andrain, "Guinea and Senegal: Contrasting Types of African Socialism," in *African Socialism*, ed. William H. Friedland and Carl G. Rosberg Jr. (Stanford, CA: Stanford University Press, 1964), 170.

36. Sékou Touré in an interview with Fernand Gigon, *Guinée, État-Pilote* (Paris: Plon, 1959), 29.

37. Sékou Touré, *La Lutte du PDG pour l'émancipation africaine* [V], 309.

38. Ahmed Sékou Touré, *The Doctrine and Methods of the Democratic Party of Guinea*, vol. 1, n.d., 172 (emphasis added).

39. A. S. Touré, *Extraits du discours tenu lors de la première conférence nationale de Labbé*, mimeo (Conakry, 1961), 17; A. S. Touré, *La Lutte du PDG pour l'émancipation africaine* [IV] (Conakry, 1959), 60.

40. A. S. Touré, *La Guinée et l'émancipation africaine* (Paris: Présence Africaine, 1959), 233.

41. A. S. Touré, *La Planification économique* (Conakry: Imprimerie Nationale, 1960), 81.

42. A. S. Touré, *L'Action Politique du PDG pour l'émancipation africaine* [iii] (Conakry, 1959), 312; A. S. Touré, quoted in *Afrique Nouvelle* (Dakar), April 27, 1960, 2.

43. Immanuel Wallerstein, "L'Idéologie du PDG," *Présence Africaine* 40 (1962): 56. I would qualify this statement by observing that Sékou Touré's "communautratic impulse" was inspired more by indigenous African traditions than by the writings of Jean-Jacques Rousseau.

44. Claude Rivière, *Guinea: The Mobilization of a People* (Ithaca, NY: Cornell University Press, 1977), 90–92.

45. Marina and David Ottaway, *Afrocommunism*, 2nd ed. (New York: Africana Publishing, 1986), 53.

46. Adamolekun, "The Socialist Experience in Guinea," 77–82; see also Ibrahima Baba Kaké, *Sékou Touré: le héros et le tyran* (Paris: Jeune Afrique Livres, 1987).

47. Pascal James Imperato, *Historical Dictionary of Mali* (Metuchen, NJ: The Scarecrow Press, 1977), 60–61; Pascal J. Imperato, *Mali: A Search for Direction* (Boulder, CO: Westview Press, 1989), 51–79; Amadou Seydou Traoré, *Modibo Kéïta: Une référence, un symbole, un patrimoine national* (Bamako: La Ruche à Livres, 2005); Sidney Taylor, ed., *The New Africans: A Guide to the Contemporary History of Emergent Africa & Its Leaders* (London: Paul Hamlyn, 1967), 288–90.

48. Modibo Kéïta was a far less prolific author than either Kwame Nkrumah or Sékou Touré. His speeches have been collected in a single volume: *Modibo Kéïta: Discours et Interventions* (Bamako, n.p., n.d.), translated into English as *Modibo Kéïta: A Collection of Speeches: September 22, 1960–August 27, 1964* (Bamako, n.p., n.d.).

49. Seydou Badian Kouyaté, "Politique de développement et voies africaines du socialisme," *Présence Africaine* 47 (Fall 1963), 67, 70, 68.

50. Seydou Badian Kouyaté, in *2eme Séminaire de l'US-RDA* (Bamako: Imprimerie Nationale, 1962); quoted in Cheick Oumar Diarrah, *Le Mali de Modibo Kéïta* (Paris: L'Harmattan, 1986), 132 (emphasis added).

51. "Modibo Keita parle . . . ," in *Jeune Afrique* 280 (May 8, 1966); quoted in Cheick Oumar Diarrah, *Le Mali de Modibo Kéïta*, 136–37 (emphasis added).

52. Kouyaté, "Politique de développement et voies africaines du socialisme," 72.

53. Seydou Badian Kouyaté, *Les dirigeants africains face à leur peuple* (Paris: François Maspéro, 1965).

54. On local government in Socialist Mali, see Nicholas S. Hopkins, *Popular Government in an African Town: Kita, Mali* (Chicago, IL: The University of Chicago Press, 1972), 9–23.

55. On socialist planning in Mali, see in particular Samir Amin, *Trois expériences africaines de développement: le Mali, la Guinée et le Ghana* (Paris: Presses Universitaires de France, 1965), 99–129; Yves Bénot, *Idéologies des Indépendances africaines*, 2nd ed. (Paris: François Maspéro, 1972), 282–86; Kenneth W. Grundy, "Mali: The Prospects of Planned Socialism," in *African Socialism*, 175–93; William I. Jones, *Planning and Economic Policy: Socialist Mali and Her Neighbors* (Washington, DC: Three Continents Press, 1976); Guy Martin, "Socialism, Economic Development and Planning in Mali, 1960–1968," *Canadian Journal of African Studies* X, no. 1 (1976): 23–47; Louis V. Thomas, *Le Socialisme et l'Afrique; vol. 2: L'Idéologie socialiste et les voies africaines de développement* (Paris: Le Livre Africain, 1966), 79–87; and Crawford Young, *Ideology and Development in Africa* (New Haven, CT: Yale University Press, 1982), 174–80.

56. Louis V. Thomas, *Le socialisme et l'Afrique*, 80–81.

57. Adi and Sherwood, *Pan-African History*, 147–51; Brockman, *An African Biographical Dictionary*, 268–70; Trevor Huddleston, "The Person Nyerere," in *Mwalimu: The Influence of Nyerere*, ed. Colin Legum and Geoffrey Mwari (London: James Currey, 1995), 1–8; "Biographical Note on Julius Nyerere," in Julius K. Nyerere, *Nyerere on Socialism* (Dar es Salaam: Oxford University Press, 1969), v–vi.

58. The numerous writings and speeches of Julius Nyerere have been collected in three main volumes: *Freedom and Unity/Uhuru na Umoja* (1967), *Freedom and Socialism/Uhuru na Ujamaa* (1968), and *Freedom and Development/Uhuru na Maendeleo* (1973), all published by Oxford University Press in Dar es Salaam (Tanzania). See also Julius K. Nyerere, *Ujamaa: The Basis of African Socialism* (Dar es Salaam: TANU, 1962), reproduced in Friedland and Rosberg Jr., eds., *African Socialism*, Appendix II, 238–47; Julius K. Nyerere, *Ujamaa: Essays on Socialism* (London: Oxford University Press, 1968); Julius K. Nyerere, *Nyerere on Socialism* (Dar es Salaam: Oxford University Press, 1969); and Julius K. Nyerere, *Man and Development/Binadamu na Maendeleo* (London: Oxford University Press, 1974).

59. Henry Bienen asserts, against all available evidence, that "Nyerere is suspicious of creeds and dogmas, and thus has been disinclined to create a blueprint for the new society. And he has not yet successfully married his ideas and symbols to programs for action." Henry Bienen, *Tanzania: Party Transformation and Economic Development*, expanded ed. (Princeton, NJ: Princeton University Press, 1970), 212.

60. "Preface," in Nyerere, *Ujamaa*, i–ii; see also "Introduction," in Julius K. Nyerere, *Freedom and Socialism/Uhuru na Ujamaa* (Dar es Salaam: Oxford University Press, 1968), 1. The Arusha Declaration of February 5, 1967, is reproduced in *Ujamaa*, 13–37; this volume also includes another seminal doctrinal statement of April 1962: "Ujamaa: The Basis of African Socialism" (1–12).

61. Nyerere, "Ujamaa: The Basis of African Socialism," in *Ujamaa: Essays on Socialism*, 12.

62. Nyerere, *Freedom and Socialism/Uhuru na Ujamaa*, 16.

63. Nyerere, "Ujamaa," 4–5.

64. Ibid., 7, 11, 12, 8.

65. Ibid., 1 (emphasis added).

66. Nyerere, *Freedom and Socialism/Uhuru na Ujamaa*, 2.

67. Nyerere, "Ujamaa," 12.

68. Nyerere, *Freedom and Socialism*, 4; Nyerere, "Ujamaa," 92, 38 (emphasis added).

69. Nyerere, *Freedom and Socialism*, 11.

70. Julius K. Nyerere, "The Arusha Declaration," in *Ujamaa: Essays on Socialism*, 14.

71. Nyerere, "The Arusha Declaration," 29, 27, 32–34. On the implementation of "Rural Socialismm," see Julius K. Nyerere, *Freedom and Development/Uhuru na Maendeleo* (Dar es Salaam: Oxford University Press, 1973), 5–11.

72. Julius K. Nyerere, "Education for Self-Reliance," in *Ujamaa: Essays on Socialism*, 44–75; Nyerere, *Freedom and Socialism*, 31–32.

73. P.L.E. Idahosa, *The Populist Dimension to African Political Thought: Critical Essays in Reconstruction and Retrieval* (Trenton, NJ: Africa World Press, 2004), 212.

CHAPTER 7

1. Crawford Young, *Ideology and Development in Africa* (New Haven, CT: Yale University Press, 1982), 12.

2. Ibid., 100–103.

3. Frantz Fanon, Letter to Roger Tayeb, November, 1961, quoted in Clément Mbom, *Frantz Fanon, aujourd'hui et demain* (Paris: Fernand Nathan, 1985), 154.

4. Frantz Fanon's major works (most of which have been translated into English) are *Peau Noire, Masques Blancs* (Paris: Éditions du Seuil, 1952), translated into English by Charles L. Markmann as *Black Skin, White Masks* (New York: Grove Press, 1967); *Les damnés de la terre*, with a preface by Jean-Paul Sartre (Paris: François Maspéro, 1961), (poorly) translated into English by Constance Farrington as *The Wretched of the Earth* (New York: Grove Press, 1968); *Pour la Révolution africaine: Écrits politiques* (Paris: François Maspéro, 1964), translated into English by Haakon Chevalier as *Toward the African Revolution: Political Essays*, 2nd ed. (New York: Grove Press, 1988); *Sociologie d'une révolution: L'an V de la révolution algérienne*, 2nd ed. (Paris: François Maspéro, 1978).

5. David Caute, *Fanon* (London: Fontana/Collins, 1970); Peter Geisman, *Fanon: The Revolutionary as Prophet* (New York: Grove Press, 1971); Irene L. Gendzier, *Frantz Fanon: A Critical Study* (New York: Vintage Books/Random House, 1973); and Mbom, *Frantz Fanon*.

6. Emmanuel Hansen, *Frantz Fanon: Social and Political Thought* (Columbus: Ohio State University Press, 1977); L. Adele Jinadu, *Fanon: In Search of the African Revolution* (London: Routledge, 1986); Guy Martin, "Fanon's Relevance to Contemporary African Political Thought," *Ufahamu* 4, no. 3 (Winter 1974): 11–34; Guy Martin, "Fanon's Continuing Relevance: A Comparative Study of the Political Thought of Frantz Fanon & Thomas Sankara," *Journal of Asian & African Studies* 5, no. 1 (Fall 1993): 65–85; Guy Martin, "Revisiting Fanon, From Theory to Practice: Democracy and Development in Africa," *The Journal of Pan-African Studies* 4, no. 7 (November 2011): 24–38; Nguyen Nghe, "Frantz Fanon et les problèmes de l'indépendance," *La Pensée* 107 (February 1963): 23–36; Marie B. Perinbam, *Holy Violence: The Revolutionary Thought of Frantz Fanon* (Washington, DC: Three Continents Press, 1982); and Renate Zahar, *Frantz Fanon: Colonialism and Alienation* (New York: Monthly Review Press, 1974).

7. Alice Cherki, *Frantz Fanon: A Portrait* (Ithaca, NY: Cornell University Press, 2006); Nigel C. Gibson, *Fanon: The Postcolonial Imagination* (Cambridge, UK: Polity Press, 2003); Nigel Gibson, *Fanonian Practices in South Africa: From Steve Biko to Abahlali baseMjondolo* (New York: Palgrave Macmillan, 2011); David Macey, *Frantz Fanon: A Biography* (New York: Picador USA/St. Martin's Press, 2000).

8. Jinadu, *Fanon*, 7.

9. Fanon, *The Wretched of the Earth*, 112–13, 164 (translation modified by the author whenever appropriate).

10. Fanon, *Toward the African Revolution*, 186.

11. Fanon, *The Wretched of the Earth*, 251–52, 254–55.

12. Hansen, *Frantz Fanon*, 178.

13. Fanon, *The Wretched of the Earth*, 78.

14. Ibid., 151–52, 154.

15. Ibid., 165.

16. Ibid., 165.

17. Ibid., 145, 155–56.

18. Ibid., 159.

19. Ibid., 149, 151.

20. Ibid., 34.

21. Ibid., 199, 196, 28.

22. Ibid., 163.

23. Ibid., 158.

24. Ibid., 158.

25. Ibid., 132.

26. Fanon, *Toward the African Revolution*, 187.

27. P. L. E. Idahosa, *The Populist Dimension to African Political Thought: Critical Essays in Reconstruction and Retrieval* (Trenton, NJ: Africa World Press, 2004), 101–56.

28. Fanon, *Les damnés de la terre*, 239–42 (author's translation).

29. Guy Martin, "Actualité de Fanon: Convergences dans la Pensée Politique de Frantz Fanon et de Thomas Sankara," *Geneva-Africa, Special 26th Anniversary Issue: Des Africains Revendiquent Leur Histoire* 25, no. 2 (1987): 103–22; Martin, "Fanon's Continuing Relevance," 65–85.

30. Sennen Andriamirado, *Sankara Le Rebelle* (Paris: Jeune Afrique Livres, 1987), 114.

31. There is a relatively abundant literature (essentially in French) on Thomas Sankara and the Burkinabè Revolution. See in particular Andriamirado, *Sankara Le Rebelle*; Sennen Andriamirado, *Il S'Appelait Sankara: Chronique d'une mort violencte* (Paris: Jeune Afrique Livres, 1989); Babou Paulin Bamouni, *Burkina Faso: Processus de la Rèvolution* (Paris: L'Harmattan, 1986); Pierre Englebert, *La Révolution Burkinabè* (Paris: L'Harmattan, 1986); Bruno Jaffré, *Burkina Faso: Les Années Sankara, de la Révolution à la Rectification* (Paris: L'Harmattan, 1989)...Ludo Martens with Hilde Meesters, *Sankara, Compaoré et la Révolution Burkinabè* (Anvers: Éditions EPO, 1989); Jean Ziegler and J. Ph. Rapp, *Thomas Sankara: Un nouveau pouvoir africain* (Lausanne & Paris: Éditions Pierre-Marcel Favre/ABC, 1986); Valère D. Somé, *Thomas Sankara: L'Espoir assassiné* (Paris: L'Harmattan, 1990). For an analysis of the Burkinabè Revolution in English, see Guy Martin, "Revolutionary Democracy, Socio-Political Conflict and Militarization in Burkina Faso, 1983–1988," in *Democracy and the One-Party State in Africa*, ed. Peter Meyns and Dan W. Nabudere (Hamburg: Institut für Afrika-Kunde, 1989), 57–77.

32. Jaffré, *Biographie de Thomas Sankara*, 8–11 (author's translation from the French, as elsewhere in this chapter).

33. The collected speeches of Thomas Sankara have been published in two volumes (one in French and one in English, both containing the same materials): *Thomas Sankara Speaks: The Burkina Faso Revolution, 1983–87*, edited and translated by Samantha Anderson, with a preface by Doug Cooper (New York: Pathfinder, 1988); Thomas Sankara, *Oser Inventer L'Avenir: La parole de Sankara, 1983–1987*, présenté par David Gakunzi (New York: Pathfinder, 1991). On Sankara's political thought, see in particular Guy Martin, "Idéologie et Praxis dans la Révolution Populaire du 4 août 1983 au Burkina Faso," *Geneva-Africa* 24, no. 1 (1986): 35–62; Guy Martin, "Ideology and Praxis in Thomas Sankara's Populist Revolution of 4 August 1983 in Burkina Faso," *Issue: A Journal of Opinion* 15 (1987): 77–90; Martin, "Fanon's Continuing Relevance," 65–85.

34. "Sankara: cet Homme qui Dérange," Interview of Thomas Sankara by Siradiou Diallo in *Jeune Afrique*, October 12, 1983, 43 (author's translation from the French, as elsewhere in this chapter, unless otherwise indicated).

35. "Sankara: cet Homme qui Dérange," Interview, 43.

36. *Déclaration du Capitaine Thomas Sankara à la 39ème sessions ordinaire de l'Assemblée Générale des Nations Unies* (Ouagadougou: Ministère des Relations

extérieures, 1984), 3. This is quite reminiscent of Fanon's concluding sentences in *Les damnés de la terre* (239–42) quoted before.

37. "We Have to Depend on Ourselves," Interview of Thomas Sankara by Patricia J. Sethi in *Newsweek*, November 19, 1984, 68.

38. "Sankara, cet Homme qui Dérange," Interview, 43.

39. Fanon, *Les damnés de la terre*, 242.

40. Jean-Philippe Rapp, Interviews with Thomas Sankara, in *Sankara: Un nouveau pouvoir africain*, 103; reproduced in *Thomas Sankara Speaks*, 185 (translation by Samantha Anderson; emphasis added).

41. Letter of Basile L. Guissou, then Burkina Faso's minister of external relations, to the author, dated August 9, 1985.

42. Ibid.

43. Conseil National de la Révolution, *Discours d'Orientation Politique pronouncé à la Radio-télévision nationale par le Capitaine Thomas Sankara le 2 octobre 1983* (Ouagadougou: Ministère de l'Information, 1983), 23; reproduced in *Thomas Sankara Speaks*, 62.

44. "Thomas Sankara: le multipartisme? Une mascarade qui nous a coûté très cher," Interview of Thomas Sankara by Mohammed Maïga in *Afrique-Asie*, October 24, 1983, 32.

45. "Sankara: cet Homme qui Dérange," Interview, 46.

46. Interview of T. Sankara by M. Maïga in *Afrique-Asie*, August 15, 1983, 19.

47. Quoted in Susan McDonald, "Burkina: Sankara in Paris," *West Africa*, February 17, 1986, 339.

48. CNR, *Discours d'Orientation Politique*, 17–19; reproduced in *Thomas Sankara Speaks*, 58–60.

49. CNR, *Discours d'Orientation Politique*, 35–37; reproduced in *Thomas Sankara Speaks*, 71–72; see also Thomas Sankara, *Women's Liberation and The African Freedom Struggle* (New York: Pathfinder Press, 1990).

50. CNR, *Discours d'Orientation Politique*, 25; reproduced in *Thomas Sankara Speaks*, 63–64.

51. CNR, *Discours d'Orientation Politique*, 38–43; reproduced in *Thomas Sankara Speaks*, 72–76.

52. See Pascal Labazée, "Réorganisation économique et résistances sociales: la question des alliances au Burkina," *Politique africaine* 20 (December 1985), 14.

53. A. Conchiglia and C. Benabdessadok, "Education: Le Retour aux Sources," *Afrique-Asie*, August 27, 1984, 54–56.

54. CNR, *Discours d'Orientation Politique*, 45; reproduced in *Thomas Sankara Speaks*, 77.

55. Interview of Thomas Sankara by Inga Nagel in *Jeune Afrique*, November 11, 1987, 38.

56. Jean-Philippe Rapp, Interviews with Thomas Sankara, in *Thomas Sankara: Un nouveau pouvoir africain*, 99; reproduced in *Thomas Sankara Speaks*, 181 (translation by Samantha Anderson, slightly modified by the author; emphasis added).

57. The author has identified eight different spellings of the name "Qaddafi" (but there are as many as 432 according to the *Sunday Times* of London). The current spelling has been retained because it is one of the most commonly used in the English language. The proper spelling—as used by the Libyan authorities in their official publications, and also used in French—would be "El Kadhafi," though "Qadhafi" is also commonly used.

58. The author is greatly indebted to Edmond Jouve (professor of political science, Université René-Descartes, Paris) for offering biographical insights on Gaddafi (whom he met personally on more than ten occasions), as well as for providing essential official documentation (notably *The Green Book*).

59. Mouammar Kadhafi, *Dans le Concert des Nations; Libres propos & entretiens avec Edmond Jouve* (Paris: Éditions de l'Archipel, 2004), 7–9, 17–39.

60. Kadhafi, *Dans le Concert des Nations*, 137 (translated from the French by the author, as elsewhere in this section).

61. *Introduction aux Explications du Livre Vert*, vol. 1 (Tripoli: Centre mondial d'Etudes & de Recherches du Livre Vert, 1984), 7.

62. Muammar El Kadhafi, *Le Livre Vert*, vol. 2: *La solution du problème économique: "Le Socialisme"* (n.p., n. d.), 90–91.

63. In this section, reference will be made to the French edition: Moammar El Kadhafi, *Le Livre Vert* (n.p., n.d.); vol. 1: *La solution du problème de la Démocratie: "Le Pouvoir du Peuple"*; vol. 2: *La solution du problème économique: "Le Socialisme"*; vol. 3: *"Les fondements sociaux de la Troisième Théorie universelle."* The text of *The Green Book* in 3 volumes is also reproduced *in extenso* as Annex I in Kadhafi, *Dans le Concert des Nations*, 143–94.

64. *Le Livre Vert*, vol. 1, 55–56.

65. *Kadhafi: 'Je suis un opposant à l'échelon mondial,'* Interviews with Hamid Barrada, Marc Kravetz, and Mark Whitaker (Paris: Éditions Pierre-Marcel Favre/ABC, 1984), 69–70.

66. *Le Livre Vert*, vol. 1, 51, 53–55, 18, 59.

67. Ibid., 57–58.

68. Ibid., 53–63.

69. Ibid., 92.

70. *Kadhafi: 'Je suis un opposant à l'échelon mondial,'* Interviews, 69.

71. *Le Livre Vert*, vol. 2, 50, 47.

72. Ibid., 19–20.

73. Ibid., 85–86, 80–81.

74. *Le Livret Vert*, vol. 3, reproduced in Kadhafi, *Dans le Concert des Nations*, 173.

75. Ibid., 174.

76. Ibid., 179.

77. Ibid., 180.

78. Ibid., 181, see also 181–88.

79. Ibid., 189.

80. Ibid., 190–91.

81. Kadhafi, *Dans le Concert des Nations*, 82–84.

82. On the difficult and often antagonistic relations between Gaddafi's Libya and the OAU, see Jean-Emmanuel Pondi, "Qadhafi and the Organization of African Unity," in *The Green and the Black: Qadhafi's Policies in Africa*, ed. René Lemarchand (Bloomington: Indiana University Press, 1988), 139–49.

83. M. Kadhafi, *Dans le Concert des Nations*, Annex V, 223–35.

84. Ibid., 85–86.

85. After receiving three Libyan delegations, Thomas Sankara visited Libya on two occasions, eventually concluding a deal worth 3.5 billion CFA francs. *Thomas Sankara Speaks: The Burkina Faso Revolution, 1983–87* (New York: Pathfinder Press, 1988), 31–32; see also Sennen Andriamirado, *Sankara Le Rebelle* (Paris: Jeune Afrique Livres, 1987), 215–17; and Bruno Jaffré, *Burkina Faso: Les Années Sankara* (Paris: L'Harmattaqn, 1989), 155–56.

86. Stephanie Nieuwoudt, "Libya to Supply Kenya with Cheaper Oil," *IPS Africa*, June 21, 2007, http://www.ipsnews.net/Africa/nota.asp?idnews=38259; John Kamau, "Kenya: Gaddafi's Fall Puts Country in a Tight Diplomatic Spot," *Business Daily* (Nairobi), posted on *allAfrica.com* on August 22, 2011.

87. "Gaddafi Gold-For-Oil, Dollar-Doom Plans Behind Libya 'Mission,'" *Russia Today* (Moscow), radio broadcast, May 5, 2011 (available on YouTube); "Is Libya Being Bombed Because Gaddafi Wants to Introduce Gold Dinar?" *SodaHead* opinions, March 24, 2011, http://Sodahead.com/united-states. These sources also point out that Libya has 144 tons of gold and Gaddafi's plan involved the sale of African oil for gold dinars.

88. Kadhafi, *Dans le Concert des Nations*, 138.

89. Lindy Wilson, "Bantu Stephen Biko: A Life," in *Bounds of Possibility: The Legacy of Steve Biko & Black Consciousness*, ed. N. Barney Pityana, M. Ramphele, M. Mpumlwana, and Lindy Wilson (New York: David Philip/Zed Books, 1991), 16.

90. Aelred Stubbs, "Martyr of Hope. A Personal Memoir," in Steve Biko, *I Write What I Like*, edited by Aelred Stubbs (San Francisco, CA: Harper & Row, 1986), 192.

91. Gail M. Gerhart, *Black Power in South Africa: The Evolution of an Ideology* (Berkeley: University of California Press, 1978), 260.

92. Millard Arnold, ed., *Steve Biko: Black Consciousness in South Africa* (New York: Vintage Books, 1979); Stubbs, "Martyr of Hope," 154–216; Wilson, "Bantu Stephen Biko," 15–77; Donald Woods, *Biko*, rev. ed. (London: Penguin Books, 1987).

93. C. R. D. Halisi, *Black Political Thought in the Making of South African Democracy* (Bloomington, IN: Indiana University Press, 1999), 128.

94. Gerhart, *Black Power in South Africa*, 285–86. The term "decolonizing the mind" was popularized by Kenyan novelist and scholar Ngugi wa Thiong'o in *Decolonizing the Mind: The Politics of Language in African Literature* (London: James Currey, 1986).

95. Biko, *I Write What I like*, 29.

96. Gerhart, *Black Power in South Africa*, 286.

97. Biko, *I Write What I Like*, 28–29.

98. *SASO Policy Manifesto*, quoted in Gerhart, *Black Power in South Africa*, 272; Steve Biko, quoted by Lindy Wilson in "Bantu Stephen Biko," 50 (emphasis in the original).

99. Wilson, "Bantu Stephen Biko," 23. On Biko's sharp critique of White liberalism, see also Gibson, *Fanonian practices in South Africa*, 44–50.

100. Biko, *I Write What I Like*, 49, 52.

101. Quoted by Gerhart, *Black Power in South Africa*, 271–72.

102. Barney Pityana, quoted in Gerhart, *Black Power in South Africa*, 274 (emphasis in the original).

103. C. R. D. Halisi, "Biko and Black Consciousness Philosophy: An Interpretation," in *Bounds of Possibility*, 103; Halisi, *Black Political Thought*, 128.

104. Gerhart, *Black Power in South Africa*, 294.

105. This episode is mentioned by Gail Gerhart in *Black Power in South Africa*, 294. On Biko's gift of leadership, Fr. Aelred Stubbs made this very personal observation: "He was able to channel into a creative and purposeful direction my diffused sense of compassion for the poor and oppressed." Fr. Stubbs goes even as far as comparing his complete *trust* in Biko to his trust in Jesus: "But I would

have to go back to Jesus himself to find a parallel to this extraordinary pastoral care which Steve had for his own. I suppose this is why I was prepared to commit myself so wholeheartedly to the care of his leadership. In this particular area I trusted him with the same *kind* of trust I have in Jesus." Aelred Stubbs, "Martyr of Hope: A Personal Memoir," in Steve Biko, *I Write What I Like* (San Francisco, CA: Harper & Row, 1986), 192, 193 (emphasis in the original).

106. Stubbs, "Martyr of Hope," 212–13. On Black theology, see also Robert Fatton Jr., *Black Consciousness in South Africa: The Dialectics of Ideological Resistance to White Supremacy* (Albany: State University of New York Press, 1986), 107–19.

107. Other prominent SASO leaders were Barney Pityana, Harry Nengwekhulu, Hendrick Musi, Petrus Machaka, Manana Ngware, and Aubrey Mokoape, plus two of Biko's Indian friends, J. Goolam and Strini Moodley. Note that in the South African context, the term "Colored" refers to all mixed-race people who, along with people originating from Southeast Asia referred to as "Malays," are mostly to be found in the Western Cape Province.

108. Gerhart, *Black Power in South Africa*, 257.

109. Steve Biko, quoted by Ibid., 264, 265.

110. Biko, *I Write What I Like*, 22.

111. Gerhart, *Black Power in South Africa*, 277–78.

112. Halisi, *Black Political Thought*, 129.

113. Biko, *I Write What I Like*, 48.

114. "Editorial," *SASO Newsletter*, September, 1970, 2; quoted in Gail Gerhart, *Black Power in South Africa*, 278.

115. O. Mannoni, *Prospero and Caliban: The Psychology of Colonization* (New York: Frederick A. Praeger, 1964); Albert Memmi, *Portrait du colonisé, précédé du Portrait du colonisateur*, with a preface by Jean-Paul Sartre (Paris: Jean-Jacques Pauvert, 1966), translated into English as *The Colonizer and the Colonized*, expanded ed. (Boston, MA: Beacon Press, 1991); Fanon, *The Wretched of the Earth* (New York: Grove Press, 1968). See also Mahmood Mamdani, *Citizen and Subject: Contemporary Africa and the Legacy of Late Colonialism* (Princeton, NJ: Princeton University Press, 1996). On the processes by which Fanon's philosophy of liberation was articulated in Biko's conception of Black Consciousness in South Africa, see Gibson, *Fanonian practices in South Africa*, 43–70.

116. Memmi, *Portrait du colonisé, précédé du Portrait du colonisateur*, 183–85 (emphasis in the original).

117. Gerhart, *Black Power in South Africa*, 281.

118. Lindy Wilson, "Banto Stephen Biko: A Life," in *Bounds of Possibility*, 76.

119. Mongale Wally Serote, "The Impact of Black Consciousness on Culture and Freedom," quoted in *Bounds of Possibility*, 9–10.

120. N. Barney Pityana et al., Introduction to *Bounds of Possibility*, 11.

121. Halisi, "Biko and Black Consciousness Philosophy," 110.

122. Stubbs, "Martyr of Hope," 214–15 (emphasis in the original).

123. Martin, "Fanon's Continuing Relevance," 65–85.

Chapter 8

1. Daniel T. Osabu-Kle, *Compatible Cultural Democracy: The Key to Development in Africa* (Peterborough, Ontario: Broadview Press, 2000), 9, 25, 27.

2. Ibid., 25.

3. Ibid., 27.
4. Ibid., 11.
5. Ibid., 79–80.
6. Ibid., 100–107.
7. Ibid., 115–272.
8. Ibid., 110–11. Note that this list is an abbreviated version of the original, which includes 14 separate items.
9. Ibid., 72.
10. Ibid., 77.
11. Ibid., 274–75.
12. Ibid., 106.
13. Ibid., 275.
14. Ibid., 107, 114.
15. Ibid., 107.
16. Ibid., 274, 278.
17. Ibid., 278.
18. Ibid., 279–80.
19. Ibid., 282.
20. Jeremiah O. Arowosegbe, "The Making of an Organic Intellectual: Claude Ake, Biographical & Theoretical Orientations," *African and Asian Studies* 11, no. 1–2 (2012): 127, see also 123–43 (emphasis in the original; the concept of "organic intellectual" is evidently borrowed from Antonio Gramsci); see also Victor Adebola O. Adetula, ed., *Claude Ake and Democracy in Africa: A Tribute* (Jos: AFRIGOV, 1997); and Guy Martin, "Claude Ake: A Tribute," in *Claude Ake and Democracy in Africa*, 39–40.
21. Arowosegbe, "The Making of an Organic Intellectual," 137.
22. Ibid., 131–35.
23. Claude Ake, *A Theory of Political Integration* (Homewood, IL: The Dorsey Press, 1967).
24. As reported by Arowosegbe, "The Making of an Organic Intellectual," 132–35.
25. Claude Ake, *Social Science as Imperialism: The Theory of Political Development* (Ibadan: Ibadan University Press, 1979).
26. Claude Ake, *Revolutionary Pressures in Africa* (London: Zed Books, 1978); Claude Ake, *A Political Economy of Africa* (Harlow, UK: Longman, 1981).
27. Cited by Arowosegbe, "The Making of an Organic Intellectual," 133.
28. Claude Ake, *Democracy and Development in Africa* (Washington, DC: The Brookings Institution, 1996); Claude Ake, *The Feasibility of Democracy in Africa* (Dakar: CODESRIA Books, 2000).
29. Ake, *The Feasibility of Democracy in Africa*, 10, see also 9–10.
30. Ibid., 11.
31. Ibid., 12–17.
32. Ibid., 16–17.
33. Claude Ake, *Democracy and Development in Africa* (Washington, DC: The Brookings Institution, 1996), 1; see also Guy Martin, "Reflections on Democracy and Development in Africa: The Intellectual Legacy of Claude Ake," *Ufahamu* 26, no. 1 (Winter 1998): 102–9.
34. Ake, *Democracy and Development in Africa*, 3–6.
35. Dipesh Chakrabarty, *Provincializing Europe: Postcolonial Thought and Historical Difference* (Princeton, NJ: Princeton University Press, 2000), 8.

36. Arowosege, "The Making of an Organic Intellectual," 140 (emphasis in the original).
37. K. A. Busia, *The Challenge of Africa* (New York: Frederick A. Praeger, 1962), 66.
38. Ake, *Democracy and Development in Africa*, 7 (emphasis added).
39. Ibid., 42 (emphasis added).
40. Ibid., 15–16.
41. Ibid., 125 (abbreviated from the original; emphasis added).
42. Ibid., 132 (abbreviated from the original; emphasis added).
43. Ibid., 139 (emphasis added). Note Ake's rare reference to "African traditions," a point on which Daniel Osabu-Kle had much more to say. We can only speculate that had Ake had the opportunity to develop his thought further, he would have stressed the centrality of African tradition and culture in a specifically African concept of democracy.
44. Ibid., 140–42 (abbreviated from the original; emphasis in the original).
45. Martin, "Reflections on Democracy and Development in Africa," 108–9.
46. This section draws exclusively from one of the author's latest books: Godfrey Mwakikagile, *The Modern African State: Quest for Transformation* (Huntington, NY: Nova Science Publishers, 2001).
47. Naomi Chazan et al., *Politics and Society in Contemporary Africa*, 3rd ed. (Boulder, CO: Lynne Rienner, 1999), 22.
48. Mwakikagile, *The Modern African State*, xi, ix, xii.
49. Ibid., 73.
50. Ibid., 220 (emphasis added).
51. Ibid., 73.
52. Ibid., 220–21.
53. Ibid., 1–186.
54. Ibid., 196. The present author observed that as of January 2002, some form of conflict persisted in more than half of the African countries (30 out of 54). Guy Martin, *Africa in World Politics: A Pan-African Perspective* (Trenton, NJ: Africa World Press, 2002), 186.
55. Mwakikagile, *The Modern African State*, 21.
56. Ibid., 58.
57. Ibid., 218.
58. Ibid., 103 (emphasis added).
59. Ibid., 207 (emphasis added).
60. Ibid., 215–16.
61. Ibid., 121.
62. Ibid., 216.
63. Ibid., 225, 222, 224.
64. Ibid., 221–22 (emphasis added; abridged from the original).
65. Ibid., 225.
66. Ibid., 226.
67. *Fundi wa Afrika* was first published in article form by Mueni wa Muiu, "Fundi wa Afrika: Toward a New Paradigm of the African State," *Journal of Third World Studies* 19, no. 2 (Fall 2002): 23–42; and Mueni wa Muiu and Guy Martin, "Fundi wa Afrika: Towards an Authentic African Renaissance," *Black Renaissance/Renaissance Noire* 4, no. 1 (Spring 2002): 83–96. A more comprehensive and elaborate version of the paradigm is found in Mueni wa Muiu and Guy Martin, *A New Paradigm of the African State* (New York: Palgrave Macmillan, 2009). It should be noted that although the present author was invited to help

develop and refine the paradigm in two publications, the original idea of *Fundi wa Afrika* rests solely and exclusively with Mueni wa Muiu.

68. Muiu, "Fundi wa Afrika," 23.
69. Muiu and Martin, "Fundi wa Afrika," 83–84.
70. Ibid., 84. Mueni borrows the term "African Predicament" from Stanislav Andreski, *The African Predicament* (New York: Atherton Press, 1968).
71. Mueni wa Muiu justifies the choice of *Fundi wa Afrika* as follows: "I decided to apply [*Fundi wa Afrika*] to study the nature of the African state after I observed the building process in a small village in eastern Kenya. The owner of the house decided what the needs of the family were which he/she explained to the builder. Throughout the building process the builder and the owner consulted each other and whenever anything needed changing the builder changed it based on the needs of the client. I noticed the same process when I took my material to a tailor to make some outfits for me. She asked me what my needs were and we consulted each other throughout the process. When everything was over we were both happy. It is then that I realized that the relationship between Africans and their institutions in indigenous Africa was similar to the building and tailoring processes." Muiu, "Fundi wa Afrika," 23–24; Muiu and Martin, *A New Paradigm of the African State*, 194.
72. Muiu and Martin, "Fundi wa Afrika," 84. In Mueni's acception, "Africa" refers to the whole continent from Cape Town to Cairo, including the Indian Ocean islands as per the 55 member-states of the African Union; "Africans" refers to any person—regardless of race or ethnicity—whose exclusive loyalty is to the African continent.
73. Muiu and Martin, *A New Paradigm of the African State*, 194.
74. Ibid., 5.
75. Fernand Braudel, *La Méditerranée et le Monde Mediterraneen à l'époque de Philippe II*, 3 volumes (Paris: Armand Colin, 1966); Fernand Braudel, *Civilization and Capitalism, 15th-18th Centuries*, 3 volumes (Berkeley: University of California Press, 1992); Charles Tilly, *Coercion, Capital and European States, AD 990–1992* (Cambridge, MA: Blackwell Publishers, 1992). Fernand Braudel (1902–85) taught at the *Collège de France* (Paris) and was the leader of the *Annales* school of historiography; Charles Tilly (1929–2008) was, at the time of his death, the Joseph L. Buttenweiser Professor of Social Sciences at Columbia University (New York).
76. Three notable exceptions in this regard are Basil Davidson, *Africa in History*, rev. ed. (New York: Simon and Schuster, 2005); Christopher Ehret, *The Civilizations of Africa: A History to 1800* (Charlottesville: University Press of Virginia, 2002); and Elikia M'Bokolo, *Afrique Noire: Histoire et Civilisations*, vol. 1: *Jusqu'au 18ème siècle* (Paris: Hatier, 1995); vol. 2: *Du 19ème siècle à nos jours*, 2nd ed. (Paris: Hatier, 2004).
77. See for example Roland Oliver and Anthony Atmore, *Africa since 1800*, 4th ed. (Cambridge, UK: Cambridge University Press, 1994).
78. Muiu and Martin, *A New Paradigm of the African State*, 4–5.
79. Ibid., 5–6.
80. Ibid., 23–47.
81. Ibid., 49–62.
82. Ibid., 63–84.
83. Ibid., 102–37.
84. Ibid., 139–89.

85. Ake, *Democracy and Development in Africa*, 3–6.
86. Mwakikagile, *The Modern African State*, 220.
87. Muiu & Martin, *A New Paradigm of the African State*, 193–94.
88. Ibid., 192.
89. Ibid., 195–205 (emphasis in the original; abridged from the original).
90. Ibid., 207–8.
91. Ibid., 208–9.
92. Ibid., 5.
93. Mueni wa Muiu & Guy Martin, *Fundi wa Afrika: Toward a New African State* (manuscript in progress).
94. Muiu and Martin, *A New Paradigm of the African State*, 192.
95. Daniel T. Osabu-Kle, *Compatible Cultural Democracy: The Key to Development in Africa* (Peterborough, Ontario: Broadives Press, 2000), 9.
96. Ibid., 11.
97. Mwakikagile, *The Modern African State*, 220.

CONCLUSION

1. Mueni wa Muiu and Guy Martin, *A New Paradigm of the African State: Fundi wa Afrika* (New York: Palgrave Macmillan, 2009), 195–216.
2. Ibid., 216.
3. Frantz Fanon *Toward the African Revolution* (New York: Grove Press, 1967), 186.
4. Frantz Fanon, *The Wretched of the Earth* (New York: Penguin Books, 1967), 255.

Bibliography

Abdel-Malek, Anouar, ed. *La Pensée politique arabe contemporaine* (Paris: Éditions du Seuil, 1970).

Abdul-Raheem, Tajudeen, ed. *Pan-Africanism: Politics, Economy and Social Change in the Twenty-First Century* (New York: New York University Press, 1996).

Abraham, Willie E. *The Mind of Africa* (Chicago, IL: University of Chicago Press, 1962).

Abrahamsen, Rita. *Disciplining Democracy: Development Discourse and Good Governance in Africa* (London: Zed Books, 2000).

Adamafio, Tawia. *By Nkrumah's Side: The Labour and the Wounds* (London: Rex Collings/Westcoast Publishing House, 1982).

Adamolekun, Lapido. *Sékou Touré's Guinea: An Experiment in Nation Building* (London: Methuen, 1976).

———. "The Socialist Experience in Guinea," in Carl G. Rosberg and Thomas M. Callaghy, eds., *Socialism in Sub-Saharan Africa: A New Assessment* (Berkeley: Institute of International Studies/University of California, 1979), 61–82.

Adandé, Alexis B. A., ed. *Intégration Régionale, Démocratie et Panafricanisme: Paradigmes Anciens, Nouveaux Défis* (Dakar: CODESRIA, 2007).

Adejumobi, Saïd, and Adebayo Olukoshi, eds. *The African Union and New Strategies for Development in Africa* (Dakar: CODESRIA, 2009).

Adetula, Victor Adebola O., ed., *Claude Ake and Democracy in Africa: A Tribute* (Jos, Nigeria: African Center for Democratic Governance/AFRIGOV, 1997).

Adi, Hakim. "African Diaspora, Development and Modern African Political Theory," *Review of African Political Economy* 29, no. 92 (July 2002): 237–51.

———. "Pan-Africanism and West African Nationalism in Britain," *African Studies Review* 43, no. 1 (April 2000): 69–82.

———, and Marika Sherwood. *Pan-African History: Political Figures from Africa and the Diaspora since 1787* (London: Routledge, 2003).

Adogamhe, Paul G. "Pan-Africanism Revisited: Vision and Reality of African Unity and Development," *African Review of Integration* 2, no. 2 (July 2008): 1–34.

Adotevi, Stanislas S. K. *Négritude et Négrologues* (Paris: Le Castor Astral, 1998 [1972]).

Afolayan, A. L. "The Rise and Fall of Development: The Discourse of African Development from an Epistemic Standpoint," in Ike Odimegwu, ed., *Perspectives on African Communalism* (Victoria, BC: Trafford Publishing, 2007), 524–45.

Agagu, Femi Omotoso A. A. *Selected Issues in African Political Thought* (Porto-Novo: L'Institut Universitaire Sonou d'Afrique, 2007).

Agbakoba, J. C. Achike. "Traditional African Political Thought and the Crisis of Governance in Contemporary African Societies," *Journal for the Study of Religions and Ideologies* 3, no. 7 (Spring 2004): 137–54.

Agbese, Pita O., and George Klay Kieh Jr., eds. *Reconstituting the State in Africa* (New York: Palgrave Macmillan, 2007).

Ake, Claude. "The Congruence of Political Economies and Ideologies in Africa," in Peter Gutkind and Immanuel Wallerstein, eds., *The Political Economy of Contemporary Africa* (Beverly Hills, CA: Sage Publications, 1976), 198–211.

———. *Democracy and Development in Africa* (Washington, DC: The Brookings Institution, 1996).

———. "Democracy and Development in Africa: The Residual Option," in Victor A. O. Adetula, ed., *Claude Ake and Democracy in Africa: A Tribute* (Jos: African Center for Democratic Governance/AFRIGOV, 1997), 4–21.

———. *The Feasibility of Democracy in Africa* (Dakar: CODESRIA, 2000).

———. *A Political Economy of Africa* (Harlow, UK: Longman, 1981).

———. *Revolutionary Pressures in Africa* (London: Zed Press, 1978).

———. *Social Science as Imperialism: The Theory of Political Development* (Ibadan: Ibadan University Press, 1979).

———. *The Social Sciences in Africa: Trends, Tasks and Challenges* (Dakar: CODESRIA, 1986).

Akokpari, John, A. Ndinga-Muvumba, and Tim Murithi, eds. *The African Union and Its Institutions* (Auckland Park: Fanele/Center for Conflict Resolution, 2008).

Alessandrini, Anthony C., ed. *Frantz Fanon: Critical Perspectives* (London: Routledge, 1999).

Alexandre, Pierre. "Marxism and African Cultural Traditions," *Survey* 43 (August 1962): 65–78.

Al Gathafi, Muammar. *The Green Book: The Solution to the Problem of Democracy; The Solution to the Economic Problem; The Social Basis of the Third Universal Theory* (Reading, UK: Ithaca Press, 2005).

Alpers, Edward A. "The Struggle for Socialism in Mozambique, 1960–1972," in Carl G. Rosberg and Thomas M. Callaghy, eds., *Socialism in Sub-Saharan Africa: A New Assessment* (Berkeley: Institute of International Studies/University of California, 1979), 267–95.

Ameillon, B. *La Guinée, bilan d'une indépendence* (Paris: François Maspéro, 1964).

Amir, Samir. *Eurocentrism* (New York: Monthly Review Press, 2nd edition, 2010).

———. *La Faillite du Développement en Afrique et dans le Tiers-Monde: Une Analyse politique* (Paris: L'Harmattan, 1989).

Amuta, Chidi. "The Ideological Content of Soyinka's War Writings," *African Studies Review* 29, no. 3 (September 1986): 43–54.

Andrade, Mario de. *Amilcar Cabral: Essai de Biographie politique* (Paris: François Maspéro, 1980).

———. "Amilcar Cabral: Profil d'un révolutionaire africain," *Présence Africaine* 86 (1973): 3–19.

Andrain, Charles F. "Guinea and Senegal: Contrasting Types of African Socialism," in William H. Friedland and Carl G. Rosberg Jr., eds, *African Socialism* (Stanford, CA: Stanford University Press, 1964), 160–74.

———. "Patterns of African Socialist Thought," *African Forum* 1, no. 3 (Winter 1966), 41–60.

Andréini, Jean-Claude, and Marie-Claude Lambert, *La Guinée-Bissau d'Amilcar Cabral à la Reconstruction nationale* (Paris: L'Harmattan, 2001).

Andriamirado, Sennen. *Sankara Le Rebelle* (Paris: Jeune Afrique Livres, 1987).

Anyang' Nyong'o, Peter. *African Politics and the Crisis of Development* (Trenton, NJ: Africa World Press, 1989).

———, ed. *Popular Struggles for Democracy in Africa* (London: Zed Books/United Nations University, 1987).

Anyanwu, Christian C. *The African and Conscientization: A Critical Approach to African Social and Political Thought with Particular Reference to Nigeria* (Bloomington, IN: Author House, 2012).

Appiah, Kwame Anthony. *In My Father's House: Africa in the Philosophy of Culture* (New York: Oxford University Press, 1992).

Appiah, Kwame A., and Henry Louis Gates Jr., eds., *Africana: The Encyclopedia of the African and African American Experience* (London: Running Press, 2003).

Arnold, Millard, ed. *Steve Biko: Black Consciousness in South Africa* (New York: Vintage Books/Random House, 1979).

Arowosegbe, Jeremiah O. "The Making of an Organic Intellectual: Claude Ake, Biographical and Theoretical Orientations," *African and Asian Studies* 11, nos. 1–2 (2012): 123–43.

Arrighi, Giovanni, and John S. Saul. *Essays on the Political Economy of Africa* (New York: Monthly Review Press, 1973).

———. "Nationalism and Revolution in Sub-Saharan Africa," in Giovanni Arrighi and John S. Saul, *Essays on the Political Economy of Africa* (New York: Monthly Review Press, 1973), 44–102.

Asante, Molefi Kete. *An Afrocentric Manifesto: Toward an African Renaissance* (Malden, MA: Polity Press, 2007).

———. *Afrocentricity: The Theory of Social Change* (Chicago, IL: African American Images, revised edition, 2003).

———. *Cheikh Anta Diop: An Intellectual Portrait* (Los Angeles, CA: University of Sankore Press, 2007).

———. *The Egyptian Philosophers: Ancient African Voices from Imhotep to Akhenaten* (Chicago, IL: African American Images, 2000).

Assensoh, A. B. *African Political Leadership: Jomo Kenyatta, Kwame Nkrumah and Julius Nyerere* (Malabar, FL: Krieger Publishing Co., 1998).

———. *Kwame Nkrumah of Africa: His Formative Years and the Beginning of His Political Career* (Ilfracombe, UK: Arthur A. Stockwell Publisher, 1989).

Atieno Odhiambo, E. S. "The Cultural Dimensions of Development in Africa," *African Studies Review* 45, no 3 (December 2002): 1–16.

Auma-Osolo, A., and N. Osolo-Nasubo. "Democratic African Socialism: An Account of African Communal Philosophy," *African Studies Review* 14, no. 2 (September 1971): 265–72.

Ayittey, George B. N. *Africa Unchained: The Blueprint for Africa's Future* (New York: Palgrave Macmillan, 2005).

———. *Indigenous African Institutions* (Ardsley-on-Hudson, NY: Transnational Publishers, 1991).

Bâ, Amadou Hampâté. *Aspects de la civilization africaine* (Paris: Présence Africaine, 2000).

Baali, Fuad. *Social Institutions: Ibn Khaldun's Social Thought* (Lanham, MD: University Press of America, 1992).

Babu, Abdul Rahman Mohamed. *African Socialism or Socialist Africa?* (London: Zed Press, 1981).

Bangura, Abdul Karim. "From Diop to Asante: Conceptualizing and Contextualizing the Afrocentric Paradigm," *Journal of Pan African Studies* 5, no. 1 (March 2012): 103–25.

———. "The Nexus among Democracy, Economic Development, Good Governance, and Peace in Africa: A Triangulative Analysis and Diopian Remedy," *Africa Peace and Conflict Journal* 4, no. 2 (December 2011): 1–16.

Bangura, Abdul Karim, "Ubuntugogy: An African Educational Paradigm That Tran-scends Pedagogy, Andragogy, Ergonagy and Heutagogy," *Journal of Third World Studies* 22, no. 2 (Fall 2005): 13–53.

Bankie, B. F., and K. Mchomble, eds. *Pan-Africanism/African Nationalism: Strength-ening the Unity of Africa and its Diaspora* (Trenton, NJ: Red Sea Press, 2002).

Barrada, Hamid, Marc Kravetz, and Mark Whitaker. *Kadhafi: Je suis un opposant à l'échelon mondial* (Lausanne & Paris: Éditions Pierre-Marcel Favre/Éditions ABC, 1984).

Baxter, Joan, and Keith Somerville. "Burkina Faso"; Part 3 in Chris Allen, Michael Radu, Joan Baxter, and Keith Somerville, *Benin, The Congo, Burkina Faso: Eco-nomics, Politics and Society* (London: Pinter Publishers, 1989): 237–86.

Beauchamp, Kay. "African Socialism in Ghana," *Spearhead* (Dar es Salaam) 1, no. 4 (February 1962): 21–25.

Bénot, Yves. *Idéologies des Indépendances africaines* (Paris: François Maspéro, 2nd edition, 1972).

———. *Les Indépendances africaines; Idéologies et réalités*, 2 vols. (Paris: François Maspéro, 1975).

———. "Idéologies, nations et structures sociales en Afrique," *Tiers-Monde* 57 (January–March 1974): 135–70.

Bidima, Jean-G. *La Philosophie négro-africaine* (Paris: Presses Universitaires de France, 1995).

Bienen, Henry. "An Ideology for Africa," *Foreign Affairs* 47, no. 3 (April 1969): 545–59.

———. "State and Revolution: The Work of Amilcar Cabral," *Journal of Modern African Studies* 15, no. 4 (1977): 555–68.

Biko, Steve. *I Write What I Like: A Selection of His Writings*, edited by Aelred Stubbs, preface by Desmond Tutu (Randburg, South Africa: Ravan Press, 1996 [1978]).

Biney, Ama. "The Legacy of Kwame Nkrumah in Retrospect," *Journal of Pan-Afri-can Studies* 2, no. 3 (March 2008): 129–59.

———. *The Political and Social Thought of Kwame Nkrumah* (New York: Palgrave Macmillan, 2011).

Birmingham, David. *Kwame Nkrumah: The Father of African Nationalism* (Athens: Ohio University Press, revised edition, 1998).

Biya, Paul. *Pour le Libéralisme Communautaire* (Paris: Éditions Pierre-Marcel Favre/Éditions ABC, 1986).

Blackey, Robert. "Fanon and Cabral: A Contrast in Theories of Revolution for Africa," *Journal of Modern African Studies* 12, no. 2 (June 1974): 191–201.

Bockel, Alain. "Amilcar Cabral, marxiste africain," *Éthiopiques* 5 (January 1976): 35–39.

Bond, Patrick, ed. *Fanon's Warning: A Civil Society Reader on the New Partnership for Africa's Development* (Trenton, NJ: Africa World Press, 2nd edition, 2005).

Bretton, Henry L. "Current Political Thought and Practice in Ghana," *American Political Science Review* 52, no. 1 (1958).

———. *The Rise and Fall of Kwame Nkrumah* (London: Pall Mall Press, 1966).

Brockman, Norbert C. *An African Biographical Dictionary* (Santa Barbara, CA: ABC-CLIO, 1994).

Brockway, A. Fenner. *African Socialism* (London: Bodley Head, 1963).

Bulhan, Hussein A. *Frantz Fanon and the Psychology of Oppression* (New York: Plenum Press, 1985).

Burke, Fred G. "Tanganyika: The Search for Ujamaa," in William G. Friedland and Carl G. Rosberg Jr., eds., *African Socialism* (Stanford, CA: Stanford University Press, 1964), 194–219.

Busia, Kofi A. *Africa in Search of Democracy* (New York: Frederick A. Praeger, 1967).

———. *The Challenge of Africa* (New York: Frederick A. Praeger, 1962).

———. *The Position of the Chief in the Modern Political System of Ashanti* (London: Oxford University Press, 1951).

Cabral, Amilcar. *Return to the Source: Selected Speeches of Amilcar Cabral*, edited by Africa Information Service (New York: Monthly Review Press, 1973).

———. *Revolution in Guinea: Selected Texts by Amilcar Cabral*, edited and translated by Richard Handyside (New York: Monthly Review Press, 1972).

———. *Unité et Lutte; I: L'Arme de la théorie* (Paris: François Maspéro, 1975).

———. *Unité et Lutte; II: La pratique révolutionnaire* (Paris: François Maspéro, 1975).

———. *Unity and Struggle*, with an introduction by Basil Davidson (London: Heinemann, 1980)

Campbell, Bonnie. *Libération Nationale and Constrtuction du Socialisme en Afrique: Angola, Guinée-Bissau, Mozambique* (Montréal: Éditions Nouvelle Optique, 1977).

CELTHO. *La Charte de Kurukan Fuga: Aux sources d'une pensée politique en Afrique* [*The Mande Charter of 1340*] (Paris: L'Harmattan/SAEC, 2008).

Césaire, Aimé. *Discourse on Colonialism*, translated by J. Pinkham (New York: Monthly Review Press, 1973).

———. *Discours sur le Colonialisme* (Paris: Présence Africaine, 5th edition, 1970 [1955]).

———. "La Pensée Politique de Sékou Touré," *Présence Africaine* 29 (December 1959/January 1960): 65–73.

———. "Sékou Touré: His Political Thought," *Spearhead* (Dar es Salaam) 1, no. 8 (July/August 1962): 9–13.

Chabal, Patrick. *Amilcar Cabral: Revolutionary Leadership and People's War* (Trenton, NJ: Africa World Press, 2003 [1983]).

———. "The Social and Political Thought of Amilcar Cabral: A Reassessment," *Journal of Modern African Studies* 19, no. 1 (1981): 31–56.

Chaliand, Gérard. *Mythes révolutionnaires du Tiers-Monde* (Paris: Éditions du Seuil, 1976).

———. *Revolution in the Third World: Myths and Prospects* (Baltimore, MD: Penguin Books, 1978).

Charles, Bernard. "Le Socialisme Africain: Mythes et Réalités," *Revue Française de Science Politique* 15, no. 5 (October 1965): 856–84.

Che-Mponda, Aleck H. "Aspects of Nyerere's Political Philosophy: A Study in the Dynamics of African Political Thought," *African Study Monographs* (University of Dar es Salaam)5 (December 1984): 63–74.

Cherki, Alice. *Frantz Fanon: A Portrait* (Ithaca, NY: Cornell University Press, 2006).

Chilcote, Ronald H. "Amilcar Cabral: A Bio-Bibliography of His Life and Thought, 1925–73," *Africana Journal* 5, no. 4 (Winter 1974–75): 289–307.

———. *Amilcar Cabral's Revolutionary Theory and Practice: A Critical Guide* (Boulder, CO: Lynne Rienner Publishers, 1991).

Cissoko, Sékéné Mody. *Un Combat pour l'Unité de l'Afrique de l'Ouest: La Fédération du Mali, 1959–1960* (Dakar: Les Nouvelles Éditions Africaines du Senegal, 2005).

Clapham, Christopher. "The Context of African Political Thought," *Journal of Modern African Studies* 8, no. 1 (April 1970): 1–13.

Cliffe, Lionel, and John S. Saul, eds. *Socialism in Tanzania: An Interdisciplinary Reader*, vol. 1: *Politics* (Nairobi: East African Publishing House, 1972).

———. *Socialism in Tanzania: An Interdisciplinary Reader*, vol. 2: *Policies* (Nairobi: East African Publishing House, 1973).

Cox, Idris. *Socialist Ideas in Africa* (London: Lawrence and Wishart, 1966).

Cronon, E. David. *Black Moses: The Story of Marcus Garvey and the Universal Negro Improvement Association* (Madison: University of Wisconsin Press, 1969).

Cruse, Harold. "The Amilcar Cabral Politico-Cultural Model," *Black World* (October 1965): 20–27.

Danabo, Pelle Darota. *From Africa of States to United Africa: Towards Africana Democracy*, PhD dissertation, University of Kansas, 2008.

Davidson, Basil. *African Civilization Revisited: From Antiquity to Modern Times* (Trenton, NJ: Africa World Press, 1991).

———. *The African Genius: An Introduction to African Cultural and Social History* (Boston, MA: Little, Brown, 1969).

———. *The Black Man's Burden: Africa and the Curse of the Nation-State* (New York: Times Books, 1992).

———. *Black Star: A View of the Life and Times of Kwame Nkrumah* (Oxford, UK: James Currey, 2007).

———. *The Liberation of Guiné: Aspects of an African Revolution*, foreword by Amilcar Cabral (Baltimore, MD: Penguin Books, 1969).

———. *Which Way Africa? The Search for a New Society* (Baltimore, MD: Penguin Books, revised edition, 1967).

Davis, John. *Libyan Politics: Tribe and Revolution* (London: I. B. Tauris, 1987).

Decraene, Philippe. "Scientific Socialism: African Style," *Africa Report* 20, no. 3 (March 1975): 46–51.

Dembélé, Demba Moussa. *Samir Amin, Intellectuel organique au service de l'émancipation du Sud* (Dakar: CODESRIA, 2011).

Desfosses, Helen, and J. Dirck Stryker. "Socialist Development in Africa: The Case of Kéïta's Mali," in H. Desfosses and J. Levesque, eds., *Socialism in the Third World* (New York: Frederick A. Praeger, 1975), 167–79.

Dia, Mamadou. *The African Nations and World Solidarity*, translated by Mercer Cook (New York: Frederick A. Praeger, 1961).

———. "African Socialism," in William H. Friedland and Carl G. Rosberg Jr., eds., *African Socialism* (Stanford, CA: Stanford University Press, 1964), 248–49.

———. *Afrique: Le Prix de la Liberté* (Paris: L'Harmattan, 2001).

———. *Nations Africaines et Solidarité Mondiale* (Paris: Presses Universitaires de France, 1960).

Diagne, Pathé. *Cheikh Anta Diop et l'Afrique dans l'histoire du monde* (Paris: L'Harmattan/Sankoré, 2002).

———. *L'Afrique, enjeu de l'histoire: Afrocentrisme, Eurocentrisme, Semitocentrisme* (Paris: L'Harmattan, 2010).

———. *Pouvoir Politique Traditionnel en Afrique Occidentale* (Paris: Présence Africaine, 1967).

Diagne, Souleymane Bachir. "Precolonial African Philosophy in Arabic," in Kwasi Waredu, ed., *A Companion to African Philosophy* (Oxford, UK: Blackwell Publishing, 2004), 66–77.

Diallo, Demba. *L'Afrique en Question* (Paris: François Maspéro, 1968).

Diarrah, Cheick Oumar. *Le Mali de Modibo Kéïta* (Paris: L'Harmattan, 1986).

Diawara, Manthia. "Toward a Regional Imaginary in Africa," in Fredric Jameson and Masao Miyoshi, eds., *The Cultures of Globalization* (Durham, NC: Duke University Press, 1998): 103–24.

Dieng, Amady Aly. *Contribution a l'étude des problèmes philosophiques en Afrique noire* (Paris: Nubia, 1983).

———. *Le Marxisme et l'Afrique Noire: Bilan d'un débat sur l'universalité du marxisme* (Paris: Nubia, 1985).

Diop, Boubacar Boris. *L'Afrique au-delà du miroir* (Paris: Éditions Philippe Rey, 2007).

———, Odile Tobner, and François-Xavier Verschave. *Négrophobie* (Paris: Éditions des Arènes, 2005).

Diop, Cheikh Anta. *The African Origin of Civilization: Myth or Reality?*, translated by Mercer Cook (Chicago, IL: Lawrence Hill Books, 1974).

———. *Black Africa: The Economic and Cultural Basis for a Federated State*, translated by Harold J. Salemson (Chicago, IL: Lawrence Hill Books/Africa World Press, revised edition, 1987).

———. *Civilization or Barbarism: An Authentic Anthropology* (Brooklyn, NY: Lawrence Hill Books, 1991 [1981]).

———. *Civilisation our Barbarie: Antrhopologie sans Complaisance* (Paris: Présence Africaine, 1981).

———. *L'Afrique Noire Pré-Coloniale* (Paris: Présence Africaine, 1960).

———. *L'Unité Culturelle de l'Afrique Noire* (Paris: Présence Africaine, 2nd edition, 1982).

———. *Nations Nègres et Culture*, 2 vols. (Paris: Présence Africaine, 3rd édition, 1979).

———. *Precolonial Black Africa* (Chicago, IL: Lawrence Hill Books, 1987).

Diop, Majhemout. *Contribution à l'étude des Problèmes Politiques en Afrique Noire* (Paris: Presence Africaine, 1958).

Doumbi-Fakoly. *Afrique: La Renaissance* (Ivry-sur-Seine: Silex/Nouvelles du Sud, 2000).

Dramani-Issifou, Z. "Islam as a Social System in Africa since the Seventh Century," in M. El Fasi and I. Hrbek, eds., *General History of Africa III* (Berkeley: University of California Press, 1988), 92–118.

Eboussi-Boulaga, Fabien. *La Crise du Muntu: Authenticité africaine et philosophie* (Paris: Présence Africaine, 1997).

———. *L'Affaire de la Philosophie africaine: Au-delà des querelles* (Paris: Karthala, 2011).

Edgar, Robert R., and Luyanda ka Msumza, eds. *Freedom in Our Lifetime: The Collected Writings of Anton Muziwakhe Lembede* (Athens: Ohio University Press, 1996).

Elungu, Pene Elungu. "La Philosophie, condition de développement en Afrique aujourd'hui," *Présence Africaine* 103 (1977): 3–18.

Emmert, Kirk. "African Socialism and Western Liberalism," *Africa Quarterly* 15, nos. 1 and 2 (April and July 1975): 5–21.

Esedebe, P. Olisanwuche. *Pan-Africanism: The Idea and Movement, 1776–1991* (Washington, DC: Howard University Press, 2nd edition, 1994).

Eze, Emmanuel C., ed. *African Philosophy: An Anthology* (Malden, MA: Blackwell Publishers, 1998).

Falola, Toyin. *Nationalism and African Intellectuals* (Rochester, NY: University of Rochester Press, 2004).

Fanon, Frantz. *Black Skin, White Masks*, translated by Charles Lam Markmann (London: Pluto Press, 2nd edition, 1986).

———. *Les Damnés de la terre*, preface by Jean-Paul Sartre (Paris: François Maspéro, 1961).

———. *Peau Noire, Masques Blancs*, preface and postface by Francis Jeanson (Paris: Éditions du Seuil, 1952).

———. *Pour la Révolution africaine: Écrits politiques* (Paris: La Décuverte, 2001 [1964]).

———. *Toward The African Revolution: Political Essays*, translated by Haakon Chevalier (New York: Grove Press, new edition, 1988).

———. *The Wretched of the Earth*, translated by Constance Farrington, preface by Jean-Paul Sartre (New York: Grove Press, 1968).

Fatton, Robert, Jr. *Black Consciousness in South Africa: The Dialectics of Ideological Resistance to White Supremacy* (Albany: State University of New York Press, 1986).

Fischer, Georges. "Quelques aspects de la doctrine politique guinéenne," *Civilisations* 9, no. 4 (1959): 457–74.

Folson, Kweku G. "The Development of Socialist Ideology in Ghana," *Ghana Social Science Journal* 1, no. 2 (November 1971): 1–20.

———. "Ideology, Revolution and Development: The Years of Jerry John Rawlings in Ghana," in Okwudiba Nnoli, ed., *Government and Politics in Africa: A Reader* (Harare: AAPS Books, 2000), 124–50.

Foltz, William J. *From French West Africa to the Mali Federation* (New Haven, CT: Yale University Press, 1965).

Fortes, M., and E. E. Evans-Pritchard, eds. *African Political Systems* (London: Oxford University Press/International African Institute, 1940).

Founou-Tchigoua, Bernard, Sams Dine Sy, and Amady Aly Dieng, eds. *Critical Social Thought for the 21st Century: Essays in Honor of Samir Amin* (Paris: L'Harmattan, 2003).

Francis, David J. *Uniting Africa: Building Regional Peace and Security Systems* (Aldershot, UK: Ashgate, 2006).

Friedland, William H., and Carl G. Rosberg Jr., eds., *African Socialism* (Stanford, CA: Stanford University Press, 1964).

Fyle, C. Magbaily. *Introduction to the History of African Civilization*; vol. 1: *Pre-Colonial Africa* (Lanham, MD: University Press of America, 1999).

Gaddafi, Muammar, with Edmond Jouve. *My Vision* (London: John Blake Publishing, 2005).

Gakwandi, Arthus S. "Towards a New Political Map of Africa," in Tajudeen Abdul-Raheem, ed., *Pan-Africanism: Politics, Economy and Social Change in the Twenty-First Century* (New York: New York University Press, 1996), 181–90.

Garvey, Amy Jacques, ed. *Philosophy and Opinions of Marcus Garvey, or Africa for the Africans* (London: Frank Cass, 2nd edition, 1967).

Gassama, Makhily, ed. *50 Ans après: Quelle Indépendence pour l'Afrique?* (Paris: Éditions Philippe Rey, 2010).

Geisman, Peter. *Fanon: The Revolutionary as Prophet* (New York: Grove Press, 1971).

Gellar, Sheldon. *Democracy in Senegal: Tocquevillian Analytics in Africa* (New York: Palgrave Macmillan, 2005).

Gendzier, Irene L. *Frantz Fanon: A Critical Study* (New York: Vintage Books, 1974).

Gerhart, Gail M. *Black Power in South Africa: The Evolution of an Ideology* (Berkeley: University of California Press, 1978).

Gibson, Nigel C. *Fanon: The Postcolonial Imagination* (Cambridge, UK: Polity Press, 2003).

———. *Fanonian Practices in South Africa: From Steve Biko to Abahlali baseMjondolo* (New York: Palgrave Macmillan/University of KwaZulu-Natal Press, 2011).

Gordon, Lewis R. "Fanon and Development: A Philosophical Look," in Lansana Keita, ed., *Philosophy and African Development: Theory and Practice* (Dakar: CODESRIA, 2011), 69–86.

Grant, Colin. *Negro with a Hat: The Rise and Fall of Marcus Garvey* (New York: Oxford University Press, 2008).

Griaule, Marcel, and Germaine Dieterlen. *Le Renard Pâle*, vol. 1: *Le Mythe Cosmogonique* (Paris: Institut d'Ethnologie, 1965).

Grohs, George K. "Frantz Fanon and the African Revolution," *Journal of Modern African Studies* 6, no. 4 (December 1968): 543–56.

Gromyko, A., and R. Bezborodova, eds. *Idéologie de la Démocratie Révolutionnaire Africaine* (Moscou: Académie des Sciences de l'URSS, 1984).

Grundy, Kenneth W. "Mali: The Prospects of 'Planned Socialism,'" in William H. Friedland and Carl G. Rosberg, Jr., eds., *African Socialism* (Stanford, CA: Stanford University Press, 1964), 175–93.

———. "Marxism-Leninism and African Underdevelopment: The Mali Approach," *International Journal* 27, no. 3 (Summer 1962): 300–304.

———. "Nkrumah's Theory of Underdevelopment: An Analysis of Recurrent Themes," *World Politics* 15, no. 3 (April 1963): 438–54.

———. "Recent Contributions to the Study of African Political Thought," *World Politics* 18, no. 4 (July 1966): 674–89.

Guissé, Y. Mbargane. *Philosophie, Culture et Devenir Social en Afrique Noire* (Dakar: Les Nouvelles Éditions Africaines, 1979).

Gyekye, Kwame. *An Essay on African Philosophical Thought: The Akan Conceptual Scheme* (Philadelphia, PA: Temple University Press, 1995).

———. *Tradition and Modernity: Philosophical Reflections on the African Experience* (New York: Oxford University Press, 1997).

Hadjor, Kofi Buenor. *Nkrumah and Ghana: The Dilemma of Post-Colonial Power* (London: Kegan Paul International, 1988).

Halisi, C. R. D. *Black Political Thought in the Making of South African Democracy* (Bloomington: Indiana University Press, 1999).

Hallen, Barry. "African Meanings, Western Words," *African Studies Review* 40, no. 1 (April 1997): 1–11.

———. "African Philosophy in a New Key," *African Studies Review* 43, no. 3 (December 2000): 131–34.

Hansen, Emmanuel, ed. *Africa: Perspectives on Peace and Development* (London: Zed Books/The United Nations University, 1987).

———. "Frantz Fanon: Portrait of a Revolutionary Intellectual," *Transition* 46 (Fall 1974): 25–36.

———. *Frantz Fanon: Social and Political Thought* (Columbus: Ohio State University Press, 1977).

———. *Ghana under Rawlings: Early Years* (Lagos: Malthouse Press/AAPS, 1991).

Harris, Joseph E. *Africans and Their History* (New York: Meridian/Penguin Books, 2nd revised edition, 1998).

Harris, Kelly. "Still Relevant: Claude Ake's Challenge to Mainstream Discourse on African Politics and Development," *Journal of Third World Studies* 22, no. 2 (Fall 2005): 73–88.

Hazard, John N. "Marxism Socialism in Africa," *Comparative Politics* 2, no. 1 (October 1969): 1–15.

Hazoumé, Guy Landry. *Idéologies tribalistes et Nation en Afrique: Le Cas dahoméen* (Paris: Présence Africaine, 1972).

Henriksen, Thomas H. "The Revolutionary Thought of Eduardo Mondlane," *Geneva-Africa* 12, no. 1 (1973): 37–52.

Hill, Frances. *Ujamaa: Mobilization and Participation in Tanzania* (London: Frank Cass, 1978).

Hill, Robert A., ed. *Walter Rodney Speaks: The Making of an African Intellectual* (Trenton, NJ: Africa World Press, 1990).

Hodgkin, Thomas. *Nationalism in Colonial Africa* (New York: New York University Press, 1957).

Holas, B. Théophile. *La Pensée africaine: Textes choisis, 1949–1969* (Paris: Geuthner, 1972).

Hopkins, Nicholas S. *Popular Government in an African Town: Kita, Mali* (Chicago, IL: University of Chicago Press, 1972).

———. "Socialism and Social Change in Rural Mali," *Journal of Modern African Studies* 7, no. 3 (October 1969): 457–67.

Hoppe, Elizabeth, and Tracey Nicholls, eds. *Fanon and the Decolonization of Philosophy* (Lanham, MD: Lexington Books, 2010).

Houngnikpo, Mathurin C. *Africa's Elusive Quest for Development* (New York: Palgrave Macmillan, 2006).

———. *Des Mots pour les Maux de l'Afrique* (Paris: L'Harmattan, 2004).

Hountondji, Paulin J. *African Philosophy: Myth and Reality* (Bloomington: Indiana University Press, 2nd edition, 1996).

———. *The Struggle for Meaning: Reflections on Philosophy, Culture and Democracy in Africa*, foreword by K. A. Appiah, translated by John Conteh-Morgan (Athens: Ohio University Press, 2002).

Hugues, Arnold, ed. *Marxism's Retreat from Africa* (London: Frank Cass, 1992).

Ibawoh, Bonny, and J. I. Dibua. "Reconstructing Ujamaa: The Legacy of Julius Nyerere in the Quest for Social and Economic Development in Africa," *African Journal of Political Science* 8, no. 1 (2003): 59–83.

Idahosa, Paul L. E. *The Populist Dimension to African Political Thought: Critical Essays in Reconstruction and Retrieval* (Trenton, NJ: Africa World Press, 2004).

———. "A Tale of Three Images: Globalization, Marginalization, and the Sovereignty of the African Nation-State," in John Mukum Mbaku and Suresh C. Saxena, eds., *Africa at the Crossroads: Between Regionalism and Globalization* (Westport, CT: Praeger Publishers, 2004), 93–120.

Ihonvbere, Julius O., ed. *The Political Economy of Crisis and Underdevelopment in Africa: Selected Works of Claude Ake* (Lagos: JAD Publishers, 1989).

Irele, F. Abiola. *The African Experience in Literature and Ideology* (Bloomington: Indiana University Press, 1990).

———. *Négritude et condition africaine* (Paris: Éditions Karthala, 2008).

———. *The Négritude Moment: Explorations in Francophone African and Caribbean Literature and Thought* (Trenton, NJ: Africa World Press, 2010).

———. "Négritude or Black Cultural Nationalism," *Journal of Modern African Studies* 3, no. 3 (October 1965): 321–48.

Irele, F. Abiola and Biodun Jeyifo, eds. *The Oxford Encyclopedia of African Thought*, 2 vols. (New York: Oxford University Press, 2010).

Jackson, John G. *Introduction to African Civilizations* (New York: Citadel Press/ Kensington Publishing, 2001).

Jahn, Janheinz. *Muntu: An Outline of the New African Culture* (New York: Grove Press, 1961).

Jalata, Asafa. "*Gadaa* (Oromo Democracy): An Example of Classical African Civilization," *Journal of Pan African Studies* 5, no. 1 (March 2012): 126–52.

Jewsiewicki, Bogumil. *Marx, Afrique et Occident: Les pratiques africanistes de l'histoire marxiste* (Montreal: McGill University/Center for Developing Area Studies, 1985).

———, and David Newbury, eds. *African Historiographies: What History for Which Africa?* (London: Sage Publications, 1986).

Jinadu, L. Adele. "Claude Ake: An Appreciation," in Victor A. O. Adetula, ed., *Claude Ake and Democracy in Africa: A Tribute* (Jos: African Center for Democratic Governance, 1987), 22–27.

———. *Fanon: In Search of the African Revolution* (London: Kegan Paul International, 1986).

———. "Ideology, Political Religion and Modernization: Some Theoretical and Empirical Explorations," *African Studies Review* 19, no. 1 (April 1976): 119–37.

———. *Social Science and the Challenge of Peace and Development in Africa: The Contribution of Claude Ake* (Uppsala: Uppsala University/Nordiska Afrikainstitutet, 2004).

———. "Some African Theorists of Culture and Modernization: Fanon, Cabral and Some Others," *African Studies Review* 21, no. 1 (April 1978): 121–38.

———. "Some Aspects of the Social and Political Philosophy of Frantz Fanon," *Pan-African Journal* 5, no. 4 (December 1972): 493–522.

Johnson, R. W. "Sékou Touré: The Man and His Ideas," in Peter C. W. Gutkind and Peter Waterman, eds., *African Social Studies: A Radical Reader* (London: Heinemann, 1977), 329–42.

Jones, William I. "The Mise and Demise of Socialist Institutions in Rural Mali," *Geneva-Africa* 11, no. 2 (1972): 19–44.

———. *Planning and Economic Policy: Socialist Mali and Her Neighbors* (Washington, DC: Three Continents Press, 1976).

July, Robert W. *The Origins of Modern African Thought: Its Development in West Africa during the Nineteenth and Twentieth Centuries* (Trenton, NJ: Africa World Press, 2004 [1968]).

Kadhafi, Mouammar. *Dans le Concert des Nations; Libres propos and entretiens avec Edmond Jouve* (Paris: Éditions de l'Archipel, 2004).

Kaké, Ibrahima Baba. *Sékou Touré: Le héros et le tyran* (Paris: Jeune Afrique Livres, 1987).

Kamto, Maurice, Jean-E. Pondi, and Laurent Zang. *L'OUA: Rétrospective and Perspectives Africaines* (Paris: Economica, 1990).

Kanouté, Pierre. "Le Socialisme africain: Expression de l'Humanisme africain," *Afrique Nouvelle* (Dakar) (November 30–December 6, 1962).

Karp, Ivan, and D. A. Masolo, eds. *African Philosophy as Cultural Inquiry* (Bloomington: Indiana University Press, 2000).

Kaunda, Kenneth D. *Humanism in Africa and a Guide to Its Implementation* (Lusaka: Zambian Information Services, 1968).

———. *A Humanist in Africa* (London: Longman, 1966).

Kaunda, Kenneth D., *Zambia Shall Be Free: An Autobiography* (London: Heinemann Educational Books, 1962).

Kaushal, Indra. *Political Ideologies in Africa* (Delhi: Sunindu Publishers, 1972).

Kavwahirehi, Kasereka. *L'Afrique, entre passé et futur: L'Urgence d'un choix public de l'intelligence* (New York: P. I. E. Peter Lang, 2009).

Kebede, Messay. "African Development and the Primacy of Mental Decolonization," in Lansana Keita, ed., *Philosophy and African Development: Theory and Practice* (Dakar: CODESRIA, 2011), 97–114.

Keita, Lansana, ed. *Philosophy and African Development: Theory and Practice* (Dakar: CODESRIA, 2011).

———. "Philosophy and Development: On the Problematic African Development—A Diachronic Analysis," in Lansana Keita, ed., *Philosophy and African Development: Theory and Practice* (Dakar: CODESRIA, 2011), 115–38

Kéïta, Modibo. "The Foreign Policy of Mali," *International Affairs* 37, no. 4 (October 1961): 436–37.

———. *Modibo Kéïta: A Collection of Speeches (22 September 1960–27 August 1964)* (Bamako: n.p., 1965).

Keller, Edmond J., and Donald Rothchild, eds. *Afro-Marxist Regimes: Ideology and Public Policy* (Boulder, CO: Lynne Rienner Publishers, 1987).

Keto, C. Tsehloane. *Revision of the African-Centered Perspective of History and Social Science in the Twenty-First Century* (Blackwood, NJ: K. A. Publishers, 1989).

Khaldûn, Ibn. *The Muqaddimah: An Introduction to History*, edited by N. J. Dawood, translated and introduction by Franz Rosenthal (Princeton, NJ: Princeton University Press/Bollingen Series, 2005 [1967]).

Kiros, Teodros, ed. *Explorations in African Political Thought: Identity, Community, Ethics*, preface by Anthony Appiah (New York: Routledge, 2001).

Kissangou, Ignace. *Une Afrique, un Espoir* (Paris: L'Harmattan, 1996).

Ki-Zerbo, Joseph. "African Intellectuals, Nationalism and Pan-Africanism: A Testimony," in Thandika Mkandawire, ed., *African Intellectuals: Rethinking Politics, Language, Gender and Development* (London: Zed Books/CODESRIA, 2005), 78–93.

———. *La natte des autres: Pour un développement endogène en Afrique* (Paris: Karthala, 1993).

———. *A Quand L'Afrique? Entretiens avec René Holenstein* (Paris: Éditions de l'aube/Éditions d'en bas, 2003).

———. *Un jour l'Afrique* (Paris: Éditions de l'aube, 2003).

Klay Kieh, George, Jr. "Reconstituting the Neo-Colonial State in Africa," *Journal of Third World Studies* 26, no. 1 (Spring 2009): 41–55.

Kodjo, Edem. *Et Demain l'Afrique* (Paris: Éditions Stock, 1985).

Kosukhin, Nikolai. *Revolutionary Democracy in Africa: Its Ideology and Policy* (Moscow: Progress Publishers, 1985).

Kounou, Michel. *Le Panafricanisme: De la Crise à la Renaissance* (Yaoundé: Éditions CLE, 2007).

Kuupole, D. D., and N. Y. M. Botchway De-Valera, eds. *Polishing the Pearls of Ancient Wisdom: Exploring the Relevance of Endogenous African Knowledge Systems for Sustainable Development in Postcolonial Africa: A Reader* (Accra: Center for Indigenous Knowledge and Organizational Development, n.d.).

Lacoste, Yves. *Ibn Khaldoun: Naissance de l'Histoire, Passé du Tiers Monde* (Paris: François Maspéro, 5th edition, 1980).

Langley, Ayodele J. *Ideologies of Liberation in Black Africa: Documents on Modern African Political Thought from Colonial Times to the Present* (London: Rex Collings, 1979).

———. *Pan-Africanism and Nationalism in West Africa, 1900–1945: A Study in Ideology and Social Classes* (London: Oxford University Press, 1973).

Lara, Oruno D. *La Naissance du Panafricanisme: Les raciness caraïbes, américaines et africaines du mouvement au XIXe siècle* (Paris: Maisonneuve and Larose, 2000).

Legesse, Asmarom. *Oromo Democracy: An Indigenous African Political System* (Lawrenceville, NJ: Red Sea Press, 2000).

Legum, Colin. *Pan-Africanism: A Short Political Guide* (London: Pall Mall Press, 1962).

———. "Socialism in Ghana: A Political Interpretation," in William H. Friedland and Carl G. Rosberg Jr., eds., *African Socialism* (Stanford, CA: Stanford University Press, 1964), 131–59.

———, and Geoffrey Mmari, eds. *Mwalimu: The Influence of Nyerere* (London: James Currey/Africa World Press, 1995).

Lemarchand, René, ed. *The Green and the Black: Qadhafi's Policies in Africa* (Bloomington: Indiana University Press, 1988).

Levtzion, Nehemia. *Ancient Ghana and Mali* (New York: Africana Publishing, 1980).

———, and Randall L. Pouwels, eds. *The History of Islam in Africa* (Athens, Oxford, and Cape Town: Ohio University Press/James Currey/David Philip, 2000).

Lewin, André. *Ahmed Sékou Touré, Président de la Guinée, 1922–1984* (Paris: L'Harmattan, 2009)

Lewis, Rupert Charles. *Marcus Garvey: Anti-Colonial Champion* (Trenton, NJ: Africa World Press, 1988).

———. *Walter Rodney's Intellectual and Political Thought* (Detroit, MA: Wayne State University Press, 1998).

Liniger-Goumaz, Max. *La Démocrature: Dictature camouflée, Démocratie truquée* (Paris: L'Harmattan, 1992).

———. *L'Eurafrique: Utopie ou Réalité?* (Yaoundé: Editions CLE, 1972).

Lofchie, Michael F. "Political Theory and African Politics," *Journal of Modern African Studies* 6, no. 1 (1968): 3–15.

Lumumba-Kasongo, Tukumbi, ed. *Liberal Democracy and Its Critics in Africa: Political Dysfunctions and the Struggle for Social Progress* (London: CODESRIA/Zed Books, 2005).

———. *Nationalistic Ideologies, Their Policy Implications and the Struggle for Democracy in African Politics* (Lewiston, NY: Edwin Mellen Press, 1991).

———. *Political Re-Mapping of Africa* (Lanham, MD: University Press of America, 1993).

Macey, David. *Frantz Fanon: A Biography* (New York: Picador USA/St. Martin's Press, 2000).

Machel, Samora. *Le Processus de la Révolution Démocratique Populaire au Mozambique: Textes du Président du FRELIMO, 1970–1974* (Paris: L'Harmattan, 1977).

———. *Mozambique: Sowing the Seeds of Revolution* (London: CEMAG, 1974).

———. "The People's Republic of Mozambique: The Struggle Continues," *Review of African Political Economy* 4 (November 1975): 14–25.

MacPherson, Fergus. *Kenneth Kaunda of Zambia: The Times and the Man* (New York: Oxford University Press, 1974).

Mafeje, Archie B. M. "Africanity: A Combative Ontology," *CODESRIA Bulletin*, no. 1 (2000): 66–71.

Mafeje, Archie B.M. *In Search of An Alternative: A Collection of Essays on Revolutionary Theory and Politics* (Harare: SAPES Books, 1992).

Magubane, Bernard. "Amilcar Cabral: Evolution of Revolutionary Thought," *Ufahamu* 2, no. 2 (1971): 71–87.

Makgoba, Malegapuru William, ed. *African Renaissance: The New Struggle* (Sandton: Mafube/Tafelberg, 1999).

Maloka, E., ed. *A United States of Africa?* (Pretoria: Africa Institute of South Africa Press, 2001).

Mamdani, Mahmood. "Africa: Democratic Theory and Democratic Struggles," *Economic and Political Weekly* 27 (1992): 2228–32.

———. *Citizen and Subject: Contemporary Africa and the Legacy of Late Colonialism* (London: Princeton University Press/James Currey, 1996).

———. "A Critique of the State and Civil Society Paradigm in Africanist Studies," in Mahmood Mamdani and Ernest Wamba-dia-Wamba, eds., *African Studies in Social Movements and Democracy* (Dakar: CODESRIA Book Series, 1995), 602–16.

———, and Ernest Wamba-dia-Wamba, eds. *African Studies in Social Movements and Democracy* (Dakar: CODESRIA Book Series, 1995).

Markovitz, Irving Leonard. *Léopold Sédar Senghor and the Politics of Négritude* (New York: Atheneum, 1969).

Martin, Guy. "Actualité de Fanon: Convergences dans la Pensée Politique de Frantz Fanon et de Thomas Sankara," *Geneva-Africa* 25, no. 2 (1987): 103–22.

———. "Africa and the Ideology of Eurafrica: Neo-Colonialism or Pan-Africanism?," *Journal of Modern African Studies* 20, no. 2 (1982): 221–38.

———. *Africa in World Politics: A Pan-African Perspective* (Trenton, NJ: Africa World Press, 2002).

———. "Claude Ake: A Tribute," in Victor A. O. Adetula, ed., *Claude Ake and Democracy in Africa: A Tribute* (Jos: African Center for Democratic Governance, 1997), 39–40.

———. "Fanon on Violence and the Revolutionary Process in Africa," *African Insight*, no. 2 (1974): 14–19.

———. "Fanon's Continuing Relevance: A Comparative Study of the Political Thought of Frantz Fanon and Thomas Sankara," *Journal of Asian and African Affairs* 5, no. 1 (Fall 1993): 65–85.

———. "Fanon's Relevance to Contemporary African Political Thought," *Ufahamu* 4, no. 3 (Winter 1974): 11–34.

———. "Francophone Africa in the Context of Franco-African Relations," in John W. Harbeson and Donald Rothchild, eds., *Africa in World Politics: Post-Cold War Challenges* (Boulder, CO: Westview Press, 2nd edition, 1995), 163–88.

———. "Idéologie et Praxis dans la Révolution Populaire du 4 août 1983 au Burkina Faso," *Geneva-Africa* 24, no. 1 (1980): 35–62.

———. *Ideology and Politics in West Africa: A Comparative Study of Ghana and Guinea (1957–1966)*, MA thesis, University of London/School of Oriental and African Studies, 1970.

———. "Ideology and Praxis in Thomas Sankara's Populist Revolution of August 1983 in Burkina Faso," *Issue: A Journal of Opinion* 15 (1987): 77–90.

———. "L'Afrique et l'idéologie de l'Eurafrique: Néo-colonialisme ou Panafricanisme?," *Africa Development* 7, no. 3 (July 1982): 5–21.

———. "Reflections on Democracy and Development in Africa: The Intellectual Legacy of Claude Ake," *Ufahamu* 26, no. 1 (Winter 1998): 102–9.

Martin, Guy. Review of Paul L. E. Idahosa's *The Populist Dimension to African Political Thought*, in *African Studies Review* 48, no. 1 (April 2005): 226–29.

———. Reviews of K. Kavwahirehi's *L'Afrique, entre Passé et Futur* and Ousmane Sy's *Reconstruire l'Afrique*, in *Africa Today* 58, no. 3 (Spring 2012): 94–98.

———. "Revisiting Fanon, from Theory to Practice: Democracy and Development in Africa," *Journal of Pan-African Studies* 4, no. 7 (November 2011): 24–38.

———. "Revolutionary Democracy, Socio-Political Conflict and Militarization in Burkina Faso, 1983–1988," in Peter Meyns and Dani W. Nabudere, eds., *Democracy and the One-Party State in Africa* (Hamburg: Institut für Afrika-Kunde, 1989), 57–77.

———. "Socialism, Economic Development and Planning in Mali, 1960–1968," *Canadian Journal of African Studies* 10, no. 1 (1976): 23–46.

Martin, Tony. *Race First: The Ideological and Organizational Struggles of Marcus Garvey and the Universal Negro Improvement Association* (Westport, CT: Greenwood Press, 1976).

———. "Rescuing Fanon from the Critics," *African Studies Review* 13, no. 3 (December 1970): 381–99.

Masolo, D. A. *African Philosophy in Search of Identity* (Bloomington: Indiana University Press/Edinburgh University Press, 1994).

———. "Western and African Communitarianism: A Comparison," in Kwasi Waredu, ed., *A Companion to African Philosophy* (Oxford, UK: Blackwell Publishing, 2004), 483–98.

Mazama, Ama, ed. *Africa in the 21st Century: Toward A New Future* (New York: Routledge, 2007).

Mazrui, Ali A. *Towards a Pax Africana: A Study of Ideology and Ambition* (Chicago, IL: University of Chicago Press, 1967).

———, and George Engholm. "Rousseau and Intellectualized Populism in Africa," *Review of Politics* 30, no. 1 (January 1968): 19–32.

Mbaku, John Mukum, and Suresh C. Saxena, eds. *Africa at the Crossroads: Between Regionalism and Globalization* (Westport, CT: Praeger Publishers, 2004).

Mbaye, Sanou. *L'Afrique au Secours de l'Afrique* (Paris: Les Éditions de l'Atelier/Éditions Ouvrières, 2009).

Mbembe, Achille. *De la Postcolonie: Essai sur l'imagination politique dans l'Afrique contemporaine* (Paris: Éditions Karthala, 2000).

———. *On the Postcolony* (Berkeley: University of California Press, 2001).

Mbiti, John S. *African Religions and Philosophy* (London: Heinemann Educational Publishers, 2nd edition, 1989 [1969]).

M'Bokolo, Élikia. *Afrique Noire: Histoire et Civilisations*, vol. 1: *Jusqu'au XVIIIe siècle* (Paris: Hatier/AUPELF, 1995).

———. *Afrique Noire: Histoire et Civilisations*, vol. 2: *Du XIXe siècle à nos jours* (Paris: Hatier/AUF, 2nd edition, 2004).

Mbom, Clément. *Frantz Fanon, aujourd'hui et demain: Réflexions sur le tiers monde* (Paris: Éditions Fernand Nathan, 1985).

Mboya, Tom. "African Socialism," in William H. Friedland and Carl G. Rosberg Jr., eds., *African Socialism* (Stanford, CA: Stanford University Press, 1964), 250–58.

———. *Freedom and After* (London: Andre Deutsch, 1963).

M'Buyinga, E. *Pan-Africanism or Neo-Colonialism? The Bankruptcy of the OAU* (London: Zed Books, 1982).

McCain, James A. "Ideology in Africa: Some Perceptual Types," *African Studies Review* 18, no. 1 (April 1975): 61–87.

McCollester, Charles. "The Political Thought of Amilcar Cabral," *Monthly Review* 24, no. 10 (March 1973): 10–21.

McCulloch, Jock. *In The Twilight of Revolution: The Political Theory of Amilcar Cabral* (London: Routledge and Kegan Paul, 1983).

McHenry, Dean E., Jr. "The Struggle for Rural Socialism in Tanzania," in Carl G. Rosberg and Thomas M. Callaghy, eds., *Socialism in Sub-Saharan Africa: A New Assessment* (Berkeley: Institute of International Studies/University of California, 1979), 37–60.

Meebelo, Henry S. *Main Currents of Zambian Humanist Thought* (Lusaka: Oxford University Press, 1973).

Memmi, Albert. *The Colonizer and the Colonized* (Boston, MA: Beacon Press, expanded edition, 1991).

———. *Portrait du Colonisé, précédé du Portrait du Colonisateur* (Paris: Jean-Jacques Pauvert, 1966).

Mendes, João. *La Rèvolution en Afrique: Problèmes and Perspectives* (n.p., 1971).

Mengisteab, Kidane. *Globalization and Autocentricity in Africa's Development in the 21st Century* (Trenton, NJ: Africa World Press, 1996).

Mennasemay, Maimire. "Political Theory, Political Science and African Development," *Canadian Journal of African Studies* 16, no. 2 (1982): 223–44.

Merle, Marcel. *Ahmed Ben Bella* (New York: Walker, 1967).

Metz, S. "In Lieu of Orthodoxy: The Socialist Theories of Nkrumah and Nyerere," *Journal of Modern African Studies* 20, no. 3 (1982): 377–92.

Mfoulou, Jean. *L'OUA, Triomphe de l'Unité ou des Nationalités? Essai d'une Sociologie politique de l'OUA* (Paris: L'Harmattan, 1986).

Milon, René. *Marxisme, Communisme et Socialisme africain* (Paris: Imprimerie Édimpra, 1961).

Mkandawire, Thandika, ed. *African Intellectuals: Rethinking Politics, Language, Gender and Development* (London: Zed Books/CODESRIA, 2005).

———. "African Intellectuals and Nationalism," in T. Mkandawire, ed., *African Intellectuals: Rethinking Politics, Language, Gender and Development* (London: Zed Books/CODESRIA, 2005), 10–55.

———. "Thinking about Developmental States in Africa," *Cambridge Journal of Economics* 25, no. 3 (2001): 289–314.

Mohan, Jitendra. "Varieties of African Socialism," in R. Milliband and J. Saville, eds., *The Socialist Register* (London, 1966), 220–66.

Mohiddin, Ahmed. "The Basic Unit of African Ideal Society in Nyerere's Thought," *Africa* (Milan) 26, no. 1 (March 1976): 3–24.

———. "Ujamaa: A Commentary on President Nyerere's Vision of Tanzanian Society," *African Affairs* 57, no. 267 (April 1968): 130–43.

Mondlane, Eduardo. *The Struggle for Mozambique* (Baltimore, MD: Penguin Books, 1969).

Monteil, Vincent. *L'Islam Noir* (Paris: Éditions du Seuil, 1964).

More, Mabogo P. "Albert Luthuli, Steve Biko and Nelson Mandela: The Philosophical Basis of Their Thought and Practice," in Kwasi Wiredu, ed., *A Companion to African Philosophy* (Oxford, UK: Blackwell Publishing, 2004), 207–15.

Mudimbe, V. Y. *The Invention of Africa: Gnosis, Philosophy and the Order of Knowledge* (London: Indiana University Press/James Currey, 1988).

Muiu, Mueni wa. "Africa in 2108: A Strategic Plan," *African Journal of International Affairs* 11, no. 2 (2008): 1–28.

Muiu, Mueni wa. "'Civilization on Trial: The Colonial and Postcolonial State in Africa," *Journal of Third World Studies* 25, no. 1 (Spring 2008): 73–109.

———. "Colonial and Postcolonial State and Development in Africa," *Social Research: An International Quarterly* 77, no. 4 (Winter 2010): 1211–1338.

———. "*Fundi wa Afrika*: Toward a New Paradigm of the African State," *Journal of Third World Studies* 19, no. 2 (Fall 2002): 23–42.

———. Review of C. R. D. Halisi's "Black Political Thought in the Making of South African Democracy," in *Africa Today* 47, nos. 3–4 (Summer/Autumn 2001), 187–91.

———, and Guy Martin. "Fundi wa Afrika: Towards an Authentic African Renaissance," *Black Renaissance/Renaissance Noire* 4, no. 1 (Spring 2002): 83–96.

———, and Guy Martin. *A New Paradigm of the African State: Fundi wa Afrika* (New York: Palgrave Macmillan, 2009).

———, and Guy Martin. "Repenser l'État, la Démocratie et le Développement en Afrique: *Fundi wa Afrika*," in Jean-Emmanuel Pondi, ed., *Repenser le Développement à partir de l'Afrique* (Yaoundé: Afrédit/Africaine d'Édition, 2011), 125–41.

Mukandabantu, Angel Mwada. "The Political Thought of Amilcar Cabral: A Review Article," *Review of African Political Economy*, nos. 27–28 (1983): 207–13.

Mungazi, Dickson A. *The Mind of Black Africa* (Westport, CT: Praeger Publishers, 1996).

Munslow, Barry, ed. *Samora Machel: An African Revolutionary* (London: Zed Books, 1985).

Murithi, Timothy. *The African Union: Pan-Africanism, Peacebuilding and Development* (Aldershot, UK: Ashgate, 2005).

Mushkat, Marion. "African Socialism Reappraised and Reconsidered," *Africa* (Rome) 27, no. 2 (June 1972): 151–78.

Mutiso, Gideon C. M., and S. W. Rohio, eds. *Readings in African Political Thought* (London: Heinemann, 1975).

Mutua, Makau wa. "Why Redraw the Map of Africa: A Moral and Legal Inquiry," *Michigan Journal of International Law* 16 (Summer 1995): 1113–76.

Mvelle, Guy. *L'Union Africaine: Fondements, organes, programmes and actions* (Paris: L'Harmattan, 2007).

———. "Union africaine et Fédéralisme: Remarques sur la problématique d'un gouvernement continental africain," *Cameroonian Review of International Studies* 2 (1st Semester 2009): 241–59.

Mwakikagile, Godfrey. *The Modern African State: Quest for Transformation* (Huntington, NY: Nova Science Publishers, 2001).

Mwansasu, Bismarck U., and Cranford Pratt, eds. *Towards Socialism in Tanzania* (Toronto: University of Toronto Press, 1979).

Mwase, Ngila. "African Goals and Ideologies: 'African Socialism' Revisited," *PULA: Botswana Journal of African Studies* 5, no. 1 (May 1985): 54–76.

Na'Allah, Abdul-Rasheed. "Literature, Culture, and Thought in Africa: A Conversation with Abiola Irele," *West Africa Review*, no. 7 (2005).

Nabudere, Dani Wadada. *The United States of Africa: Challenges and Prospects* (Pretoria: Africa Institute of South Africa, 2010).

Ndaw, Alassane. *La Pensée Africaine: Recherches sur les fondements de la pensée négro-africaine* (Dakar: Les Nouvelles Éditions Africaines, 1983).

Ndiaye, Guédel. *L'Échec de la Fédération du Mali* (Dakar: Les Nouvelles Éditions Africaines, 1980).

Nellis, John R. *A Theory of Ideology: The Tanzanian Case* (London: Oxford University Press, 1972).

Ngandu Nkashama, Pius. *La Pensée politique des mouvements religieux en Afrique: Le cas du Congo-Kinshasa* (Paris: L'Harmattan, 1998).

Ngodi, Etanislas. "Intellectuels, panafricanisme et démocratie en Afrique: Bilan and persectives," in Alexis B. A. Adandé, ed., *Intégration Régionale, Démocratie and Panafricanisme* (Dakar: CODESRIA, 2007), 55–78.

Ngoma-Binda, P. *Philosophie et pouvoir politique en Afrique: La théorie inflectionnelle* (Paris: L'Harmattan, 2004).

Niane, Djibril Tamsir. *Soundjata ou L'Épopée Mandingue* (Paris: Présence Africaine, 3rd edition, 1960).

———. *Sundiata: An Epic of Old Mali*, translated by G. D. Pickett (Harlow, Essex: Longman, 1965).

Nicolas, Guy. *Dynamique de l'Islam au Sud du Sahara* (Paris: Publications Orientalistes de France, 1981).

Nkrumah, Kwame. *Africa Must Unite* (New York: International Publishers, new edition, 1970)

———. *The Autobiography of Kwame Nkrumah* (London: Thomas Nelson and Sons, 1959).

———. *Consciencism: Philosophy and Ideology for De-Colonization* (New York: Monthly Review Press, revised edition, 1970).

———. *Handbook of Revolutionary Warfare* (London: Panaf Books, 1968).

———. "African Socialism Revisited," *African Forum* (Winter 1966): 200–208.

———. *Neo-Colonialism: The Last Stage of Imperialism* (London: Heinemann, 1965).

———. *Revolutionary Path* (New York: International Publishers, 1973).

———. *Towards Colonial Freedom* (London: Heinemann, 1962).

———, and *The Spark* editors. *Some Essential Features of Nkrumaism* (New York: International Publishers, 1965).

Nwala, T. U. *Igbo Philosophy* (Lagos: Literamed Publications, 1985).

Nyang, Sulayman S. "The Political Thought of Amilcar Cabral: A Synthesis," *Odu: Journal of Yoruba and Related Studies* 13 (January 1976): 3–20.

Nyerere, Julius K. *Freedom and Development; Uhuru na Maendeleo: A Selection from Writings and Speeches, 1968–1973* (London: Oxford University Press, 1973).

———. *Freedom and Socialism; Uhuru na Ujamaa: A Selection from Writings and Speeches, 1965–1967* (London: Oxford University Press, 1968).

———. *Man and Development: Binadamu na Maendeleo* (London: Oxford University Press, 1974).

———. *Nyerere on Socialism* (Dar es Salaam: Oxford University Press, 1969).

———. *Ujamaa: Essays on Socialism* (London: Oxford University Press, 1968).

———. "Ujamaa: The Basis of African Socialism," in Okwudiba Nnoli, ed., *Government and Politics in Africa: A Reader* (Harare: AAPS Books, 2000), 151–58.

Nzongola-Ntalaja, Georges. "Amilcar Cabral et la Théorie de la Lutte de Libération nationale," in *Pour Cabral: Symposium International Amilcar Cabral*, Praia, Cape Verde, January 17–20, 1983 (Paris: Présence Africaine, 1987), 132–41.

———. "Pour une alternative africaine à la pensée unique," in Bernard Founou-Tchigoua, Sams Dine Sy, and Amady A. Dieng, eds., *Pensée sociale critique pour le XXIe Siècle: Mélanges en l'honneur de Samir Amin* (Paris: L'Harmattan, 2003), 445–59.

———. "Amilcar Cabral and the Theory of the National Liberation Struggle, in G. Nzongola-Ntalaja, *Revolution and Counter-Revolution in Africa: Essays in*

Contemporary Politics (London: Zed Books/Institute for African Alternatives, 1987), 31–41.

————. *Revolution and Counter-Revolution in Africa: Essays in Contemporary Politics* (London: Zed Books/Institute for African Alternatives, 1987).

Obenga, Théophile. *African Philosophy: The Pharaonic Period, 2780–330 B.C.* (Popenguine, Senegal: Per Ankh, 2004).

————. *Cheikh Anta Diop, Volney et le Sphinx: Contribution de Cheikh Anta Diop à l'Historiographie mondiale* (Paris: Présence Africaine/Khepera, 1996).

Oculi, Okello. "Ake, the Critical Theorist," in Victor A. O. Adetula, ed., *Claude Ake and Democracy in Africa: A Tribute* (Jos: African Center for Democratic Governance, 1997), 28–30.

————. *Discourses on African Affairs: Directions and Destinies for the 21st Century*, preface by Ngugi wa Thiong'o (Trenton, NJ: Africa World Press, 2000).

Odimegwu, Ike F. H. "African Personality and Nationalism in Nkrumah's Philosophy of Liberation," *UCHE: Journal of the Department of Philosophy* (University of Nigeria, Nsukka) 14 (December 2008): 91–103.

————, ed. *Perspectives on African Communalism* (Victoria, BC: Trafford Publishing, 2007).

Odinga, Oginga. *Not Yet Uhuru: The Autobiography of Oginga Odinga* (New York: Hill and Wang, 1967).

Ofuatey-Kodjoe, W. *Pan-Africanism: New Directions in Strategy* (Lanham, MD: University Press of America, 1986).

Oghale Agbele, Emma. *Selected Themes in African Political Thought* (Lagos: Eregha, 1998).

Okolo, M. S. C. *African Literature as Political Philosophy* (Dakar: CODESRIA, 2007).

Okumu, Washington A. J. *The African Renaissance: History, Significance and Strategy* (Trenton, NJ: Africa World Press, 2002).

Oladipo, Olusegun. *The Idea of African Philosophy* (Ibadan: Hope Publications, 1998).

Oliver, Roland, ed. *The Middle Age of African History* (New York: Oxford University Press, 1967).

Oluoch Imbo, Samuel. *An Introduction to African Philosophy* (Lanham, MD: Rowman and Littlefield, 1998).

Onuoba, Bede. *The Elements of African Socialism* (London: Andre Deutsch, 1965).

Onyewuenyi, Innocent C. *The African Origin of Greek Philosophy: An Exercise in Afrocentrism* (Charleston, SC: BookSurge Publishing, 2005).

Osabu-Kle, Daniel T. *Compatible Cultural Democracy: The Key to Development in Africa* (Peterborough, Ontario: Broadview Press, 2000).

Osha, Sanya. *Kwasi Wiredu and Beyond: The Text, Writing and Thought in Africa* (Dakar: CODESRIA, 2005).

Ottaway, Marina and David. *Afrocommunism* (New York: Africana Publishing, 2nd edition, 1986).

Owomoyela, Oyekan. *The African Difference: Discourses on Africanity and the Relativity of Cultures* (New York: Peter Lang/Witswatersrand University Press, 1996).

Owusu, Maxwell. "Democracy and Africa—A View from the Village," *Journal of Modern African Studies* 30, no. 3 (September 1992): 369–96.

————. "Evolution in the Revolution: Nkrumah, Ghana and African Socialism," *Africa Today* 26, no. 2 (1979): 71–76.

————. *Uses and Abuses of Political Power: A Case Study of Continuity and Change in the Politics of Ghana* (Chicago, IL: University of Chicago Press, 1970).

Padmore, George. "A Guide to Pan-African Socialism," in William H. Friedland and Carl G. Rosberg Jr., eds., *African Socialism* (Stanford, CA: Stanford University Press, 1964), 223–37.

———. *Pan-Africanism or Communism?* (New York: Anchor Books/Doubleday, 1972).

Pajot, Florian. *Joseph Ki-Zerbo: Itinéraire d'un intellectuel africain au XXème siècle* (Paris: L'Harmattan, 2007).

Palmberg, Mai, ed. *Problems of Socialist Orientation in Africa* (Uppsala: Scandinavian Institute of African Studies, 1978).

Perinbam, B. Marie. *Holy Violence: The Revolutionary Thought of Frantz Fanon* (Washington, DC: Three Continents Press, 1982).

Person, Yves. "Le Socialisme en Afrique noire et les Socialismes africains," *Revue française d'études politiques africaines* 27 (July 1976): 15–68.

Pityana, Barney N., Mamphela Ramphele, Malusi Mpumlwana, and Lindy Wilson, eds. *Bounds of Possibility: The Legacy of Steve Biko and Black Consciousness* (London & Cape Town: Zed Books/David Philip, 1991).

Poe, D. Zizwe. *Kwame Nkrumah's Contribution to Pan-Africanism: An Afrocentric Analysis* (New York: Routledge, 2003).

Pondi, Jean-Emmanuel, ed. "Qadhafi and the Organization of African Unity," in René Lemarchand, ed., *The Green and the Black: Qadhafi's Policies in Africa* (Bloomington: Indiana University Press, 1988), 139–49.

———. *Repenser le Développement à partir de l'Afrique* (Yaoundé: Afrédit/Africaine d'Édition, 2011).

Prah, Kwesi K. *Beyond the Colour Line: Pan-Africanist Disputations* (Florida Hills: Vivlia Publishers, 1997).

———. "Culture: The Missing Link in Development Planning in Africa," in Lansana Keita, ed., *Philosophy and African Development: Theory and Practice* (Dakar: CODESRIA, 2011), 155–68.

Pratt, Cranford. "The Political Thought of Julius Nyerere," *Tanzanian Affairs* 22 (October 1, 1985).

Rabemananjara, Jacques. *Nationalisme et Problèmes Malgaches* (Paris: Présence Africaine, 1958).

Ray, Donald I. *Ghana: Politics, Economics and Society* (London & Boulder, CO: Franes Pinter Publishers/Lynne Rienner Publishers, 1986).

Richardson, Max W. *The Myths and Realities of African Socialism*, MA thesis, Texas Technological College, 1968.

Rivière, Claude. *Guinea: The Mobilization of a People* (Ithaca, NY: Cornell University Press, 1977).

Robinson, David. *Muslim Societies in African History* (Cambridge, UK: Cambridge University Press, 2004).

Rodney, Walter. *The Groundings with My Brothers* (London: Bogle-L'Ouverture Publications, 1969).

———. *How Europe Underdeveloped Africa* (Washington, DC: Howard University Press, 1982).

———. "Tanzanian Ujamaa and Scientific Socialism," *African Review* 1, no. 4 (April 1972): 61–76.

———. *Walter Rodney Speaks: The Making of an African Intellectual*, introduction by Robert Hill, foreword by Howard Dodson (Trenton, NJ: Africa World Press, 1990).

Rooney, David. *Kwame Nkrumah: The Political Kingdom in the Third World* (New York: St. Martin's Press, 1989).

Ropivia, Marc-Louis. *Géopolitique de l'Intégration en Afrique noire* (Paris: L'Harmattan, 1994).

Rosberg, Carl G., and Thomas M. Callaghy, eds., *Socialism in Sub-Saharan Africa: A New Assessment* (Berkeley: Institute of International Studies/University of California, 1979).

Rudebeck, Lars. *Guinea-Bissau: A Study of Political Mobilization* (Uppsala: Scandinavian Institute of African Studies, 1974).

———. "Socialist-Oriented Development in Guinea-Bissau," in Carl G. Rosberg and Thomas M. Callaghy, eds., *Socialism in Sub-Saharan Africa: A New Assessment* (Berkeley: Institute of International Studies/University of California, 1979), 322–44.

Sago, Julius. "The Ideological Battle in Africa," *The Spark* 19 (April 1963).

Sané, P. A. "Réflexions sur le socialisme africain," *Revue Libanaise de Sciences Politiques* 1 (January–June 1970): 75–94.

Sankara, Thomas. *Oser Inventer L'Avenir: La Parole de Sankara, 1983–1987* (New York. Pathfinder/L'Harmattan, 1991).

———. *Thomas Sankara Speaks: The Burkina Faso Revolution, 1983–87* (New York: Pathfinder, 1988).

Santos, Eduardo dos. *Ideologias politicas africanas* (Lisbon: Centro de estudos politico-sociais, 1968).

Saul, John S. "African Socialism in One Country: Tanzania," in G. Arrighi and J. S. Saul, eds., *Essays on the Political Economy of Africa* (New York: Monthly Review Press, 1973), 237–335.

———. "FRELIMO and the Mozambique Revolution," in G. Arrighi and J. S. Saul, eds., *Essays on the Political Economy of Africa* (New York: Monthly Review Press, 1973), 378–405.

———. "On African Populism," in G. Arrighi and J. S. Saul, eds., *Essays on The Political Economy of Africa* (New York: Monthly Review Press, 1973), 152–79.

Sayah, Jamil. *Philosophie politique de l'Islam: L'Idée de l'État, de Ibn Khaldoun à Aujourd'hui* (Paris: L'Atelier de l'Archer, 2000).

Seidman, Ann, and Frederick Aanang, eds. *Twenty-First Century Africa: Towards a New Vision of Self-Sustainable Development* (Trenton, NJ: Africa World Press/African Studies Association Press, 1992).

Sekyi-Otu, Ato. *Fanon's Dialectic of Experience* (Cambridge, MA: Harvard University Press, 1996).

Senghor, Léopold Sédar. *La Poésie de l'Action*, conversations with Mohamed Aziza (Paris: Éditions Stock, 1980).

———. *Liberté I: Négritude et Humanisme* (Paris: Éditions du Seuil, 1964).

———. *Liberté II: Nation et Voie Africaine du Socialisme* (Paris: Éditions du Seuil, 1971).

———. *On African Socialism* (New York: Frederick A. Praeger, 1964).

Serequeberhan, Tsenay. "Theory and the Actuality of Existence: Fanon and Cabral," in Kwasi Wiredu, ed., *A Companion to African Philosophy* (Oxford, UK: Blackwell Publishing, 2004), 225–30.

Shinnie, Margaret. *Ancient African Kingdoms* (London: Edward Arnold, 1965).

Sigmund, Paul E., Jr., ed. *The Ideologies of the Developing Nations* (New York: Frederick A. Praeger, 1963).

Sindjoun, Luc. *L'État Ailleurs: Entre noyau dur et case vide* (Paris: Economica, 2002).

———. *Science politique réflexive et Savoirs sur les pratiques politiques en Afrique noire* (Dakar: CODESRIA, 1999).

Sisoko, Fa-Digi. *The Epic of Son-Jara*, notes, translation, and introduction by John William Johnson (Bloomington: Indiana University Press, 1992).

Sithole, Ndabaningi. *African Nationalism* (London: Oxford University Press, 2nd edition, 1968).

Skinner, Elliott P. *The Mossi of the Upper Volta: The Political Development of a Sudanese People* (Stanford, CA: Stanford University Press, 1964).

———, ed. *Peoples and Cultures of Africa: An Anthropological Reader* (Garden City, NY: Doubleday/Natural History Press, 1973).

Skurnik, W. A. E., ed. *African Political Thought: Lumumba, Nkrumah and Touré* (Denver, CO: University of Denver/Graduate School of International Studies, 1968).

———. "Léopold Sédar Senghor and African Socialism," *Journal of Modern African Studies* 3, no. 3 (October 1965): 349–69.

Smith, Stephen. *Négrologie: Pourquoi l'Afrique meurt* (Paris: Hachette/Calmann-Lévy, 2003).

Snyder, Frank G. *One-Party Government in Mali: Transition toward Control* (New Haven, CT: Yale University Press, 1965).

———. "The Political Thought of Modibo Kéïta," *Journal of Modern African Studies* 1 (May 1967): 79–106.

Sow, Alpha I., O. Balogun, H. Aguessy, and P. Diagne. *Introduction à la Culture Africaine* (Paris: Unesco/10–18, 1977).

Soyinka, Wole. *Politics, Poetics and Postcolonialism* (New York: Cambridge University Press, 2004).

Sprinzak, Ehud. "African Traditional Socialism: A Semantic Analysis of Political Ideology," *Journal of Modern African Studies* 11, no. 4 (December 1973): 629–47.

Sy, Ousmane. *Reconstruire l'Afrique: Vers une nouvelle gouvernance fondée sur les dynamiques locales* (Paris: Éditions Charles Léopold Mayer/Éditions Jamana, 2009).

Syahuka-Muhindo, A. "The Rwenzururu Movement and the Democratic Struggle," in Mahmood Mamdani and Ernest Wamba-dia-Wamba, eds., *African Studies in Social Movements and Democracy* (Dakar: CODESRIA Book Series, 1995), 491–543.

Taiwo, Olufemi. *How Colonialism Preempted Modernity in Africa* (Bloomington: Indiana University Press, 2010).

Tempels, Placide. *Bantu Philosophy* (Orlando, FL: HBC Publishing, 2010 [1949]).

———. *La Philosophie Bantoue* (Paris: Présence Africaine, 1949).

Temu, Arnold, and Bonaventure Swai. *Historians and Africanist: History: A Critique; Post-Colonial Historiography Examined* (London: Zed Press, 1981).

Thiam, Habib. "The African Road to Socialism," *Review of International Affairs* 16 (December 1965): 12–15.

Thiong'o, Ngugi wa. *Decolonizing the Mind: The Politics of Language in African Literature* (London: Heinemann/James Currey, 1986).

———. "Europhone or African Memory: The Challenge of the Pan-Africanist Intellectual in the Era of Globalization," in Thandika Mkandawire, ed., *African Intellectuals: Rethinking Politics, Language, Gender and Development* (London: Zed Books/CODESRIA, 2005), 155–64.

Thomas, Louis V. *Le socialisme et l'Afrique*, vol. 1: *Essai sur le socialisme africain* (Paris: Le Livre africain, 1966).

———. *Le socialisme et l'Afrique*, vol. 2: *L'Idéologie socialiste and les voies afrticaines de développement* (Paris: Le Livre africain, 1966).

Thompson, Vincent Bakpetu. *Africa and Unity: The Evolution of Pan-Africanism* (London: Longman, 1969).

Thukrai, K. B. "Tanzanian Socialism with Special Reference to 'Arusha Declaration.'" *Journal of African and Asian Studies* 2, no. 1 (Autumn 1968): 53–68.

Touré, Ahmed Sékou. *Africa on the Move* (London: Panaf Books, 2010).

———. *Expérience Guinéenne et Unité Africaine*, preface by Aimé Césaire (Paris: Présence Africaine, 1961).

———. *L'Afrique en Marche* (Conakry: n.p., 4th edition, 1967).

———; *L'Afrique et la Révolution* (Paris: Présence Africaine, 1965).

———. *Le Pouvoir Populaire* (Conakry, n.p., 3rd edition, 1972).

———. *The United States of Africa* (Conakry: n.p., 1982).

Towa, Marcien. *Essai sur la Problématique philosophique dans l'Afrique actuelle* (Yaoundé: Editions CLE, 2nd edition, 1979).

———. *Léopold Sédar Senghor: Négritude ou Servitude?* (Yaoundé: Editions CLE, 1976).

———. *L'Idée d'une Philosophie négro-africaine* (Yaoundé: Editions CLE, 1979).

Traoré, Amadou Seydou. *Modibo Kéita: Une référence, un symbole, on patrimoine national* (Bamako: La Ruche à Livres, 2005).

Trimingham, J. Spencer. *A History of Islam in West Africa* (London: Oxford University Press, 1970).

Tshiyembe, Mwayila. *État Multinational et Démocratie africaine: Sociologie de la renaissance politique* (Paris: L'Harmattan, 2001).

Turnbull, Colin M. *The Lonely African* (New York: Clarion Book/Simon and Schuster, 1962).

UNESCO. *Le concept de pouvoir en Afrique* (Paris: Les Presses de l'Unesco, 1981).

Vaillant, Janet G. *Black, French, and African: A Life of Léopold Sédar Senghor* (Cambridge, MA: Harvard University Press, 1990).

Van Hensbroek, Peter Boele. *Political Discourses in African Thought, 1860 to the Present* (Westport, CT: Praeger Publishers, 1999).

———. "Some Nineteenth Century African Political Thinkers," in Kwasi Wiredu, ed., *A Companion to African Philosophy* (Oxford, UK: Blackwell Publishing, 2004), 78–89.

Van Lierde, Jean, ed. *Lumumba Speaks: The Speeches and Writings of Patrice Lumumba, 1958–1961*, translated by Helen R. Lane, introduction by Jean-Paul Sartre (Boston, MA: Little, Brown, 1972).

———, ed. *La Pensée politique de Patrice Lumumba*, preface by Jean-Paul Sartre (Paris: Présence Africaine, 2nd edition, 2010).

Van Sertima, Ivan, ed. *Great African Thinkers*, vol. 1: *Cheikh Anta Diop* (New Brunswick, NJ: Transaction Publishers, 1986).

Vansina, Jan. *How Societies Are Born: Governance in West Central Africa before 1600* (Charlottesville: University of Virginia Press, 2004).

Van Walraven, Klaas. *Dreams of Power: The Role of the Organization of African Unity in the Politics of Africa, 1963–1993* (Aldershot, UK: Ashgate Publishing/African Studies Center, 1999).

Wallerstein, Immanuel. *Africa: The Politics of Unity* (New York: Vintage Books/Random House, 1967).

———. "The Political Ideology of the PDG," *Présence Africaine* 12 (First Quarter, 1962): 30–41.

———. "The Range of Choice: Constraints on the Policies of Governments of Contemporary African States," in Michael F. Lofchie, ed., *The State of the Nations:*

Constraints on Development in Independent Africa (Berkeley: University of California Press, 1971), 19–33.

Walters, Ronald W. *Pan Africanism in the African Diaspora: An Analysis of Modern Afrocentric Political Movements* (Detroit, MI: Wayne State University Press, 1993).

Wamala, Edward. "Government by Consensus: An Analysis of a Traditional Form of Democracy," in Kwasi Wiredu, ed., *A Companion to African Philosophy* (Oxford, UK: Blackwell Publishing, 2004), 435–42.

Wauthier, Claude. *L'Afrique des Africains: Inventaire de la Négritude* (Paris: Éditions du Seuil, 1964).

———. *The Literature and Thought of Modern Africa* (Washington, DC: Three Continents Press, 2nd edition, 1979).

Wilson, Henry S., ed. *Origins of West African Nationalism* (New York: Macmillan/ St. Martin's Press, 1969).

Wiredu, Kwasi, ed. *A Companion to African Philosophy* (Oxford, UK: Blackwell Publishing, 2004).

———. *Conceptual Decolonization in African Philosophy* (Ibadan: Hope Publications, 1995).

———. *Philosophy and an African Culture* (New York: Cambridge University Press, 1980).

———. "Toward Decolonizing African Philosophy and Religion," *African Studies Quarterly* 1, no. 4 (1998).

Woddis, Jack. *New Theories of Revolution: A Commentary on the Views of Frantz Fanon, Regis Debray and Herbert Marcuse* (New York: International Publishers, 1972).

Worsley, Peter. "Frantz Fanon: Evolution of a Revolutionary," *Monthly Review* 21, no. 1 (May 1969): 22–49.

Wright, R. "Machel's Marxist Mozambique," *Munger Africana Library Notes* 34 (1976).

Yai, Olabiyi B. "Théorie et pratique en philosophie africaine: Misère de la philosophie spéculatinve," *Présence Africaine* 108 (1978): 69–91.

Yefru, Woseme. *21st Century Africa: A Paradigm Shift* (Needham Heights, MA: Pearson Custom Publishing, 1999).

Yetna, Jean-Pierre. *Vérités et Contre-vérités sur l'Afrique* (Chennevières-sur-Marne: Éditions Dianola, 2002).

Young, Crawford. *Ideology and Development in Africa* (New Haven, CT: Yale University Press, 1982).

———. "Nationalism, Ethnicity and Class in Africa: A Retrospective," *Cahiers d'Études Africaines* 26, no. 3 (1986): 421–95.

Young, Kurt B. "*Africa Must Unite* Revisited: Continuity and Change in the Case for Continental Unification," *Africa Today* 57, no. 1 (Fall 2010): 43–63.

———. "Pan-African Nationalism in Theory and Practice," *The International Journal of Africana Studies* 15, no. 1 (Spring 2009): 11–56.

———. "Towards a Holistic Review of Pan-Africanism: Linking the Idea and the Movement," *Journal of Nationalism and Ethnic Politics* 16, no. 2 (2010): 141–63.

———. "Un-Trapping the Soul of Fanon: Culture, Consciousness and the Future of Pan-Africanism," *Journal of Pan African Studies* 4, no. 7 (November 2011): 137–61.

———, guest ed. *Veneration and Struggle: Commemorating Frantz Fanon*, special issue of *Journal of Pan African Studies* 4, no. 7 (November 2011).

Zahar, Renate. *Frantz Fanon: Colonialism and Alienation* (New York: Monthly Review Press, 1974).

Zartman, I. William. *International Relations in the New Africa* (Lanham, MD: University Press of America, 1987).

Zeleza, Paul Tiyambe. "African Studies and the Disintegration of Paradigms," *Africa Development* 19, no. 4 (1994): 179–93.

———. *Manufacturing African Studies and Crises* (Dakar: CODESRIA Book Series, 1997).

———. *Rethinking Africa's "Globalization"*; vol. 1: *The Intellectual Challenges* (Trenton, NJ: Africa World Press, 2003).

Ziegler, Jean. *Thomas Sankara: Un nouveau pouvoir africain; entretiens avec Jean-Philippe Rapp* (Lausanne and Paris: Éditions Pierre-Marcel Favre/Éditions ABC, 1986).

INDEX

CPSIA information can be obtained
at www.ICGtesting.com
Printed in the USA
LVHW081145090123
736735LV00002B/211